ADVANCING MUSIC FOR A
CENTURY

ADVANCING MUSIC FOR A

CENTURY

The First Hundred Years of Northwestern University's School of Music

Heather Rebstock

NORTHWESTERN UNIVERSITY

Produced by the Department of University Relations and the School of Music,
Northwestern University, Evanston, Illinois.

Designer: Angela Kokes
Assistant Designer: Linda Lake

Editor: Kingsley Day
Editorial Assistant: Brooke Von Gillern Fermin

Publications Director: Anne Egger

TYPESET IN NEW BASKERVILLE AND FRANKLIN GOTHIC

SEPARATIONS AND PREPRESS BY COLOR CRAFT LITHO, ELK GROVE VILLAGE, ILLINOIS

PRINTED ON GARDA PAPER BY QUANTUM COLOR GRAPHICS, MORTON GROVE, ILLINOIS

ISBN 0-9709021-0-7
Library of Congress 2001087151

Jacket front: Dean Peter Christian Lutkin conducting the North Shore Music Festival in 1909
Pages 6–7: University Hall in the 1920s
Pages 8–9: Students celebrating after Northwestern's football victory over Notre Dame in 1940
Pages 10–11: A 1934 band concert on Deering Meadow

CONTENTS

Acknowledgments

I am very grateful to all who helped make this book a reality. I thank Dean Bernard J. Dobroski, who believed in the project from the start and gave me the support to complete it. I'm grateful to my partners in the project — designer Angela Kokes and editor Kingsley Day — for their consistently excellent work.

Thanks to the School of Music staff — particularly Kay Price, Esther Bush, Hindrek Ott, Dorothy Wyandt, and Kristine Batey — for answering my endless questions. And I thank University archivist Patrick Quinn for sharing his encyclopedic knowledge of Northwestern University and Evanston.

I'm grateful to the many alumni who took the time to write and set records straight, especially Anita H. Kastner (26, G29), Thora Simons Bonnell (29), Link Igou (30, G33, G46), Avanelle Jackson Poehler (30), Lois M. Hackney (32), George Waln (34, G38), Agatha Otto Mauthe (35), Charles M. Fisher (37), Don Vandenberg (38, G43), C. Oliver Fuller (39, G47), Dorothy Ruth Arnold Hall (39), Elaine D. Schuessler (39, G40), Betty Bridge Greene (41), Julaette H. Jones (G41), Julia Caldwell Mitchell (41), Claire Vander Griend Thomas (41, G42), Loren McDonald (G42), Newton Dwight Strandberg (42, G47, 56), Leona Edidin Swirsky (44), Jeanne Moreau Holst (45), Conrad F. Wedberg Jr. (45), Donald Bryce Thompson (46), Elsie Fardig Cordoba (48), Delores Wheeler Dickinson (48), Harold A. Hedlund (48), Frederick Grade (49), Elva Waldon Nibbelink (50, G51), Mary Rutledge Alexander (51), Vida Chenowith (51), Donald Kington (51), Myrra Stevenson Johnson (52), Izola E. Collins (G53), Thomas Schaettle (53, G54), John Romano (G54), Jim Bestman (58, G59), Richard Ditewig (G63), Don Looser (G63), John R. Heidinger (G65), William Von Gillern (70), Dawn Woodworth Von Gillern, Teresa Cowin Muir (79), Don Rebstock (86), Andrew Herman (88), Jennifer Gore Walters (91), Tim Woods (G91), Rebecca Kenneally (96), Ellen Blanchard (99), Brooke Von Gillern Fermin (99), Leile Laura Wickland, and Lotta Winkler, as well as non–School of Music alumni Andrew Von Gillern (Weinberg 95) and David Fermin (McCormick 98).

Many current and former School of Music faculty members provided stories and information. I especially thank Richard Alderson, Stephen Alltop, Jill Bailiff, John Buccheri, the late Clifton Burmeister, Walter Carringer, Lynden DeYoung, Michael Ehrman, Richard Enright, Grigg Fountain, Norman Gulbrandsen, Kurt Hansen, Gary Kendall, Walfrid Kujala, Frances Larimer, Thomas Miller, Dominic Missimi, James Moore, Frederick Ockwell, Don Owens, the late John P. Paynter, the late Jack Pernecky, Stephen Peterson, Dudley Powers, Don Roberts, Ray Still, Alan Stout, Stephen Syverud, the late Samuel Thaviu, Leona Wilkins, Thomas Willis, and the late Elizabeth Wysor.

I am indebted to my researchers — Ellen Blanchard, Kim Castleberry, Brooke Von Gillern Fermin, Linda Garton, Mark Hilbert, Kate Hunger, Maureen Ischay, Rebecca Kenneally, Diane Littlefield, Sarah Thomas, and Jennifer Walters. Thanks also to Janet Olson, Kevin Leonard, and Allen Streicker of the University Archives staff; Lilias Circle of Pi Kappa Lambda; Joann Joiner and Elizabeth Soete of University Development; and Eric Lutkin, Verna Lutkin, Lynne M. Lamy, Osea Noss, and Marietta Paynter.

I thank my sister Brooke for her partnership and constant support during the project. I thank my husband, Don. Most of all, I thank God for inspiring and empowering Peter Christian Lutkin to build Northwestern's School of Music and for enabling me to tell the story.

Heather Rebstock
April 1, 2002

Introduction

Time. Songs mourn its passing, youths revel in its infancy, and the wise recognize its brevity. Birthdays and anniversaries celebrate its gifts, and historians record its stories. Music could not exist without it.

In these pages, the School of Music at Northwestern University tells the story of its journey through time. Advancing Music for a Century *begins before the beginning, with music lessons at Northwestern Female College in the mid-1800s. From those modest origins arose a conservatory within the women's department at Northwestern University and eventually, in 1895, a school. As the School of Music moved through the 20th century, it rose in stature as it sought to fulfill its mission and its place in the world.*

Most importantly, Advancing Music for a Century *is a tribute to people. Just as musicians mold music, so the faculty, staff, and students at Northwestern's School of Music have made the institution what it is today. From the school's first dean, Peter Christian Lutkin, a man of great vision and faith, to staff members today who answer our phones, each and every person at the School of Music has played — and continues to play — a vital role.*

So with this tribute I thank everyone who has played in our song, as well as those who add new verses as they continue to help shape the School of Music. Special thanks go to Northwestern president Henry S. Bienen, provost Lawrence B. Dumas, senior vice president for business and finance Eugene S. Sunshine, and vice president for university relations Alan K. Cubbage, without whose support the book could not have been published. I'm also grateful for the generous support of Dorothy Fox Johnson (29) and Betty Van Gorkom (42).

And now I welcome you to the pages of Advancing Music for a Century. *Whether you're reminiscing, browsing, or reading for pure pleasure, enjoy our story, the story of Northwestern University's School of Music. It is a story that, like time, continues on.*

Bernard J. Dobroski
Dean, School of Music
Northwestern University

CHAPTER 1

The Origins of the School of Music

before 1895

CHAPTER 1

The Origins of the School of Music

before 1895

We are the music-makers,
And we are the dreamers of dreams . . .
Yet we are the movers and shakers
Of the world forever, it seems.
— *from* Ode *by Arthur O'Shaugnessy (1844–81)*

The story of Northwestern University's School of Music is a story of dreamers — dreamers who had a vision, who loved to make music, and who moved ideas and shook norms to attain sometimes unthinkable aspirations. Thankfully for the School of Music, these dreamers harbored within themselves the work ethic, perseverance, and tenacity that drove them to realize their ambitions.

It all began in 1855 with a little music instruction at Northwestern Female College, one of a handful of U.S. institutions providing women with a collegiate education. Though the actual birth of the School of Music was still 40 years away, the rise of music in this new women's institution helped to shape not only the music school but also Northwestern University as a whole. And now, six deans and thousands of students later, Northwestern's School of Music continues to scale new heights, its status the product of an often intriguing history.

Stirrings

Founded in 1855 by Colonel J. Wesley Jones and his brother William P. Jones Jr., Northwestern Female College emerged at a time when many still questioned the necessity of education for women. Opportunities for women to continue their schooling were largely limited to a few private colleges and female seminaries — known as "fem-sems" — that began appearing in the East and Midwest in the 1830s. Like most private academies founded after the Revolutionary War, fem-sems usually offered music lessons as a course of study for young ladies.

Many fem-sems called themselves "colleges," but according to historian Dwight F. Clark, their curriculums were not on par with other collegiate offerings. Although Oberlin College welcomed both women and men when it opened in 1833, as did the University of Iowa in 1847 and Ohio's Antioch College in 1853, women were afforded few other opportunities for a true college education until after the Civil War.

Sons of a minister, J. Wesley and William P. Jones Jr. had been early advocates of extending higher education to women. In his speech "A Plea for Women's Education," William argued that if women, as mothers, were to be the educators of America's youth, then they must themselves be thoroughly educated. Declaring that "civilization has traveled only so fast as the intellectual advance of women," he went

A Family Affair

William P. Jones Jr. was only 22 when he and his older brother, Colonel J. Wesley Jones, had an idea that the colonel later called "the dream of our youthful minds." They envisioned a women's university "where all that was taught at Harvard and Yale Universities should be placed within the reach of womanhood." A graduate of Allegheny College in Pennsylvania who had served as principal of the Peoria Female Seminary, William Jones first sought to realize his dream by converting public opinion to the idea. He traveled throughout Illinois, speaking mostly in pulpits, to seek encouragement and pupils.

For funding he relied on Colonel Jones — a McKendree College graduate who had made his fortune out West during the 1849 gold rush. The colonel had also studied law in Springfield, Illinois, and owned an investment business in Brooklyn. The two brothers journeyed to the Eastern states to drum up support for their school, observe other educational institutions, and study their methods. During the visit they met Matthew Vassar, who — caught up in their excitement for women's higher education — tried to persuade them to establish a college on his lands. The brothers declined because, as the colonel later wrote, "we were enamored with the great and glowing West." But their trip inspired Vassar to found Vassar College and Henry Durant to found Wellesley College.

The two Jones brothers returned to Evanston to co-found Northwestern Female College, and the rest of the family assisted in erecting a four-story building to house the school. All four Jones brothers, including teenagers Charles and Joseph, and their father, the Reverend William P. Jones, dug the cellar and built the foundation walls. When the college opened in 1855 with William Jr. as president, he had only one assistant, Mary E. Hayes, who soon became his wife.

When the building burned to the ground a year later and no insurance could be collected, the Jones family pitched in once again to rebuild it. Charles and Joseph Jones transported the students to and from classes on the outskirts of town when school resumed that winter.

ABOVE

Clockwise from upper left: Northwestern Female College founders William Jr. and Colonel J. Wesley Jones; Mary E. Hayes, William's sole assistant when the school opened, whom he married shortly afterward

on to say, "When we consider the vast responsibilities, the unbounded influences that go with the mother beginning at the instant of conception continuing not only until death but as long as she is remembered, it is deplorable, it is almost frightful to think how totally unfit the majority of mothers are for their position."

In founding Northwestern Female College, the Jones brothers hoped to "afford young ladies ample facilities for a thorough collegiate education near home and amid such rural seclusion as will secure every possible guaranty for health, morals, and refinement." And when they bought an Evanston city block — now bounded by Greenwood Street and Chicago, Lake, and Sherman Avenues — from Northwestern University through its business manager, Philo Judson, they planted the seeds for Northwestern University's School of Music.

The Female College first held classes in a room over James B. Colvin's general store at the northeast corner of Davis Street and Orrington Avenue in the fall of 1855; that winter it moved into its new four-story building. Total enrollment was 84, including preparatory students; at Northwestern University, which held its first classes that same year, only ten men were enrolled, including four also enrolled at Garrett Biblical Institute. The Female College offered classes in "business, academic, and ornamental branches," according to the 1855–56 catalog.

Among the Female College's earliest teachers were women who gave piano and guitar lessons; the 1855–56 catalog lists Mrs. Clara J. Jones and Mrs. S. A. Kilbourn as instructors of music. Enrollment in the music program grew from 13 that year to 63 in 1865 — the year Nicholas Cawthorne, an organist at Chicago's

First Presbyterian Church, joined the school as professor of music. According to the 1865–66 catalog, the college's course of study in music was "intended to furnish a solid musical education, both in practice and theory." Instruction was given in the following branches: system of notation, harmony, and composition, "with reference to musical forms and instrumentation." Choral singing "practices," music theory, and organ were also offered; students received two lessons a week on their chosen instrument.

Three years later, Oscar Mayo — described in the catalogs as a "thorough teacher and composer of music" — took the helm of the music program. Music was growing in stature at the Female College, and with his arrival the program became a music conservatory within the school. "The great importance of the study of music is fully appreciated," read the 1868–69 catalog. "And also the fact that parents generally are beginning to understand the folly of employing any but *masters* of music to instruct their daughters, even when in merely the *elements* of the study. It requires longer to unlearn the faults of imperfect instruction than if the learner had never begun. This institution will hesitate at no expense necessary to make its Music Department everything that can be desired, and it will look to the country, and especially to the citizens of Chicago and Evanston, for the encouragement the effort deserves."

By this time the country was recovering from the Civil War. Interest in instrumental music was growing with the proliferation of town bands. More colleges began admitting women to their degree programs. And in Evanston there was new attention to women's education.

ABOVE
The Chicago, Milwaukee, and St. Paul Station in Evanston in the 1800s

BELOW LEFT
Celebrating the Fourth of July (c. 1876) in Evanston's Fountain Square

BELOW RIGHT
People and squirrels weren't the only creatures on campus; a cow grazes in front of Lunt Library (now Lunt Hall) in the 1890s.

In the late 1860s a group of Evanston women met to establish a college offering more advanced undergraduate education for women, a college "for women, whose trustees should be women, and whose faculty should be women," according to early Northwestern University historian Arthur Herbert Wilde. In the fall of 1868, these women formed the board for the Evanston College for Ladies and persuaded the village to set aside a block of land between Orrington and Sherman Avenues as a building site. By January 1869 they had a state charter for the school, and the building's cornerstone was laid on July 4, 1871.

ABOVE

Male students on dorm steps, 1875

BELOW

View of campus from atop Woman's College in the late 1800s

OPPOSITE

Architect's drawing of the Evanston College for Ladies building, complete with a spire that was never built

Though the building was still under construction that fall, the Evanston College for Ladies began holding classes in the Northwestern Female College building. The initial enrollment was promising: 236 women, 99 of whom were also enrolled at Northwestern University, which had begun admitting women in 1869.

Meanwhile, William P. Jones, as president of Northwestern Female College, saw little hope for his young school's future. According to an article written years later by his daughter Lydia Jones Trowbridge for Northwestern's *Alumni News,* he realized that "no college without an endowment could meet the demands of the time. The [Northwestern Female College] building was large and attractive in its new furnishings, but the time was past when all a class needed was a room, a blackboard, and a globe. That was about all the University had even then. . . . Both institutions needed laboratories and other scientific equipment. For Northwestern Female College, they were out of the question. It was too late now to amass an endowment fund."

So Jones, whom his daughter described as "sincerely desirous of giving women every opportunity to demonstrate their ability," opened negotiations with the board of the Evanston College for Ladies. Trowbridge wrote that he "offered to withdraw and leave the field to them" on two conditions: "that his surrender of the Female College . . . be recognized as a free-will offering, untainted by any money consideration save the one dollar required by law; and that the Evanston College for Ladies perpetuate the history of Northwestern Female College as its own, and adopt the graduates as its own senior alumnae."

Jones agreed to a merger with Evanston College for Ladies on January 21, 1871, and Northwestern Female College graduated its last class that June. The following fall, Northwestern Female College's remaining students transferred to Evanston College for Ladies.

ASSISTANT. ___ EVANSTON COLLEGE FOR LADIES ___ G.P.RANDALL.

Together from the Beginning

Perhaps Northwestern Female College and Northwestern University were destined to unite. The cornerstones of the first Northwestern University and Northwestern Female College buildings were reportedly laid the same day.

On June 15, 1855, Northwestern University trustees, faculty, and students as well as many Evanston residents and about 300 other guests gathered at Hinman Avenue and Davis Street. There, amid great ceremony, Bishop Matthew Simpson placed the cornerstone for the frame building that much later came to be known as Old College. (The building was moved to the University's present campus in 1871.)

Colonel J. Wesley Jones wrote that by this time he, his father, and his three brothers had dug out the foundation and had built "two courses" of cemented grout wall for the Northwestern Female College building. On the morning of the University's cornerstone laying, the Jones brothers and some of their friends hauled a cornerstone to their own construction site — a large rock, 3 feet long and 15 inches wide, that they had found

one day while bathing in the lake. Colonel Jones wrote that "while the exercises of the University, its speeches, and feast were going on, we boys and a few sympathizing friends were working like beavers" — fitting a space for the stone as well as writing up their plan for the school.

Colonel Jones, who during one of his trips had formed what he termed an "intimate acquaintance" with Bishop Simpson, went to the University's site and approached him at the end of the gala dinner. He wrote, "I took him to one side and told him of our great efforts to prevent a disappointment of the people and added that we wanted him to lay our cornerstone for the Northwestern Female College and to invite all the people down to the ceremony at the close of the feast. He was delighted and enthusiastic. Without speaking to anyone, at the proper time he mounted the rostrum and called the attention of the people to 'a most pleasing surprise.'" The bishop's announcement was met with interest and applause, and many in the crowd gathered up their belongings and headed for the Female College site.

During its 16-year existence, Northwestern Female College graduated 72 students (compared with 41 at Northwestern University). The school erected its own building and rebuilt it after it was destroyed by fire. The Female College had operated without any public aid other than a $1,300 loan. It had provided loans to 27 students and had given discounts to 31 ministers' daughters and 79 needy students.

Despite absorbing Northwestern Female College, Evanston College for Ladies had financial problems of its own. The Chicago Fire of 1871 left many donors unable to fulfill their pledges to the school, so in 1873 Northwestern University's trustees took over the college's property and assumed its financial obligations, including completion of the building — the same building still in use today as the Music Administration Building. The Evanston College for Ladies became the Woman's College of Northwestern University.

Music in the First Year

In Northwestern Female College's inaugural year (1855), 13 of the 84 students majored in music, a subject offered by the department of modern languages and ornamental branches. While most of them came from Illinois, a few hailed from as far away as Boston and Bennington, Vermont. Students had to pay an extra $10 per quarter for lessons, which used Auguste Bertini's piano method. By 1860 an additional $1.50 per quarter was required for the privilege of daily practicing.

Music Lessons in 1865

The following is a sampling of repertoire for student pianists at Northwestern Female College.

First year First term: *Richardson's Method,* with "simple pieces of sheet music" introduced in the second quarter. Second term: music by Baumbach and Grove.

Second year First term: Duvernoy's *Studies* and such pieces as "Monastery Bells" and "Carnival of Venice." Second Term: Czerny's *Etudes de la velocité* and such pieces as "Tam o'Shanter" by Warren.

Third year Czerny's Etudes, the *Tradella* Overture by Flotow, *Dr. Callcott's Musical Grammar.*

Fourth year Cramer's *Studies;* sonatas and symphonies by Beethoven, Clementi, and others; *Theory and Practice of Music Composition* by Adolph Bernhard Marx.

The Conservatory of Music

Oscar Mayo remained as head of the music conservatory through Northwestern Female College's merger with Evanston College for Ladies and the latter's incorporation into Northwestern University. The conservatory's continued existence as part of the Woman's College was written into the final contract between Evanston College for Ladies and the University. Music was one of five departments in the Woman's College, along with modern languages, fine arts, health, and home and industrial arts. According to catalogs from the 1870s, the aim of the conservatory was to provide the West with a "thorough and symmetrical musical education" focusing on singing and piano playing; "to the highest and most artistic cultivation of these two branches, the best energies and talent of the conservatory will be directed."

ABOVE
This postcard bears the inscription "Spooning is Tabooed at Northwestern."

Mayo recruited teachers with top-notch qualifications for their day, which meant they had studied in Europe. During the conservatory's first year as part of the Woman's College, S. G. Pratt from the Berlin Conservatory taught piano, and James Gill from the Leipzig Conservatory taught singing and harmony. Hans Balatka, conductor of the Philharmonic Society (precursor to the Theodore Thomas Orchestra, which in turn was the predecessor of the Chicago Symphony Orchestra), directed choral music and quartet singing in the 1870s; born in Moravia, he had studied and conducted in Vienna before coming to America. Noted church and concert organist Louis Falk, trained in his native Germany, also graced the faculty list, in addition to serving as head organ teacher at Chicago Musical College.

The plan of instruction embraced both private lessons and a conservatory system, under which a teacher met with several pupils simultaneously for group lessons. Music teachers gave free lectures, private soirees, and public performances. The course of study required four years; graduating students received the diploma of the conservatory or, for those who failed to pass the requirements, a certificate of ability.

Fire!

The new Northwestern Female College building survived less than a year. Completed and formally dedicated January 1, 1856, it caught fire on December 20, 1856, described as one of that winter's "fiercest" days. A heavy storm had covered the ground and trees with ice. Evanston had no fire department, so town residents plus students and staff of the University and Garrett Biblical Institute formed a bucket line to douse the flames. Fortunately the fire claimed no lives, but the building was totally destroyed. William P. Jones "made heroic efforts," writes Estelle Frances Ward in her 1924 history of Northwestern, but he had to have his frozen clothes cut off and nearly died from pneumonia after being outside for so long.

Letters of condolence poured in from parents, who wanted their children to continue their education at the school. Classes resumed right away in a local farmhouse, with scarcely a student missing. On February 25, 1857, classes moved to the Buckeye Hotel, located on the east side of Ridge Avenue just north of Noyes Street.

Meanwhile, thanks to heroic efforts by the Jones family, the debris from the original building was cleared within 24 hours. Money poured in to fund construction of a new building, one story higher than its predecessor. Colonel Jones later reported that the work "never ceased" until the new building was completed nine months later.

From 1927 to 1938, Willard served as a dorm for freshmen women. Other Northwestern dorms housed mixed classes, and many educators commented on Willard's novel arrangement; *School and Society* published an article entitled "Willard Hall: An Experiment in Housing Freshmen Women at Northwestern University."

In the fall of 1938, after approximately $20,000 in alterations, the building reopened as a student union. An *Evanston Review* article dated November 3, 1938, called it a temporary solution to providing a student center for extracurricular activities. The building housed lounges, recreation rooms, a cafeteria, and office space for 50 campus organizations as well as six administrative offices and classrooms for the psychology, art, and mathematics departments. One special feature of the student union was a music lounge equipped with a phonograph, a collection of classical recordings, and a library of books about music.

In 1940, with the construction of Scott Hall as the University's new student union, Willard Hall reverted to housing the School of Music, although the math department remained in the building until 1941. In 1988 the interior and exterior were renovated with financial assistance from the Evanston Preservation Commission and the Preservation League of Evanston — the first preservation award ever granted to Northwestern.

ABOVE

Fire strikes Willard Hall

OPPOSITE, TOP

*A typical Willard Hall dorm room in 1888,
when fire regulations were apparently lax or
nonexistent*

OPPOSITE, BOTTOM

*A formal dining room in the basement of
Willard Hall*

The First Willard Hall Resident

"I came to Evanston the first time in 1872," reminisced William Shannon — an 1879 graduate of Garrett Biblical Institute — in the June 14, 1929, *Evanston News-Index.* "When I started school here, Willard Hall had been built only to the first floor and the Chicago Fire had wiped out the possibility of subscriptions for the further progress of the building at that time. Later it started again, and in order to have someone in the building, the college sent me over there to live. I was all alone in that building. "Frances Willard, whom everyone had heard of in those days, sent for me one day and gave me a very full idea of my responsibility in guarding that structure in the building stages from careless matches or cigars left by workers."

In 1876 the University dismissed Mayo, and Leipzig-trained Oren Edwin Locke left his position as director of the Boston Conservatory to succeed him. Locke remained committed to maintaining excellence in instruction but reworked the conservatory's curriculum and narrowed its mission. In his first year as director, the school's catalog stated, "In no department of education, perhaps, have the American people advanced so rapidly during the past 15 or 20 years as in music. From being looked upon as a mere accomplishment, of no practical value, it has come to be regarded as an almost indispensable part of everyone's education, and its power in refining and elevating all classes in society is universally felt and acknowledged. But while the interest taken by the people in music and musical culture has so greatly increased, the means for its acquirement have, until within a few years, been wholly disproportionate to their demands. The call for teachers of music has been very great, yet the number of good teachers has always been very small. . . . The aim of the Conservatory of Music is to afford facilities in the West for a solid musical education in all its branches, practical and theoretical, to those who intend to fit themselves for the profession either as artists or teachers."

Locke's tenure also saw the beginning of Northwestern's emphasis on the well-rounded musician. The 1879–80 catalog states that "the value of music as an element of culture depends very largely upon the other elements of culture, literary and scientific, acquired with it. It is, therefore, advised that pupils in music pursue at the same time some other study or studies in one of the departments of the University." But the bulletin did offer "an exclusively musical education . . . to those who desire it."

Sight-singing, music history, and notation were among the required courses for music majors. When Locke arrived, music offerings included private and class (limited to three students as of 1880) instruction in notation, harmony and counterpoint, vocal culture, sight-singing, and chorus singing as well as piano, organ, violin, and other orchestral instruments. In 1879–80 classes were divided into four distinct courses of study: for pianists, vocalists, organists, and orchestral instrumentalists. The following year the orchestral course was expanded to include military band instruments, with lessons in flute, clarinet, oboe, cornet, flügelhorn, alto horn, trombone, baritone, and tuba. Among those on Locke's staff was future School of Music dean Peter Christian Lutkin, who taught for two years after joining the faculty in 1879.

Conservatory attendance peaked at 230 in 1886–87 but dropped thereafter until 1891, when Locke resigned. With declining enrollment came uncertainty about the conservatory's future. The 1890–91 University catalog did not even list music as a separate school or department, noting merely that "to accommodate those who wish to give special attention to music, provision is made for the election of that branch in the Course of Modern Literature."

BELOW

A student picnic group in 1890

Studies at the Conservatory around 1880

Piano: Plaidy's *Technical Studies,* Duvernoy's op. 120, Loeschhorn's op. 66, Schmitt's op. 16, Czerny's *Six Exercises in Octaves,* op. 553, Heller's op. 45 and op. 46, Czerny's *Daily Exercises and Method of Legato and Staccato,* Cramer's 50 Etudes, Kullak's *Method of Octaves,* Bach's two- and three-part inventions and *Well-Tempered Clavier,* Clementi's *Gradus ad Parnassum,* Moscheles's op. 70, Harberbier's *Etudes Poésies,* Chopin's op. 10 and op. 25, Rubinstein's *Selected Etudes and Preludes*

Organ: Rink's *Organ School,* Thayer's *Pedal Techniques,* Volkmar's *Pedal Studies,* Buck's *Studies in Pedal Phrasing,* fugues from Bach's *Well-Tempered Clavier,* Mendelssohn sonatas, and selections from compositions by the "best writers for the organ," including Richter, Merkel, Smart, Buck, Freyer, and Best

Violin: Music and studies by Henning, Wichtl, Alard, DeBeriot, Dancla, Kayser, Kreutzer, Langhaus, Mazas, Rode, Wolfahrt, Krommer, Prume, Viotti, and Pleyel

Dissonance in the Early Years

Housing the music program in Willard Hall was a constant "source of more or less annoyance to the inmates of that building," wrote Northwestern president Henry Wade Rogers in his 1892 report.

And complain they did. In 1895, Emily Huntington Miller, principal of the Woman's Department, wrote a letter to the Board of Trustees imploring them to find or build another place for the music department. "With the growth of this department and the increase of recitals, rehearsals, and other attractions offered . . . a point has been reached where it seems to me there can be no question of removing it to other quarters, or abandoning Woman's Hall as a home for students. The perpetual

din of piano, organ, violin, and vocal practice from seven in the morning until six at night is a tax upon nervous endurance sufficiently heavy. But when you add to that the distraction of evening rehearsals, both vocal and instrumental, the perpetual going and coming of outsiders through the halls, the fact that there is neither quiet nor privacy possible to us must be easily understood. . . . A conservatory of music on the grounds of Woman's Hall, that should combine, as does the

Swift Hall of Oratory, one story of practice rooms, a fine recital hall above it, and a woman's gymnasium in the basement, would be a double blessing to our students, leaving them the quiet necessary to good work and providing available means for regular physical exercise, which the young women so greatly need and which they cannot take to any advantage in a gymnasium shared by young men."

The building ceased serving as a dormitory in 1938.

Locke's resignation left the music program in chaos; the number of students had reached an all-time low, and most of the faculty had left. In his year-end report to the Board of Trustees on June 23, 1891, Northwestern president Henry Wade Rogers noted that "the opportunities for the study of music in the University are not in all respects what they should be." He suggested moving part or all of the conservatory to the University's Chicago campus, home of the Colleges of Law, Medicine, Pharmacy, and Dentistry. He also envisioned expanding the conservatory by absorbing one or more of Chicago's "large and flourishing" music schools, such as Music College, the American Conservatory of Music, the Chicago Academy of Music, and Sherwood Conservatory.

While recognizing the tenuous state of the conservatory, Northwestern's trustees felt it should continue. Cornelia Gray Lunt — daughter of Northwestern founder Orrington Lunt, a member of the University's Board of Trustees from 1896 to 1920, and an avid advocate of the arts — suggested replacing Locke with Wisconsin-born Peter Christian Lutkin, who by then was teaching in Chicago after three years of study in Vienna, Paris, and Berlin. Organist and choirmaster at St. Clement's Episcopal Church, he also headed "Mr. P. C. Lutkin's School of Music" at his home at 1909 South Indiana Avenue in Chicago. The board agreed to Lutkin's appointment, and he accepted — little expecting he would remain at Northwestern for the next 40 years.

ABOVE
A dorm room in Willard Hall
BELOW
University Hall in 1880

CHAPTER 2

The Lutkin Years

1895–1928

CHAPTER 2

The Lutkin Years

1895–1928

PREVIOUS PAGES
The North Shore Music Festival at the original Patten Gymnasium in the late 1920s

ABOVE
Peter Christian Lutkin

BELOW
Original holiday greetings from the Lutkins

When he took charge of the conservatory in 1891, Peter Christian Lutkin was already familiar with its programs; he had taught organ and piano there from 1879 to 1881. But when he arrived in Evanston for the second time in 1891, he brought with him a new philosophy of music study and a determination to make his ideas a reality. Under his direction the music program improved so dramatically that by 1895 Northwestern's trustees would vote to re-organize it as the School of Music — with Lutkin as its first dean. He held that position longer than any who followed, essentially creating the school as it exists today.

With a vision of music education far exceeding that of his predecessors, Lutkin greatly advanced the conservatory's philosophy of the well-rounded musician. Though catalogs of the 1880s had urged music students to pursue studies in other academic areas, he went further by making College of Liberal Arts courses an integral element of the music curriculum.

Lutkin was a well-established musician by the time he returned to Northwestern. As a child he had sung solo alto for three years in the vested choir of Chicago's Episcopal Cathedral of Saints Peter and Paul, becoming the first boy in the western United States to sing oratorio solos. As an organist he shared keyboard duties at his church by age 12; four years later he was named the cathedral's official organist, a position he held until leaving to study in Europe in 1881.

His formal training had begun in 1871 with organ, theory, and piano lessons under Chicago teachers Regina Watson, Clarence Eddy, and Frederic Grant Gleason. In Europe he studied piano with Oscar Raif, organ with August Haupt, and composition with Woldemar Bargiel, half brother of Clara Schumann and a student of both Robert Schumann and Felix Mendelssohn. In 1882 the Royal Academy of Arts in Berlin admitted him to its music department as its only foreign student. Also while in Europe, he took piano and composition lessons from Theodor Leschetizky in Vienna and Moritz Moszkowski in Paris.

On returning to Chicago, Lutkin became choirmaster and organist at St. Clement's Episcopal Church. In 1888 he assumed directorship of the theoretical department at Chicago's American Conservatory of Music. A year later he opened his own music school at his home in Chicago, offering classes in theory, counterpoint, fugue, and composition as well as lessons in voice culture, violin, and violoncello.

ABOVE
The class of 1895 (note the shoe soles)
BELOW
Lunt Library, seen from the north, in 1912

The School of Music Is Born

Arriving at Northwestern at — in his words — "the eleventh hour," Lutkin recruited a new staff and completely revamped existing programs. He later recalled that after his overhaul, "Not a vestige of the former regime was to be found in the way of information regarding its students, patrons, graduates, courses, or internal discipline."

ABOVE

A fraternity social in the early 1900s

RIGHT

Students obviously wrote home; this 1897 postcard pictures a chemistry laboratory, tennis courts, and the registrar's office.

CHEMICAL LABRATORY

TENNIS COURT

REGISTRARS OFFICE

When Oren Locke resigned as conservatory director in 1891, music offerings were limited to lessons in harmony, voice, and selected instruments; students could earn credit for these pursuits but could not major in music. All this was to change with Lutkin, under whose supervision the school offered courses in both the theoretical and practical study of music — including harmony, counterpoint, composition, piano, organ, singing, and various orchestral instruments. History and harmony classes were expanded, and courses were added in musical form, analysis, sight-reading, and ensemble playing. After the department became a school, classes in public school methods and pedagogy followed.

In designing the music program, Lutkin aimed to offer all levels and aspects of music, "from the elementary stages to the highest proficiency." Instrumental and vocal study returned to the private, one-on-one lesson format. The curriculum was organized into four courses of study: the "course for amateurs," for those desiring merely to sample music; the "two-year normal teachers' course" and "two-year normal artists' course," for students "intending to become professionals"; and the four-year course, which led to a bachelor of music degree and prepared students for all aspects of the music profession — composer, theorist, artist, teacher, and critic.

MEMORIAL HALL.

SCIENCE HALL.   DEARBORN OBSERVATORY.

UNIVERSITY HALL.

Students could begin "amateur" studies at any time, with goals to be determined according to their individual interests and abilities. Those pursuing a professional career were required to take nine terms of theoretical work and nine terms of lessons in their instrumental major. The bachelor of music course of study was open only to those who had completed the teachers' or artists' course.

At the end of Lutkin's first year, the future of music at Northwestern seemed promising. The annual concert had taken place as usual, and graduation was held at Evanston's First Methodist Church with performances by piano and vocal students, the Glee Club, and the Cecilian Choir. Lutkin wrote that "the experience of the year amply demonstrated that there was not only room for a school of music, but that a properly conducted institution would be well patronized."

Nevertheless, enrollment stood at only 40 — a matter of personal concern to Lutkin, who, like his predecessors, depended entirely on tuition to pay salaries, including his own, and to buy musical instruments and advertising. As he explained in a 1905 essay on the school's history, before 1892 "the head of the department assumed all responsibility both educationally and financially. . . . The standing and worth of the school, therefore, depended entirely on the ability of the man in charge." Lutkin wanted a salaried position for the program's head "so that his energies could be entirely elevated to the educational side of his work." He argued that "any commission basis, which would perhaps prove remunerative in the end, would necessarily smatter of commercialism and might lead to a conflict of interests that would prove prejudicial to the interests of the school." Lutkin also proposed making music a course of study in the College of Liberal Arts and awarding professorial rank to the head of the program.

LEFT
A page from the 1890 Syllabus, *the University yearbook, shows Memorial Hall, Science Hall, Dearborn Observatory, and University Hall.*
BELOW
The 1914 Northwestern Songbook, *edited by Osbourne McConathy*

But apparently seeing little hope that his proposals would be approved, and with the trustees still contemplating the complete elimination of the music program, Lutkin declined reappointment at the end of 1891–92. President Henry Wade Rogers, in his year-end report to the Board of Trustees of June 14, 1892, wrote that Lutkin "has labored under great embarrassments but has succeeded in raising the standards of instruction very considerably, and has discharged in an admirable manner the duties pertaining to his position." He added that Lutkin had refused reappointment because he found it "impossible to give adequate attention to the affairs of the conservatory for another year." The report recommended that the whole music program be discontinued, either temporarily — until sufficient funds could be raised — or permanently.

"I do not believe that the interests of the college will be materially affected should the conservatory be discontinued," said Rogers's report. "In considering this question, the board needs to remember that the reputation of the University as an educational institution depends not on the number of departments we have but on the character of those departments. Unless we can maintain a conservatory of music which has a high standard of excellence, its connection with the University will not enhance but rather detract from the reputation of the institution. The annual income from the conservatory, amounting to $3,886.55, is not sufficient to maintain it creditably. To do this will require for some years to come an appropriation from the general funds, and this will involve a crippling of the College of Liberal Arts, whose needs at the present time are great and urgent." Rogers pointed out that the conservatory needed a "well-paid corps of instructors" and a building of its own — its Woman's College location having become "a source of more or less annoyance to the inmates of that building."

OPPOSITE

A campus path in 1920

ABOVE

Some things never change. This winter shot appeared in the 1917 Syllabus.

Instead of terminating the music program, however, the board approved Lutkin's proposal to make the conservatory a department in the College of Liberal Arts — but only after he relented and agreed to sign a three-year contract. He was named professor of music and relieved of the financial responsibility of running the program. Lutkin credited the support of trustee James H. Raymond for his remaining at Northwestern and for the eventual success of his proposals.

With educational and financial reorganization under way, the music program at Northwestern began to develop credibility and expand its enrollment. Pleased with this progress, the trustees voted on June 26, 1895, to remove the music department from the College of Liberal Arts and to elevate its status to that of a school. They named Lutkin the first dean of the School of Music.

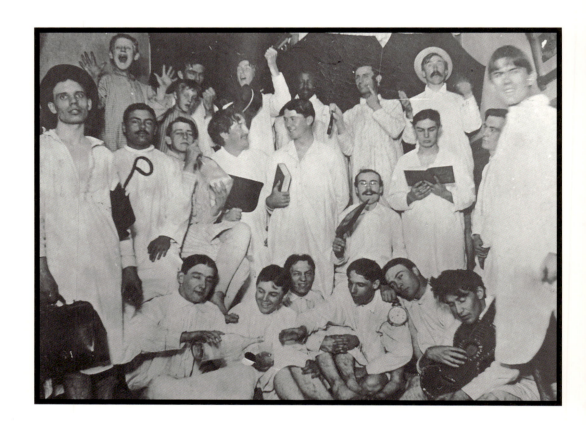

Dimes and Dollars: Tuition in the Early Years

While the amounts seem minuscule in today's dollars, nothing came cheaply in the early days, particularly the privilege of studying with master teachers. While children of ministers received a 25 per-cent discount, many School of Music students had to pay extra for lessons and even to practice. Beginning in 1896–97, a $5 matriculation fee was charged to all students entering the certificate or diploma course. For those students and for all full-tuition College of Liberal Arts students, classes in harmony, counter-point, and composition were free. In 1900 two half-hour lessons per week with Arne Oldberg cost $35 for each of the school year's two semesters. Those in the certificate program taking voice lessons with Karleton Hackett paid $45 per term. Piano and organ lessons were $35 each term. In 1908 active membership in the Evanston Musical Club cost $3 a year, and lockers could be rented for 35 cents per term. Piano practice cost $3 per quar-ter for one hour daily and $10 for four hours. By 1927–28 course fees included theoretical studies and private lessons.

ABOVE, TOP
Fraternity members studying in 1903

ABOVE, BOTTOM
Football greats Jesse Van Doozer and
A. B. Potter, star backs in 1895

Hail to Purple, Hail to Gold

More than 100 years ago, Northwestern adopted the same colors as Purdue and the University of Iowa. As Northwestern University archivist Patrick M. Quinn tells it, the growing popularity of intercollegiate athletics after the Civil War led the University to select an official color to distinguish its teams. In the fall of 1879, following the lead of many Eastern universities, a committee — unable to settle on a single color — selected black and gold. But the committee soon discovered that other schools had already chosen black and gold, so it changed the Northwestern colors to purple and gold. The University's teams wore those colors until 1892, when another committee — again paralleling the customs of Eastern universities — adopted one official color: purple.

Early Evanston

Situated 12 miles north of downtown Chicago, the area now known as the city of Evanston sprang up in the mid-19th century along Lake Michigan and "the ancient highway to the north," today called Green Bay Road. This primitive 250-mile trail from Fort Dearborn to Fort Howard — later Chicago to Green Bay — was first traversed by native Americans, especially the Potawatomies, who had occupied the swampy ground for generations. Regular stagecoach service on the route began in 1836.

TOP LEFT
The beach was a popular place to socialize.
BOTTOM LEFT
Relaxing on a fallen tree by the lake in 1898

Legend has it that the first non-Indian settler, Stephen J. Scott, landed on Evanston's shore quite by accident. On a ship from Buffalo in 1826, Scott got into an argument with the captain, who proceeded to dump Scott, his family, and their baggage on the wilderness shore. Scott built a cabin but had no valid claim to the land. In 1829 the federal government negotiated the Treaty of Prairie du Chien with the Chippewa, Ottawa, and Potawatomie Indians to obtain some of the land. By 1833 the Potawatomies signed the second Treaty of Chicago, giving up the remainder of their land in Illinois. Chicago was incorporated as a town on August 12, 1833, with a population of 350.

The future Evanston was a rural community, settled mainly by farmers from the Eastern states and Europe seeking land to support their growing families. These early settlers included immigrants from famine-struck Ireland and war-torn Germany.

In the 1840s only a few houses dotted the area, which was primarily devoted to such land-related enterprises as lumbering and farming. But by 1850 there were enough settlers to establish a township, named Ridgeville at a town meeting that April. Meanwhile, the eventual founders of Northwestern University, Garrett Biblical Institute, and Northwestern Female College purchased land for purposes of their own. Northwestern University was granted its charter in January 1851.

The town of Evanston — named to honor Northwestern founder John Evans — was incorporated on December 29, 1863. For the remainder of the century its boundaries were extended by land annexations. Population rose markedly after the Chicago Fire of 1871 and reached 19,259 by 1900. Evanston quickly developed a

ABOVE, TOP
The Henry Butler Livery & Boarding Stable at 1719 Maple. It was demolished as part of construction of the Northwestern University/ Evanston Research Park.

ABOVE, BOTTOM
Two early Evanston residents outside a log house, built by Carl Fiseman, on Niles Center Road in what is now Skokie

reputation for its educational opportunities; according to early historians, it had an "admirable" school system in addition to Northwestern and Garrett. From early in its history, Evanston boasted well-paved streets lit by both gas and electricity, in addition to maintaining its own water system.

Prohibition of the sale of alcoholic beverages within the city limits was strictly enforced until 1972; Northwestern wrote into its charter that "no spirituous, vinous, or fermented liquors shall be sold under license, or otherwise, within four miles of the location of the said university, except for medicinal, mechanical, or sacramental purposes." The Women's Christian Temperance Union, an expression of the nationwide women's crusade against liquor, remained a major influence in the city for decades.

ABOVE, TOP
Davis Street, looking east toward Centennial Square and Fountain from Benson Avenue, 1887
ABOVE LEFT
The Evanston train station in 1897
ABOVE RIGHT
A map of Evanston, July 1854

ABOVE
Evanston's Fountain Square in 1900
RIGHT
*Scene from a postcard dated September 19,
1911*
FOLLOWING PAGES
A snowy Sheridan Road in 1920

Curriculum

Once the music department had become a school, Lutkin continued the work he had begun: expanding programs and surrounding himself with an accomplished and knowledgeable faculty. Instrumental teaching methods were based on the leading German schools of the day; singing methods followed Italian models. One-on-one instruction continued to be the norm, having supplanted the class-based conservatory system.

Louis Norton Dodge (03), a freshman in 1897 who later became a professor at the school, wrote in an article about its history that "one of the forces making for a strong school has been her elaborate courses and lectures in music history." These early classes were largely the work of Sadie Knowland Coe, who had studied in Berlin under Heinrich Barth and Moritz Moszkowski. Arriving at the school in 1893, she taught comprehensive courses that focused on music within its historical context, the development of the oratorio and opera, and the lives and works of classical and modern composers. (According to a memoir by her husband, George Coe, she initially received no compensation for these classes.) Coe complemented her courses with a series of historical lectures "in chronological order with musical illustrations." By the 1897–98 school year, music history was extended to a two-hour course, and it remained a major part of the curriculum throughout Lutkin's tenure.

ABOVE
The School of Music faculty in 1905 (from top left):
Peter C. Lutkin, Harold E. Knapp, Sadie K. Coe,
Arne Oldberg, Karleton Hackett

BELOW
Student music making in the early 1900s

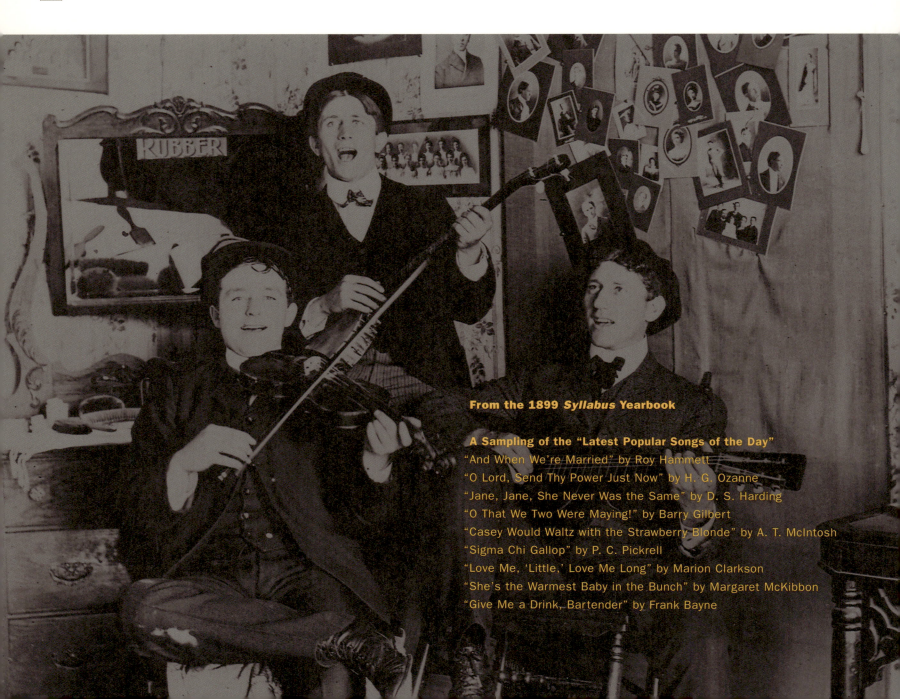

From the 1899 *Syllabus* Yearbook

A Sampling of the "Latest Popular Songs of the Day"
"And When We're Married" by Roy Hammett
"O Lord, Send Thy Power Just Now" by H. G. Ozanne
"Jane, Jane, She Never Was the Same" by D. S. Harding
"O That We Two Were Maying!" by Barry Gilbert
"Casey Would Waltz with the Strawberry Blonde" by A. T. McIntosh
"Sigma Chi Gallop" by P. C. Pickrell
"Love Me, 'Little,' Love Me Long" by Marion Clarkson
"She's the Warmest Baby in the Bunch" by Margaret McKibbon
"Give Me a Drink, Bartender" by Frank Bayne

The dean also placed considerable emphasis on music theory, requiring that students take twice as many hours of harmony courses as in comparable music conservatories elsewhere. In 1897–98 the administration added classes in musical analysis and sight-reading; by 1903 the latter was divided into separate classes for vocalists and instrumentalists. Theory courses included Harmony, Musical Form, Counterpoint, Analysis, and Canon and Fugue.

In keeping with the school's mission of producing well-rounded graduates, music students were required to complete a set of core courses in the College of Liberal Arts. They could receive as many as 27 hours of elective credit for classes in the college. Lutkin also sought to develop a love for music among students outside the school. He offered a music appreciation class for nonmajors and modified the school's sight-singing classes to better accommodate Garrett Biblical Institute students. He invited College of Liberal Arts students to take free classes in harmony, counterpoint, composition, and musical history and analysis "in the hope of creating a more widespread interest in the theory of music." Any University student could attend free music history lectures as well as all concerts, solo and ensemble class presentations, and recitals.

ABOVE

Biking at Northwestern is nothing new. A man rides a bicycle on campus in the early 1900s.

BELOW

Dean Lutkin's tuning forks

51

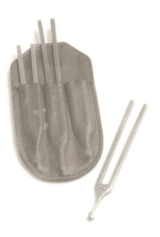

"There Would Be Some Mightily Surprised People"

(from the 1918 Syllabus*)*

If Mr. Dodge quit telling jokes.

If Dean Lutkin got a close shave.

If John Dean appeared in knee trousers. Mirabile visu!

If Mr. Beecher spoke a cross word.

If the students began to appreciate Mr. Knapp.

If Mr. McConathy ceased being sarcastic.

If Irving's dreams of a new music school came true.

If Marie Briel stopped talking about "my recital."

If the menu at the (suppressed by the censor).

If our social calendar contained more than one item per year.

Choruses

Since much of America had its musical roots in a choral tradition of singing schools, it is no surprise that choruses at Northwestern have enjoyed a longer history than their instrumental counterparts. Lutkin's special interest in choral music made singing groups an important element of the school's early years.

Glee Clubs

Lutkin organized the first Northwestern Men's Glee Club in 1891 and coached it for two years. The first campus musical group he founded, it remained active until 1898–99, when it was suspended for a year because of inappropriate behavior while on tour. But the ensemble resumed its activities the following year and continued uninterrupted until a 1918–19 hiatus during World War I.

Though originally administered by the College of Liberal Arts, the club drew many of its early members from the law, dental, and pharmacy schools. Club leadership changed frequently, with directors including W. H. Knapp, Walter Allen Stults, and Rollin Pease. In 1926 the group came under School of Music auspices when Glenn Cliffe Bainum was named director; he led it to first place in the All Western Collegiate Glee Club Contest and third place in the National Intercollegiate Glee Club Contest at Carnegie Hall. Over the years the club toured the Pacific coast and Haiti and performed in Orchestra and Carnegie Halls.

The Women's Glee Club, alternatively referred to as the women's club or girls' club, enjoyed fewer opportunities to perform but made an annual February-March concert tour. In 1941 it joined forces with the Men's Glee Club to give joint concerts under George Howerton. Both groups remained in existence until the early 1970s. In 1972 the University Chorus combined glee clubs, other students, faculty, staff, and community residents into a large ensemble that still performs major works. The Women's Glee Club became the Women's Chorus.

A Cappella Choir

Lutkin's most famous choral group started out as a favor and blossomed into a national trend. In December 1906 the wife of Alfred Emerson asked the dean to provide examples of polyphonic music for a lecture she planned to give at the Evanston Women's Club. Lutkin later reported that he reluctantly gathered a group of about 14 singers for the occasion. The performance was so successful that on March 24, 1907, he declared the choir a permanent group and requested money to buy it formal caps and gowns. According to John M. Rosborough (05), a student in the group, "During the first few rehearsals, [Lutkin] was much bored, but after several weeks of practicing he could not give it up."

Hence the first collegiate a cappella choir in the United States was born. The group often sang outside Evanston and as early as 1911 was invited to sing with the Chicago Symphony Orchestra. Other performances were hosted by social organizations, churches, clubs, and private groups in the Chicago area; the choir also gave benefit concerts for the Northwestern University Settlement and at Chicago's Hull House.

In the fall of 1907 the group increased to 22 members; in 1916 it boasted 30 members and often sang eight-part pieces. By 1929 membership

KURT HANSEN (G83) *was a Chapel Choir member from 1964 to 1968 and again from 1972 to 1985, when he also served as a vocal assistant to director Grigg Fountain. Assistant to the chaplain for liturgy and the arts from 1978 to 1985, he remains at the School of Music as a lecturer in voice. His maternal grandfather, John Mahard Rosborough (05), received an honorary master of music degree from Northwestern in 1920, the same year that Carl Beecher earned one of the School of Music's first master's degrees.*

My grandfather was Dean Lutkin's first accompanist and a very close friend of Carl Beecher. He went on to study with Josef Lhévinne in Germany at the same time as Beecher and then to serve as dean of the School of Music at the University of Nebraska for 25 years. He had a nationally renowned a cappella choir that performed at Franklin D. Roosevelt's first inauguration. My mother and father met in his choir, and, needless to say, my grandfather had a huge influence on my decision to come to Northwestern. I remember as a boy hearing him talk about Carl Beecher as that "nice boy," since he was four years my grandfather's junior. They maintained their friendship throughout Dean Beecher's tenure and would send students back and forth to each other. I have my grandfather's sheepskin for his master's degree hanging on the wall of my studio.

had grown to 52, and by 1930 to 60 — with a reserve choir of 25 who literally waited in the wings for a chance to perform. The group sang by memory (according to alumna and former faculty member Emily Boettcher), and most reserve members memorized all choir repertoire in eager anticipation that a regular member might fall by the wayside. This was entirely possible, as tardiness for a performance was cause for expulsion; in addition, singers with a cold were not allowed to go on tour. "It has been reported with fair authenticity," wrote the *Daily Northwestern*, "that director Krone spends busy hours at choir rehearsals with one eye on the score, one eye on the clock, one ear to pick out flat tones, and the other to catch any incidental sniffles."

The choir soon gained national prominence, and students clamored to become members, though scholarships were occasionally offered to entice male voices. By the 1920s many other colleges were founding such choirs; most of the directors were Northwestern graduates, such as Rosborough at the University of Nebraska.

Although he retired as dean in 1928, Lutkin continued to lead the A Cappella Choir until his death in 1931. Oliver S. Beltz then served as director until 1935, when he was succeeded by Max T. Krone. Under Krone the group won national attention in 1937 with an 11-concert East Coast tour that ended with a nationally broadcast performance at Carnegie Hall.

Choruses

The tour cost $10,000, underwritten entirely by alumni donations and ticket sales. Performing with the group was blind pianist Alec Templeton. The tour began on April 14 at Chicago's Orchestra Hall; the performance was almost sold out and received outstanding reviews. The group was similarly received at every subsequent stop, including Carnegie Hall. "Severely attired in academic robes of purple and silver," said the *New York Sun*, the group showed itself "uncommonly well-trained."

The A Cappella Choir did not always sing a cappella. In its 40th anniversary year the group performed Mahler's *Resurrection* Symphony with the Chicago Symphony Orchestra and appeared in a production of Smetana's opera *The Bartered Bride* at Cahn Auditorium.

George Howerton led the group from 1939 to 1954. During this time it joined the CSO on numerous occasions, was heard on several radio broadcasts, and continued to perform on tour around the country. When Howerton's responsibilities as dean forced him to leave the group in 1954, William Ballard assumed the directorship, which he held until 1970, the choir's last year. During his one-year sabbatical in 1968, he was replaced by Margaret Hillis; she was later named to the faculty and went on to conduct the A Cappella Choir's successor, the Concert Choir.

Other Choirs

Around 1893 Lutkin founded the Northwestern University Choral Association, a choral society for University students. Highlights of the group's first two years included performances of Haydn's *Creation* and Chadwick's *Ode* at the Columbian Exposition.

School of Music students at the turn of the century could also sing in the Evanston Musical Club, another choral group founded by Lutkin. In existence from 1894 to 1922 with Lutkin as its only director, the group drew members from both the University and the Evanston community. Ranging in membership from 100 to 200, the club sang Brahms's *German Requiem*, Mendelssohn's *Elijah*, Mozart's *Requiem*, and other major works. Occasionally its ranks were bolstered by the Ravenswood Musical Club, which Lutkin directed from 1897 to 1905. After the North Shore Music Festival was launched in 1909, most Evanston Musical Club members sang in the festival chorus, which eventually superseded the club.

The Concert Choir, led by Margaret Hillis from 1970 to 1977, sang both a cappella and large-scale accompanied works during its short existence. It disappeared when Hillis left to become the first director of the Chicago Symphony Chorus. In 1978 the choir was replaced by the University Chorale and University Singers, with Robert A. Harris as director of the choral department.

The Chapel Choir, led by George Howerton, began singing for Sunday chapel services at Lutkin Hall in 1947. Ewald Nolte succeeded him as director in 1954. The chapel services — and the choir — moved to Alice Millar Chapel when it opened in 1963; Grigg Fountain served as the group's director from 1961 until his retirement in 1985. Larry Cook led the choir until 1993, when he was succeeded by Stephen Alltop.

RIGHT
The School of Music orchestra in concert on April 3, 1912
BELOW
The Northwestern Band in 1900
OPPOSITE
An early Northwestern orchestra program

When the School of Music was established in 1895, organists — like all other instrumental majors — were part of the "two-year normal artists' program"; many divided their studies between organ and piano. A full term of weekly half-hour organ lessons cost $15 to $30.

For organists, applied study had a strong practical component. As early as the 1880s, course catalogs stressed the importance of learning to play for church services. Later catalogs, touting the advantages of studying music in Evanston, cited the opportunities to play in area churches and work with excellent choirs. As preparation for careers as church organists, organ and church music majors were encouraged (though not required) to take theology classes. Under Lutkin's leadership, the School of Music cooperated closely with the Garrett Biblical Institute and the Western Theological Seminary in the field of church music.

Around the turn of the century, Lutkin added lessons in choir accompaniment and began requiring a course in organ repertoire. By 1920 organists had to show piano proficiency in scales, arpeggios, accompanying, and simple sight-reading. They also received instruction in hymn and anthem playing, oratorio accompanying, transposition, improvisation, and choral services.

In 1926 — two years before Lutkin stepped down as dean — his dream of an organ and church music program began to materialize. That year, thanks to a $100,000 donation from the Carnegie Corporation to develop a church and choral music program, church music became a separate department. Organ students could pursue a bachelor of music degree in either organ performance or church and choral music.

The course catalog described the performance major as "designed to provide a thorough and sufficient education both for the concert and church field, the latter being particularly stressed." Organ study was open only to those who had completed the necessary piano requirements and included "a fundamental study of the manual touch, pedal technique, the independence of the hands and feet, and elementary and advanced registration." Other performance options included an organ minor or an organ major at the graduate level.

Organists pursuing the church and choral music

Louis Norton Dodge (03) did clerical work on catalogs, receiving $235 for his work. He also taught in the preparatory department during his student years but after graduating was promoted to the regular faculty as instructor of harmony and piano.

61

OUR PETER

(FROM THE 1918 *SYLLABUS*)

Now Peter Lutkin keeps music school
At a place called Northwestern, and makes this his rule,
If the pupils are slow and get off the track,
He gives the piano a terrible whack.

Now Pete has a heart as big as a ton,
And a sweet disposition, but they are all one.
A growl he has and terrible frown,
And when he does use them, he sure lets you down.

Fortunate man with a machine so big,
An Overland car (faith, a fast-going rig!),
A mansion on Church Street, a dog and a cat,
A silver goatee and a small gray cravat!

Here's luck to friend Peter, he is a world beater,
The baton to swing or the chorus to rap;
This boy is a winner, and thru the dear sinner,
Northwestern will never escape from the map!

ABOVE
String professor Harold Knapp's scrapbook

degree, also open to piano and voice majors, took courses in the history of church music and studied hymns, anthems, canticles, services, masses, cantatas, and oratorios. In addition, they were instructed in church service playing, supervision, and programming as well as choral and organ composition, community singing, and choral training.

Lutkin encouraged his organ students to obtain a degree in church music. He wrote in his book *Music in the Church* that the "fundamental mistake" of his own education was that he "pursued his work purely from the secular side and no attention had been paid to it as a ministry of the church." He added that "church organists should be primarily churchmen and secondarily musicians, but sad to relate the reverse is the rule and there are all too many organists whose interest in religion has reached the vanishing point." Many students followed his advice and went on to major church positions throughout the Chicago area.

Over the years the school added organ facilities. In 1894 a new two-manual Kimball pipe organ was rented and placed in the chapel of the Woman's Hall for student use. Music Hall, the new music school building that opened in 1897, had a two-manual pipe organ with pedals by 1902 and a three-manual pipe organ and a reed organ by 1916. When the church music department came into existence, catalogs boasted of four organs available for practice: a two-manual reed organ and a pipe organ in Music Hall, a two-manual pipe organ at Garrett, and a three-manual Cassavant Frères organ in Fisk Hall. The Fisk instrument, donated to Northwestern in 1909 by a group of College of Liberal Arts alumni, was moved to its current home in Lutkin Hall in 1941.

Faculty

The faculty was crucial to the fledgling school's development — attracting students, raising the school's stature, and sometimes winning national attention. In its first year, the school fielded teachers in theory, piano, organ, voice culture, violin, violoncello, viola, flute, clarinet, oboe, bassoon, cornet, and French horn.

Lutkin sought instrumental teachers who ranked among the best in their fields. Already on the faculty was Harold E. Knapp, who had studied at the Leipzig Conservatory. As director of the violin department, he built up the string program, initiating and sustaining the School of Music Orchestra. Other early professors, in addition to Sadie Knowland Coe and Lutkin himself, included Knapp's brother William Henry Knapp, singer Karleton Hackett, and pianist and composer Arne Oldberg. Late in his deanship Lutkin set the course for the Northwestern bands' next quarter-century when he hired Glenn Cliffe Bainum as director of bands.

Faculty members often taught both applied and academic subjects. Coe and her successor, Victor Garwood, taught piano as well as music history; Hubbard William Harris taught piano and theory; Oldberg taught composition and orchestration as well as piano; and Lutkin taught theory, piano, and organ. Deeply devoted to his faith, Lutkin also maintained ties to his church and gave lectures on church music and other subjects. By developing and leading Northwestern's well-known A Cappella Choir, he secured his place in choral history.

A talented pianist and prolific composer, Oldberg had studied with pianist Theodor Leschetizky and composer Joseph Rheinberger. While at Northwestern he wrote compositions for various campus groups, including the University String Quartet. Oldberg's activities as pianist and composer took him far beyond Evanston. He performed throughout the country and wrote compositions played by countless ensembles, including the Theodore Thomas Orchestra and the Chicago, Philadelphia, and Minneapolis Symphony Orchestras. Occasionally Oldberg conducted and performed his own works. In 1907 he and then-student Carl Beecher performed his Piano Concerto no. 1 in G Minor on a faculty recital. Beecher went on to write songs that were performed by noted singers. For many years he taught up to 50 hours a week.

Such exertions were not unheard of; Karelton Hackett and George Alfred Grant-Schaefer, later director of the vocal department, each taught 52 hours a week. Showing similar dedication, Coe taught students in her living room for nearly three years until classroom space was available.

Through faculty concerts, recitals, and lecture series, the school reached out to the Evanston community. During the 1899–1900 session, Coe gave lecture-recitals on recent American compositions, Wagner, women's music, and other subjects. As chair of the musical section of the Evanston Woman's Club for four years, she arranged a series of programs by woman composers and often recruited students as performers. Lutkin spoke widely on church music and choral singing, founded the nationally acclaimed North Shore Music Festival in 1909, and composed much music for his church and Northwestern's A Cappella Choir — including his famous choral benediction "The Lord Bless You and Keep You." He also organized the Evanston Musical Club, a 300-voice choir of students and townspeople that helped link the community with the school. The result of an 1894 merger between a Maennerchor — organized by Lutkin two years earlier — and a female chorus, it performed two oratorio and two part-song concerts each year under Lutkin's direction.

63

Pi Kappa Lambda

It all started in Evanston. Organized at Northwestern University in 1918, Pi Kappa Lambda continues to pursue its primary objective of recognizing and encouraging the highest level of musical achievement and academic scholarship. Membership in the honor society is highly competitive; upperclass students under consideration must rank in the top echelons of their classes. The society believes that recognizing and honoring those who have enhanced their talents by serious, diligent, and intelligent study will inspire others to do the same.

The society's beginnings date to the spring of 1916, when the School of Music's alumni association — as part of its plan to stimulate and reward exceptional musical achievement — appointed a committee to consider organizing an honor society. Upon investigation, the committee — which at Lutkin's request included Walter Allen Stults, Carl Milton Beecher, and Louis Norton Dodge — discovered that music was the only fine art in the country not represented by a national honor society. So the three embarked on founding Pi Kappa Lambda, choosing as its name the three Greek letters corresponding to the initials of Peter Christian Lutkin. It remains the only music honor society recognized by the American Council of Honor Societies.

Pi Kappa Lambda now has local chapters in more than 200 colleges and universities throughout the United States. Stults and School of Music deans George Howerton and Thomas Miller have served as national presidents. Northwestern's Alpha chapter has conferred honorary memberships on such musical luminaries as Milton Babbitt, Victor Babin, Elliott Carter, Ardis Krainik, Lotte Lehmann, Gerald Moore, Gustave Reese, Ned Rorem, Sir Georg Solti, and Vitya Vronsky.

Peter Christian Lutkin's Pi Kappa Lambda pin
LEFT
The Phi Mu Alpha Lowlanders play in the Quads in 1954. Originally organized at the request of director of bands John P. Paynter to perform at a 1953 football game, the Lowlanders allegedly borrowed skirts from neighboring sororities. "It was a happy group," recalls member John Romano (G54). "I'm not too sure about the quality of the sound, but we did have fun."

Mu Phi Epsilon *was founded in 1903 at the Metropolitan College of Music; the Sigma chapter was established at Northwestern in 1914. Originally an honorary sorority, it disappeared from campus around 1930 but returned in 1948 as a professional sorority, continuing here until 1968. The group aimed to promote the best in musicianship, scholarship, and friendship among its members. In addition to sponsoring guest artists, Mu Phi Epsilon supported Gad's Hill Center in Chicago and raised funds for a memorial scholarship lodge at Interlochen in honor of Gad's Hill's founder.*

Delta Omicron, *a national music sorority, was founded at the Cincinnati Conservatory in 1909. The Lambda chapter was established at Northwestern in 1923 and remained active until 1932; it resurfaced in 1939 and initiated its last member in 1957. According to Syllabus references from the 1940s, the sorority's goals were to "arouse and encourage the appreciation of good music and performance among musicians during their student days" and "to do any and all things conducive to the service, betterment, and ultimate welfare of women in music." In addition to weekly meetings and monthly*

musicales given by members, the chapter presented programs by notable musicians and outstanding alumni. Pledge requirements included a B average in music classes and the potential for superior musical accomplishment. The chapter awarded two annual scholarships, one to an outstanding member and another to a female music student not affiliated with the sorority.

Phi Mu Alpha

Officially installed and first recognized as a Northwestern University organization on April 29, 1910, the Iota chapter of Phi Mu Alpha Sinfonia was the ninth such chapter in the country. It now ranks as the nation's largest and third oldest continually active chapter of Phi Mu Alpha.

Eight men were initiated into the Iota chapter in 1910. By 1991 it reached an all-time high of 90. Open to all men interested in music, it now has an equal number of music and nonmusic majors.

Phi Mu Alpha Sinfonia's primary purpose is to encourage and promote the highest standards of creativity, performance, education, and research in music in the United States. Members hold quarterly recitals, including the All-American Recital (cosponsored by Sigma Alpha Iota), devoted exclusively to American composers. The chorus sings at occasional basketball games and other functions, such as the inauguration of Northwestern president Henry S. Bienen. Phi Mu Alpha and Sigma Alpha Iota also present Harmony Fest, a showcase of a cappella groups from around the country.

The current School of Music faculty includes 28 Sinfonians. Noteworthy chapter alumni have included director of bands Glenn Cliffe Bainum; his successor, John P. Paynter (50, G51), who served as Iota chapter president; and composer-conductor-educator Howard Hanson (16), who in 1954 received the second Man of Music Award, Sinfonia's highest national honor.

Sigma Alpha Iota

"To study and practice the goodness of life, the beauty of art, and the meaning of music." So Esther Requarth's poem "Symphony" sums up the purpose of Sigma Alpha Iota. The international music fraternity's Beta chapter had its genesis when 10 Northwestern music students and student teachers organized a local music sorority and named it Emanon ("no name" spelled backwards). Membership grew rapidly, and many activities were developed, including a glee club directed by an Emanon member. Dean Lutkin had heard of SAI's 1903 founding at the University of Michigan and was instrumental in Emanon's joining the organization as Beta chapter on December 3, 1904.

After graduation from Northwestern, five Beta chapter cofounders formed the alumnae chapter Alpha Beta, which in 1945 was renamed the Evanston North Shore Alumnae group. In 1948 it became the Evanston alumnae chapter.

Beta chapter's distinguished history includes hosting national conventions in 1908 and 1913 and helping start other chapters. Beta cofounder Myrtle Falcon designed the SAI coat of arms, and the chapter began the SAI Ring of Excellence, first given for excellence in scholarship and now the national organization's highest honor. The SAI national executive board has named Beta the most outstanding chapter in its province for several years and honored it with the 1994 College Chapter Achievement Award.

In 1991 Beta chapter became one of the few SAI chapters to acquire a house. Beta is also one of the few with a choir that rehearses weekly and performs regularly; the Beta chamber choir sings at various campus functions and delivers singing telegrams on Valentine's Day. In 1994–95 the chapter recorded *The Red Book Tape,* a collection of songs composed by past and present members. Chapter members participate in Northwestern's annual Dance Marathon, support philanthropic projects, and hold quarterly recitals.

ABOVE, TOP RIGHT
Fun at a Sigma Alpha Iota function
ABOVE, CENTER LEFT
Sigma Alpha Iota–Phi Mu Alpha concert on
December 6, 1951
ABOVE, BOTTOM
The Phi Mu Alpha stage band in the 1950s

Northwestern Music High School?

In 1902 Lutkin recommended that branches of the School of Music be started in Wilmette and on Main Street in Evanston to serve as feeders for the school. Rooms were rented for one year, primarily serving the preparatory department.

Placement

Long before the establishment of the school's placement office, the faculty aided students' job searches. The 1896–97 catalog stated that "the dean is frequently able to secure positions as teachers or performers for capable students and graduates." By 1903 that comment had been expanded: "The School is in receipt of a considerable number of inquiries for well-equipped teachers, and is always glad to recommend capable graduates. As a rule, either highly gifted and trained specialists are asked for, or candidates who are able to teach two or more branches, such as piano and voice, piano and organ, voice and violin, etc. . . . The more broadly educated and advanced the student is, the more likelihood there is of his securing a good position."

After the program in public school music was instituted, the school described it as part of a job-seeking strategy. "Attention is called to the practical advantages of the course in public school music methods," stated the 1907 catalog. "A position as supervisor of music may frequently be found useful as a means of establishing one's self in a community where later a more profitable following as teacher of piano

LEFT
The auditorium on the third floor of Music Hall, the first building constructed expressly for the School of Music

BELOW
A 1901 photograph of Music Hall, which now houses the Department of Human Resources

Music Hall

The old Music Hall, now home of the Department of Human Resources at 720 University Place, was built in 1897. Dedicatory concerts presented April 26–28 of that year included a faculty chamber music recital, a student recital, and an all-school concert featuring the University String Quartet, the Evanston Musical Club, and the School of Music Orchestra in selections by Peter Christian Lutkin,

Hubbard William Harris, and Harold Knapp. The April 26 opening concert was followed by a reception in the first-floor gymnasium room.

The lower two floors consisted of practice rooms, classrooms, and offices; the top floor housed the band department and a 350-seat concert hall equipped with large dressing rooms, a grand piano, a two-manual pipe organ with pedals, and opera chairs.

or voice culture may be developed. Such a position serves the double purpose of supplying an immediate income, and the opportunity of coming in contact with the musical public."

By 1914 the school's placement services were formally organized as the Musical Employment Bureau; teaching positions remained the focus. In 1924, under the new leadership of future dean John Walter Beattie, the name changed to Placing of Teachers, and so it remained until after Beattie retired.

Campus Expansion

Lutkin's tenure as dean lasted more than a quarter of a century, and in that time the University underwent many changes. In 1921 Northwestern established the Medill School of Journalism. The football team, originally called the Fighting Methodists, played so ferociously in a 1924 game against the University of Chicago that a Chicago sportswriter said it looked like a bunch of wildcats — and a new team name was born. Dyche Stadium was completed in 1926. Sororities and fraternities flourished in the roaring '20s, and the construction of Women's Quadrangles (now the South Quads) in 1927 added 14 sorority houses and two women's dormitories, Hobart and Rogers Houses.

The proof of Lutkin's administrative, musical, and educational accomplishments was apparent in the School of Music's enrollment, which increased from 89 in 1891–92 to more than 200 in 1894–95. By 1917 attendance neared 700, and in the mid-20s it reached 887. Increased enrollment led to the construction of Music Hall in 1897. The building (now home of the Department of Human Resources) housed practice rooms, classrooms, offices, and a 350-seat concert hall. The school continued to use the top floor of Willard Hall. In 1915 Music Practice Hall, dubbed the "Beehive," was built to alleviate practicing congestion in Music and Willard Halls.

Yet even more important to the school than numbers and buildings was Lutkin's conviction that music education meant more than attaining proficiency as a performer. Rather, Lutkin perceived music as integral to experiencing a full life and sought to prepare students for such a life by equipping them with a balanced array of skills and knowledge.

Throughout Lutkin's years of affiliation with the school, from his assumption of the conservatory directorship in 1891 to his death in 1931, Northwestern's music program rose steadily in quality and reputation. Lutkin saw a similar trend in the nation at large, as he wrote in the 1931 *Syllabus:* "The hopeful sign is the increased attention given to good music in the grade and high schools. In some sections of the country most surprising work is done by choruses, orchestras, and bands. When these admirable results become general in our lower schools and when the college continues the good work, then America will have promise of becoming a really musical nation."

Music Practice Hall (Beehive)

Little-known fact: The University moved the Beehive.

This humming practice enclave was built in 1915 on the south side of Emerson Street between Orrington Avenue and Sheridan Road. That site was chosen so as not to interfere with Lutkin's plans for the systematic development of the Willard music campus, but construction of the South Quads forced the building's removal 10 years later. The decision to move it to its present location at the northeast corner of Elgin Road and Sherman Avenue was an economic one: Replacing the Beehive, which originally cost $7,000, would have cost $25,000 in 1925, while moving it cost only $5,000.

The building contained 28 soundproof six-by-nine-foot rooms, each nine feet high. According to the April 29, 1916, issue of *Scientific American,* the building was "absolutely unique — the first in the world of its kind" because of its soundproof doors. Invented by Irving Hamlin, secretary at the School of Music from 1902 to 1926, the doors were described in the October 13, 1915, issue of the *American Architect* as odor-proof, weatherproof, and airtight, "the four joints between door and frame receiving forcible closure." Other novel features included forced warm-air ventilation, hermetically sealed windows, and soundproof floors, partitions, and ceilings.

The Rock

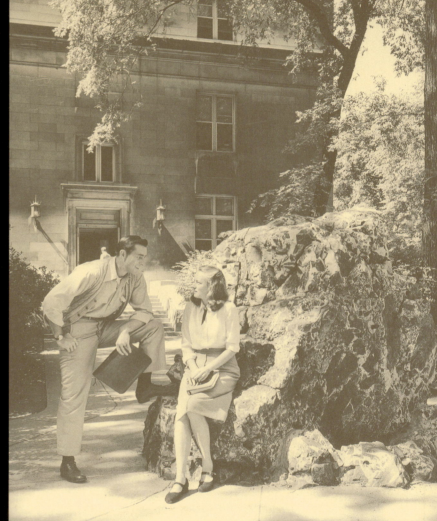

ABOVE LEFT
The Rock in 1910, eight years after its installation on campus

ABOVE RIGHT
Students gather by the Rock in 1947.

RIGHT
In the fall of 1996, students from Shepard Residential College participate in the nightly ritual of painting the Rock.

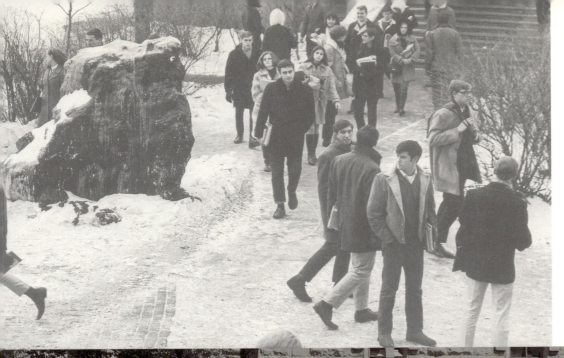

"Meet you at the Rock" has been a typical parting phrase of Northwestern students for almost a century. A gift from the class of 1902, the six-foot-tall landmark — brought to campus from Devil's Lake, Wisconsin — was originally installed as a water fountain, made to look like a natural spring. Plumbing was later added but was removed in the late 1930s after the pipes froze during the winter. Tradition once dictated that the freshman class paint the Rock every spring, only to spend the next day scrubbing it clean as sophomores stood guard. In more recent decades the Rock has been painted almost every night by one campus group or another. In the 1960s it often bore peace symbols and social-issue slogans; today's messages are frequently advertisements and group statements. In 1989, amid much protest, the Rock was moved a few feet east to its current location just south of University Hall. Supposedly under its hundreds of layers of paint lies Baraboo quartz, naturally flecked with Northwestern purple.

The North Shore Music Festival

It started as Peter Christian Lutkin's dream.

ARTISTS FOR THE 1919 MUSIC FESTIVAL

Always eager to expand the School of Music's programs and offerings, Lutkin noticed in his travels that other communities presented an event Northwestern had yet to attempt — a large-scale music festival. In the journal *The Larger Choral Groups,* he wrote that although he conceived of such an event years before organizing it, the lack of a suitable concert hall kept him from acting on his dream. But in 1908 work began on Northwestern's 4,000-seat Patten Gymnasium (later replaced by the smaller building now bearing that name). As Northwestern trustee and Evanston Musical Club president John R. Lindgren put it, "Here is Dean Lutkin's music hall."

Lutkin founded the Chicago North Shore Festival Association in 1908 and launched the first festival in 1909. The annual event quickly gained national recognition. Lutkin wanted the festival to serve two functions: to educate and enrich students, and to benefit Evanston citizens by focusing attention on the city. From 1922 through 1926 the Festival Association also sought to promote American music by sponsoring a competition in orchestral composition, offering a $1,000 prize. The contest ended when another local group offered a bigger prize.

Over the years the Chicago North Shore Music Festival — as it came to be called — drew crowds not only from Evanston but also from throughout the greater Chicago area. The inaugural concert of the first four-concert festival drew 4,000 people to hear mezzo-soprano-contralto Ernestine Schumann-Heink and the Chicago Symphony Orchestra under Frederick Stock. Subsequent festivals regularly featured the CSO, with occasional appearances by the Minneapolis Symphony Orchestra and the New York Philharmonic. Other festival soloists included Alma Gluck, Amerlita Galli-Curci, Louise Homer, John McCormack, Lawrence Tibbett, Marguerite D'Alvarez, Giovanni Martinelli, and Lili Pons.

After its third year the festival expanded from four concerts to five. Performers included a 600-member adult chorus and a 1,500-voice children's choir drawn from the Evanston public school system. The adult chorus swelled to 1,000 when performing such works as Haydn's *Creation,* Mendelssohn's *Elijah,* and Handel's *Messiah.* Members of the chorus were drawn from the Evanston Musical Club, the Ravenswood Musical Club, Northwestern's A Cappella Choir, and other singers from the University, Evanston, and adjoining suburbs. The 1914 choir was said to extend about 250 feet from one end to the other. Choral rehearsals for the spring event were held twice a week beginning in February. Lelah Lutkin, the dean's wife, provided him with a dry shirt and coat after every concert and rehearsal. Because there was no air conditioning in Patten, the heat could be oppressive; the only exception was the 1921 festival, when air was blown through ventilators over five tons of ice to cool the gymnasium.

Some of Lutkin's favorite masterworks performed at the festival were *Elijah* (presented in 1909, 1915, 1924, and 1927), Bach's *Passion According to St. Matthew,* and Brahms's *German Requiem.* To add a contemporary flair, the festival also featured Frederick Stock's *Psalmic Rhapsody,* Henry Hadley's *Ode to Music* and *The New Earth,* and Horatio Parker's *Hora Novissima, St. Christopher,* and *Harold Harfagar.*

Lutkin conducted the festival for the last time in 1930, and in his honor that year's event was dubbed the "Peter C. Lutkin Jubilee." Frederick Stock then took over the conducting reins. When Lutkin died in 1931, his will left the festival $10,000; but despite this legacy, the festival fell prey to financial problems during the Great Depression and was discontinued in 1933. After a four-season hiatus, it was revived in 1937 under the direction of Stock and band director Glenn Cliffe Bainum. But the 1939 festival in Dyche Stadium proved to be the last.

71

LOIS M. HACKNEY (32) Great soloists for the 1931 North Shore Music Festival included Lily Pons, Percy Grainger, and Ignaz Paderewski. Paderewski requested that he be provided a place of undisturbed quiet for the 15 minutes immediately preceding his concert. Back in the classroom the following Monday, Dean Carl Milton Beecher told us that his faith in immortality had been restored by Paderewski's performance, for he couldn't believe that "so great a gift as Paderewski's can be lost to the world with his death."

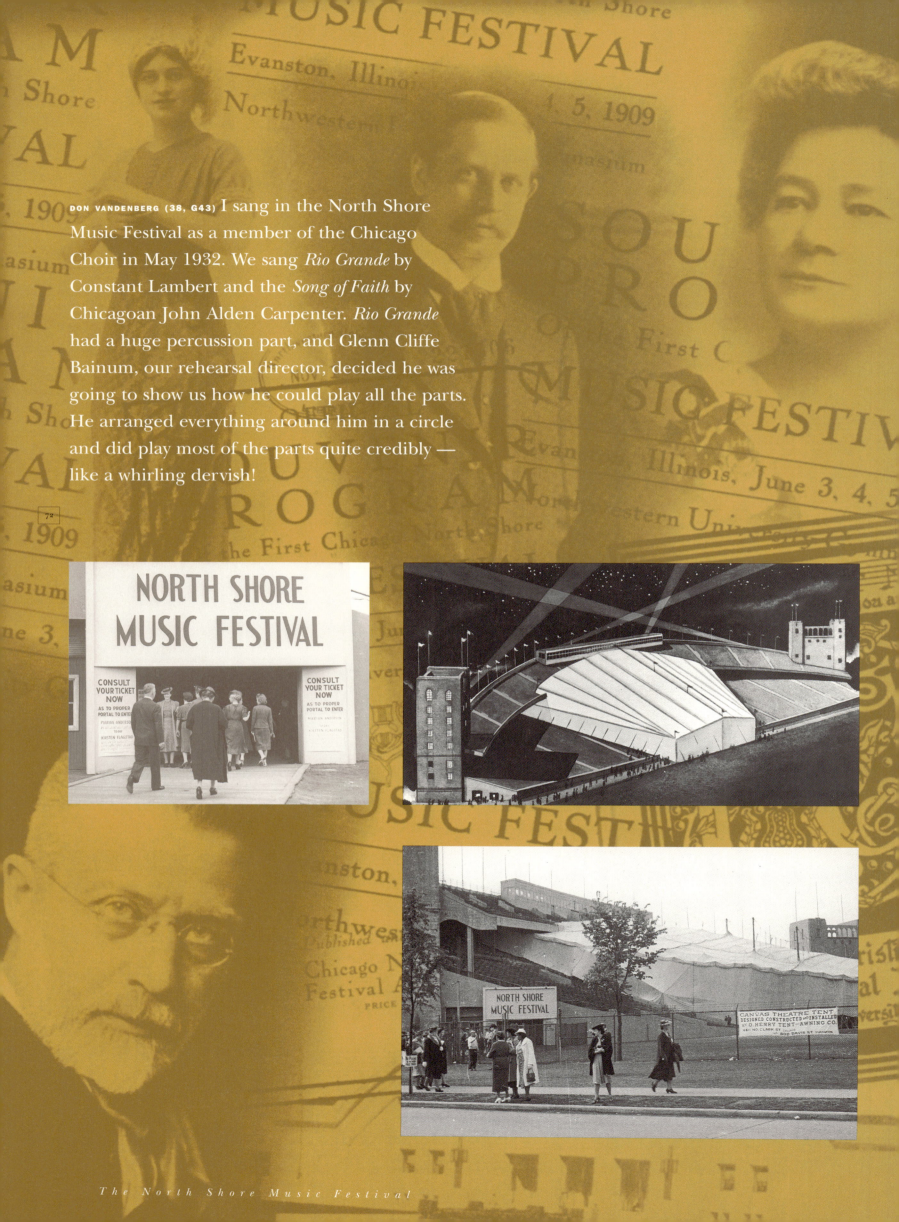

DON VANDENBERG (38, G43) I sang in the North Shore Music Festival as a member of the Chicago Choir in May 1932. We sang *Rio Grande* by Constant Lambert and the *Song of Faith* by Chicagoan John Alden Carpenter. *Rio Grande* had a huge percussion part, and Glenn Cliffe Bainum, our rehearsal director, decided he was going to show us how he could play all the parts. He arranged everything around him in a circle and did play most of the parts quite credibly — like a whirling dervish!

After the 1929 festival, Lutkin wrote a letter to the Chorale, thanking the members for all their hard work on a Bach mass: "Another great festival is at an end — the finest of them all! . . . The stately stride of the Kyrie, the ecstatic joy of the Gloria, the haunting beauty and deep sincerity of the Crucifixus, and the overwhelming outbursts of glorious sounds in the stupendous Sanctus were all of a high quality and moved me to the depths of my being. I cannot sufficiently thank you for the crowning glory of my musical career. . . . Truly I am ready to chant my Nunc Dimittis: 'Lord, now lettest Thou Thy servant depart in peace, for mine eyes have seen Thy Glory.'"

ABOVE; OPPOSITE, TOP LEFT AND BOTTOM
Audiences flock to the 1939 North Shore Music Festival at Dyche Stadium (now Ryan Field).
OPPOSITE, TOP RIGHT
The proposed choral theater for the 1939 festival at Dyche Stadium
FOLLOWING PAGES
Dyche Stadium overflows for a performance in the 1939 festival.

ELAINE D. SCHUESSLER (39, G40) I was the music school student who replaced Marian Anderson on last-minute notice at the very last North Shore Music Festival in the big tent over Dyche Stadium. Dean Beattie had organized a select all-boy chorus from Evanston and North Shore schools to sing spirituals. Miss Anderson was to have done solo portions. As I was a contralto, the dean took me along for some of the last rehearsals, not realizing that the morning of the Saturday afternoon concert I would be auditioned and pronounced "acceptable" to replace the indisposed Miss Anderson. It was a fairy-tale experience that was proclaimed newsworthy in the *Chicago Tribune!*

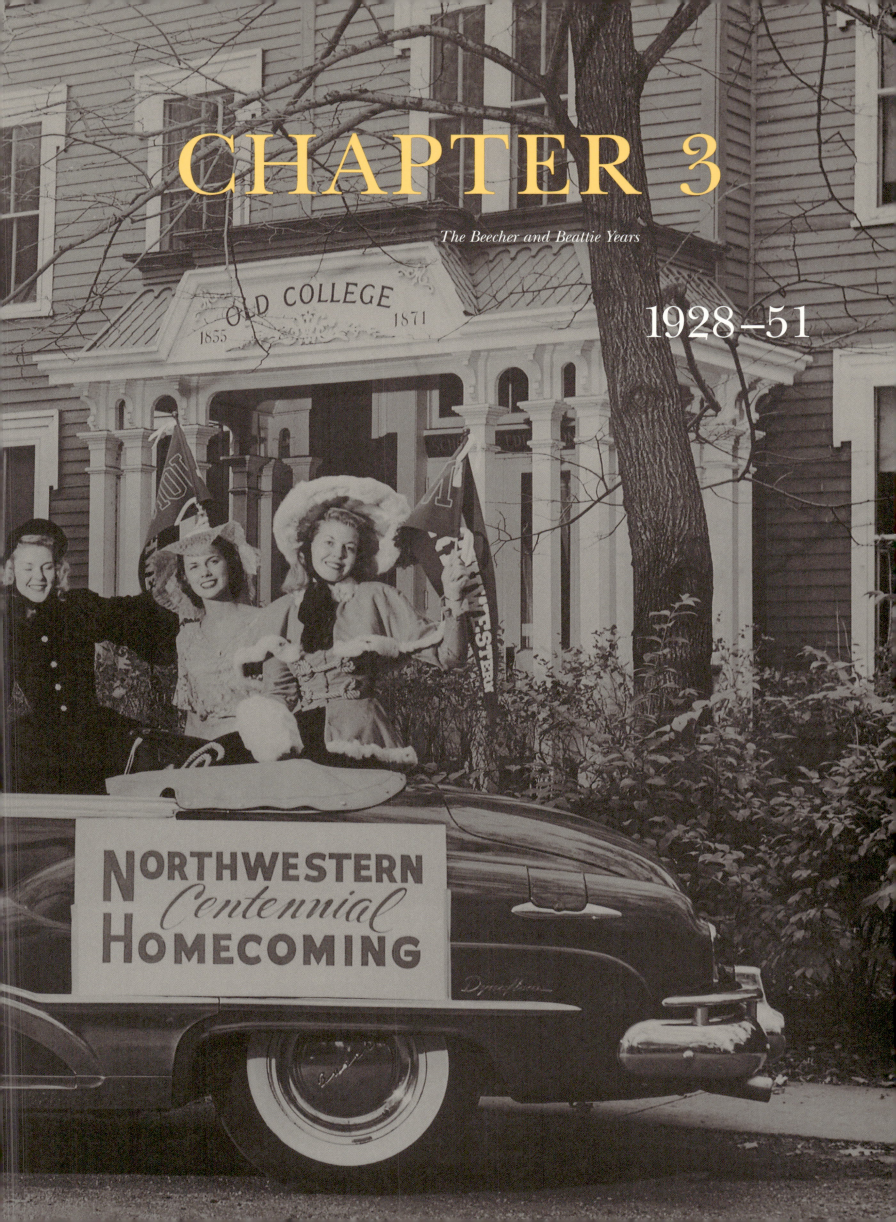

CHAPTER 3

The Beecher and Beattie Years

1928–51

CHAPTER 3

The Beecher and Beattie Years

1928–51

Rumor has it that after Peter Christian Lutkin retired to become dean emeritus in 1928, the new dean, Carl Milton Beecher — though in charge of most administrative operations since 1925 — deferred to his predecessor by declining to be called "dean" until after Lutkin's death in 1931. The facts perhaps justified his feelings.

When Lutkin left, he turned over an institution he had largely built himself. The school had been growing rapidly; as graduates assumed teaching and administrative positions around the country, word of the school's excellence spread nationwide. Total full- and part-time enrollment reached 995 by 1927–28, and the summer session attracted another 364 students. Both sessions saw an increase in male students — who, according to Lutkin, aspired to positions as college administrators, public school supervisors, and community band and chorus directors. The music education program flourished as a result of the nation's growing need for music teachers. The new church and choral music department also drew large numbers of students, especially in the summer. School of Music ensembles multiplied in number and ranks and now included the University's band and glee clubs, which became part of the school in 1926. A placement bureau had been established under John Beattie in 1925; a library, begun as a small collection of books gathered by Sadie Coe, had grown to include a large assortment of literary and musical works. And it didn't hurt the school's reputation when graduates like composer, conductor, and educator Howard Hanson (16) began to make names for themselves.

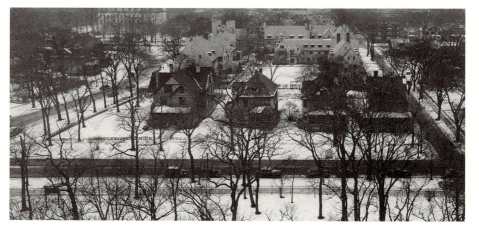

PREVIOUS PAGES

Homecoming in 1951, the year of the Northwestern centennial

ABOVE

View of the campus to the west across Sheridan Road in the early 1930s, before the construction of Scott Hall and Cahn Auditorium, with Willard Hall in the background at left

OPPOSITE

South Beach in 1949

Nationally, Americans suffered through the Great Depression and World War II. Yet it was also a time of invention and growth, with airplanes, cars, radios, and kitchen appliances galore.

At Northwestern, school spirit soared. Students hung out at the Huddle on Orrington Avenue. The first Waa-Mu Show — *Good Morning, Glory* — was produced in 1929. Benny Goodman played at the Junior Prom, and the first black sorority, Alpha Kappa Alpha, was recognized by the Panhellenic Council. Construction continued despite the Depression, with Deering Library completed in 1932 and Scott Hall, Cahn Auditorium, and Lutkin Hall to follow.

Carl Milton Beecher

Lutkin's handpicked successor to lead the School of Music, Beecher had been associated with the school since 1899. At a time when students received a graduate in music degree after completing a four-year course, the Illinois native won distinction in 1908 as the first student to earn a bachelor's degree (then a five-year program) from the School of Music — a feat not duplicated until eight years later. After further compositional and piano study in Europe, he returned in 1913 to be appointed a piano and theory instructor at his alma mater. In 1916 he became a full professor, adding ensemble playing and aesthetics to his teaching plate. He wrote several compositions that were published in both the United States and Europe, and he appeared in concert occasionally as a pianist, usually with Arne Oldberg. In 1925 the trustees named him administrative director of the music school, freeing Lutkin to focus on teaching and festival preparation.

Students called Beecher witty, enthusiastic, and interested in a wide variety of subjects. Link Igou (30, G33, G46) wrote, "Beyond any doubt the most influential person to me at Northwestern was Carl Beecher. He taught Aesthetics, a yearlong research course. Its approach to the relationship of the arts and of all the arts to the whole history of civilization became the main focus of my life."

Under Beecher's direction, the school continued to mature. While the Depression slowed growth in attendance a bit, Northwestern's reputation remained strong. Summer session, run by John Beattie, was particularly popular, growing in

AVANELLE JACKSON POEHLER (30) *shared her School of Music memories just a few months before her death on January 2, 1997. She had entered Northwestern during the Prohibition era; Lutkin was still dean, and she took a class he taught.*

Dean Lutkin kept the roll on cards, and if you cut class, your card was put on the top and you were called on first in the next class. The question was usually a very tough one, and when you didn't know the answer, he'd say, "See, it doesn't pay to cut my class!" He conducted the North Shore Festival Chorus sitting on a high stool and had jokes written in the music to tell at rehearsals.

I became a member of Mu Phi Epsilon and, in my senior year, Pi Kappa Lambda. I remember we had a dinner for PKL at the Congress Hotel; the waiters grabbed our plates whether we were through or not, and it had cost us two dollars, a goodly sum then! I also persuaded Dean Beecher to have a music school formal dance and to have a picture taken for the University yearbook.

The School of Music was small enough that you knew everyone, at least by sight. Louis Dodge taught counterpoint, and he'd put an example on the board and ask, "Is it daisies or monkeys?" He could rework an example five or six times. Luther Noss was one of the "back row" students in the class, and we'd play tic-tac-toe while Professor Dodge was grading other people's work. I sang in the Women's Glee Club, and we gave concerts in neighboring towns — usually with the Men's Glee Club — under Glenn Cliffe Bainum, who was a wonderful conductor. I remember when I tried out he said, "You have a very musical name," and I said, "Thank you." Quick as a flash he said, "Don't thank me, thank your parents!"

A School of Music teacher (who shall remain nameless) and his wife lived in the apartment next to the one my mother and I occupied. The bathrooms were side by side, and we could hear them bottling home brew. I worked at Wieboldt's part-time, and once on the "complaint" phone the wife called and said the pickle jug had cracked and she wanted a new one. I met the teacher coming out his door with his arms full of bottles one noon, and he was very evasive! The cooks in several of the sorority houses were making home brew, too, and getting the waiters to peddle it. Going out to the "west campus" (Skokie) on dates was great sport.

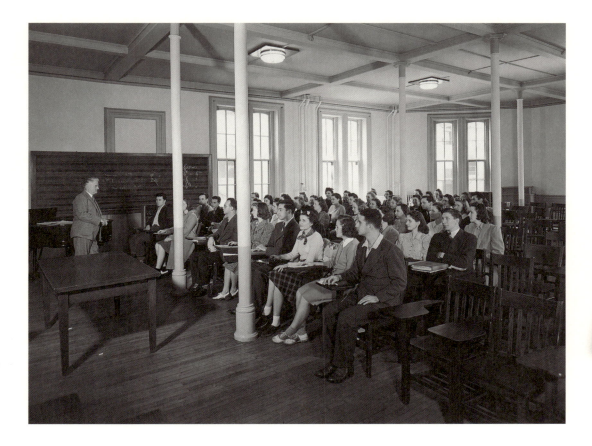

size and offerings through the 1930s. As programs and enrollment grew, space became a desperate need, as did organs. A 1930 grant from the Presser Foundation raised hopes for a new music building, though the Depression forced postponement of those plans.

Bachelor's degrees replaced diplomas and certificates, and a postgraduate program leading to a master's degree was established. The school's entrance requirements were revised to equal those of the College of Liberal Arts. The faculty was organized into departments, with leaders for each department. Garrett Biblical Institute students took courses in the church and choral music department, and the music school in turn supervised musical activities there and at the Western Theological Seminary.

Beecher was appointed dean in 1928 — the year Lutkin retired — but resigned in 1934, taking an indefinite leave to pursue research and composing projects in the South Pacific. John Walter Beattie, professor of public school music, was named acting dean and then promoted to dean in 1937 after Beecher decided not to return.

John Walter Beattie

A graduate of Denison and Columbia Universities, Beattie served as supervisor of music for public schools in Xenia, Ohio, and Grand Rapids, Michigan, and as Michigan's state supervisor of music before joining the Northwestern faculty in 1925. Under his tenure as dean, the School of Music strengthened its reputation as a leader in music education. Summer session, under his supervision from 1926 to 1951, prospered and even defied national attendance trends during the Depression. The school began offering more scholarships, as Lutkin had long advocated. The number of music school applicants and nonmajors taking music courses increased as well, due mainly to improved public-school music programs.

Nationally known as a music education expert, Beattie prepared Northwestern students for teaching careers, helped them get their first jobs, and often followed their careers. Despite his accession to the deanship, he continued to direct the placement bureau, which he had founded in 1925, and his widespread contacts benefited graduates throughout their careers. He was often able to

TOP LEFT
Dean Beattie holding class in the 1940s in what used to be a dining room in Willard Hall

TOP RIGHT
Glenn Cliffe Bainum's copy of the marching band book The Trumpet and Drum

BOTTOM
Students strolling on campus in 1930

exercise control over which teaching jobs graduates received and how long they held the positions. Clifton Burmeister, Beattie's successor as head of music placement, recalls that the dean would arrive at music conferences with one pocket full of slips of paper bearing the names of students needing jobs. When others approached him with slips of paper bearing job openings, he would either match the opening with one of his applicant slips or stuff the job notice in a different pocket.

ABOVE, TOP
Dean Beattie on July 31, 1937
ABOVE, BOTTOM
Dean Beattie's 1903 Phi Gamma Delta pin (left) and his 1925 Phi Mu Alpha pin.
LEFT
Dean Beattie's Glee Club jacket
BELOW
A piano lesson in 1940

MARY RUTLEDGE ALEXANDER (51)
Dean Beattie lived across the street from my family in Evanston and introduced the violin to me when I was seven years old. He was not only a great teacher and leader in the field of music but a fine man. When I signed my first teaching contract in 1951, the director of secondary education in the district where I planned to teach told me that the reputation of the Northwestern School of Music and Dean Beattie's recommendation had made the difference.

CONRAD F. WEDBERG JR. (45)
One day Dean John Beattie called me into his office, asking, "Can you play 'The Star Spangled Banner' in A-flat?" I told him I probably could.

"Let me hear it," said the dean, and he took me across the hall to a room with a piano. When I finished, he said, "That's OK, but don't use all those parallel fifths!

"What I want you to do," he continued, "is to wear your midshipman's uniform and play 'The Star Spangled Banner' at the Chicago Rotary Club luncheon meeting next week for all to sing following the benediction."

On the appointed day, Dean Beattie drove us to Chicago. Homer Vanderblue, dean of Northwestern's

School of Commerce, sat with Dean Beattie in the front seat while I sat in the back. Needless to say, as a freshman I was terribly intimidated in the company of these two erudite and revered deans. I knew I could not converse at their level.

To my surprise, however, the conversation began with Dean Beattie pronouncing that he was the most handsome dean on the Northwestern

campus. Dean Vanderblue objected strongly, asserting that he was the most handsome! This argument continued for the next 15 miles, each man proclaiming prettier eyes, a better figure, more flowing hair, etc.

After spending all my working life in academia, I still believe this was the most hilarious conversation I ever heard between deans.

83

World War II

In the 1930s Northwestern students protested the growing war fever, but when the United States entered World War II in 1941, the male student population plummeted as men left Northwestern to enlist. At the same time, the U.S. Army and Navy took over Patten Gymnasium, Swift Hall, Lunt Hall, Foster House, many fraternity houses, and other buildings on both campuses for military training and housing. The Evanston campus housed 3,500 uniformed personnel; among those training at the Chicago campus was John F. Kennedy. The war ended a campus construction boom as the University remodeled existing buildings to furnish housing and space for growing military units. In the School of Music, attendance hit all-time lows, and most ensembles suffered from the dearth of men.

During the war Northwestern offered special admission requirements and programs to accommodate soldiers. Such concessions included admitting "intellectually and socially mature high school students" at the end of their junior year and allowing them to start in June rather than September. A full summer quarter of 11 weeks enabled students to complete work for a bachelor's degree in two and a half to three years rather than the normal four. Special programs, such as the Naval ROTC, prepared men for war.

Following the surrender of Japan in September 1945, a large influx of veterans descended on Northwestern. In the September 27, 1945, issue of the *Daily Northwestern*, the women editors cheered, "Ah, Peace — Ah, Men. . . . Those strange, two-legged creatures wearing trousers which you may have seen around campus are MEN. Fraternities — still without houses — are coming out of hibernation. And for the feminine element, too, the lean years are over. Peace is wonderful!"

With veterans returning to college en masse through the GI Bill, School of Music enrollment swelled to 600 full-time and 100 part-time students. By 1949 the numbers had risen to 744 full-time and 118 part-time. To accommodate the flood of students, the University set up temporary Quonset housing, and many of these "huts" were situated right outside the Music Administration Building.

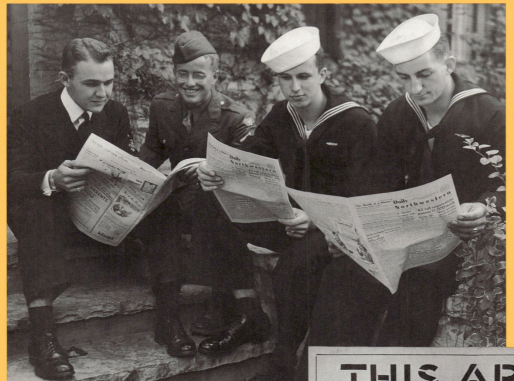

OPPOSITE, BACKGROUND
Calisthenics on Roycemore (now Long) Field. Now used for soccer, it is bordered by Lincoln, Orrington, Sheridan, and Milburn.

OPPOSITE, INSET
A Navy V-12 unit stands at ease after inspection.

ABOVE
An athlete in uniform. The inscription on the photo reads, "My adopted mascot Bud — really a good little buddy."

LEFT
Checking out the Daily Northwestern *around 1943*

BELOW
A campus sign in 1943

THIS AREA
RESERVED
FOR MEN
IN UNIFORM

NO CIVILIANS
PERMITTED

ABOVE
Doing her part: A Northwestern student signs up to give blood to the Red Cross blood bank on February 5, 1943, in Scott Hall.
RIGHT
Another wartime scene on campus
BELOW
Homecoming game halftime ceremony honoring Northwestern's war dead, October 21, 1944

JEANNE MOREAU HOLST (45)

I did two stints as song girl in Waa-Mu, one at the new Patten Gym because World War II restrictions precluded using Cahn Auditorium. It was a fabulous show and very unusual, with a Hawaiian theme around the pool. We were shaking our hips to get the war won.

TOP LEFT

Quonset housing, erected by Steelcraft Mfg. Co. of Cincinnati, Ohio, to alleviate the campus housing shortage, provided shelter for approximately 1,000 veterans and faculty members. Construction of the huts was completed in 90 days. Those pictured here stood at Ridge Avenue and Central Street; another hut village was built in front of the Music Administration Building.

TOP CENTER

Another Quonset village near Patten Gym in 1946

TOP RIGHT

Marine veteran William Roessner (left) and Navy veteran Herbert E. Blaz move into their Steelcraft hut in front of the Music Administration Building in 1946.

ABOVE

A campus ceremony honoring soldiers who died in World War II

ABOVE

Hijinks on campus, 1948

BELOW

Student residents hang out in Willard Hall in 1936.

Curriculum

When Beecher took over in 1928, students could choose from four major courses of study: applied music, theory and composition, church and choral music, and music education. Though courses in all areas underwent modifications during the 1930s and '40s, the music education and church and choral music departments experienced the greatest growth.

Under Dean Beattie, Northwestern gained widespread recognition for training music teachers, a growing profession after World War I. As more and more high schools added music to their curriculums, more and more teachers were needed at those levels, and Northwestern attracted many aspiring educators.

In his 1939–40 report to the president, Beattie said that the School of Music's reputation in music education was so great that "we have been accused of featuring the public school music department to the detriment of those concerned primarily with performers." He argued, though, that the school merely mirrored a national trend. "There has been a gradual lessening of interest in musical careers as performers, due to technological changes which have made such careers extremely hazardous," he wrote, noting that talking motion pictures had replaced many theater organists and pit orchestras. The combination of cars, radios, and movie theaters had put the "old-time lyceum and chautauqua, which had employed thousands of musicians," out of business. Stressing the importance of maintaining a strong music education department at Northwestern, he continued, "Since our School of Music was among the first to set up courses for the preparations of school music teachers, we have been able to maintain a tremendous advantage over those musical institutions which try to follow the old conservatory system of preparing performers."

To earn a bachelor's degree in music education, students in the early 1930s took six courses in psychology, two in conducting and orchestration, and two in orchestral instruments as well as Elementary Music Methods, Intermediate Music

CHARLES M. FISHER (37) One thing that captured my attention more than the required academics was the NU Male Quartet, made up of fellow students Amby Holford, Bob Biggs, Ralph Kent, and myself. I sang bass and acted as vocal arranger and manager. We weren't bad and sang many professional gigs, appearing regularly with the floor show at the Edgewater Beach Hotel. Following an audition that landed us a spot on the nationally broadcast *Amateur Hour,* we were offered a contract to tour with Horace Heidt and his Alamite Brigadeers.

Our insensitivity to scholarship was amply demonstrated in the spring of 1937, during a formal evaluation of the School of Music by a VIP committee from the National Association of Schools of Music. As a climax to the day's events, the music school was putting on its best face in a recital by outstanding student performers. Because ensembles were scarce that semester, our quartet was asked to fill the final spot on the program, and we submitted three highly respectable male-voice selections by Brahms.

We decided that in case our effort was well received, we would have another number ready, and (even though this was before the era of standing ovations for every dog and pony show) there was just enough time for us to hurry back onstage for an encore before the applause died — an unprecedented occurrence for this seriously formal occasion.

While the faculty looked on apprehensively, without announcement we enthusiastically lit into my recent "spectacular" arrangement of the then-popular Irving Berlin song "We Saw the Sea." This seemed to us to be a great choice, and the somewhat tentative smiles of the NASM contingent we misinterpreted as encouragement; so we went all out, accompanying our final 16 bars with a spirited, if somewhat grotesque, sailors' dance.

At the time I attributed Dean Beattie's extremely red face to his high blood pressure, but the scolding we subsequently received gave me a new understanding of the expression "livid with rage." For some reason the preservation of NASM accreditation and the sanity of the faculty seemed of utmost importance to the dean, and there was some question as to whether I would be allowed to graduate; but on the promise that I would not return to Northwestern for graduate work, I was finally awarded a bachelor's degree that spring.

Three of the quartet members went on to obtain advanced degrees and enjoyed significant university professorships in music. The fourth, tragically, switched to real estate and became disgustingly wealthy.

ABOVE

After World War II ended, the center of Evanston was streamlined and a monument was erected to honor those who had died in the war.

Methods, High School Music Methods, Principles of Supervision, School Music Problems, Comparative Methods, and practice teaching. Mandatory College of Liberal Arts courses nearly doubled from the previous decade and included one in public speaking.

The church and choral music program continued to grow during Beecher's and Beattie's tenures as well. Church music majors carried heavy academic loads, fulfilling the same applied-music requirements as performance majors (with organ or voice as primary instrument) but also taking classes on the history and practice of church music "from early Christian to modern times." They studied hymns, anthems, canticles, services, masses, cantatas, and oratorios as well as the art of creating an effective service program. Expected to be able to compose and arrange for choir and organ, they also had to learn the necessary skills for developing and conducting a community ensemble. The department attracted many long-time organ faculty members during this era, including Horace Whitehouse (1927–46), George McClay (1928–68), Theodore Lams (1930–71), Adalbert Huguelet (1946–67), Ewald Nolte (1947–56), Barrett Spach (1947–64), and Thomas Matthews (1948–61).

Beginning in 1933, Northwestern annually hosted the Choral Music Institute, often held in conjunction with the yearly convention of the National Association of Choir Directors. Founded and directed by Oliver S. Beltz, then chair of the church and choral music

91

Nice Work if You Can Get It

DOROTHY RUTH ARNOLD HALL (39)

I drove over to Evanston with some trepidation one warm day in July 1935. Dean Beattie was a busy man, but he heard me out — no money, needed a scholarship, etc.

He sent me to the main campus to see if someone would give me a National Youth Administration job and to see somebody else about a scholarship; the dean would arrange for the first semester. Back and forth I went, but it worked! NYA was the program organized by President Roosevelt to help students work to pay for

school; I got $20 a month for working as a secretary for the YMCA in its old building. An approved freshman off-campus rooming house at $4 a week (including breakfast) was paid for by a clerking job at National Tea, a grocery chain, down by the fountain.

It was a 10-hour day followed by a long walk back to North Orrington, but one thought little of walks in those days.

That first year was completed with the help of other jobs, from waitressing to clerical work

and accompanying. With additional scholarships, the next three years followed, plus a semester working in the Registrar's Office while completing four missing credits from the first semester. Those were busy but happy years, including A Cappella Choir and the choir's 1937 tour with Max T. Krone. We visited several Eastern cities, including Pittsburgh, Washington, Philadelphia, and New York, where we performed at Carnegie Hall and on NBC Radio in the RCA Building.

As for walking, we could beat the buses back on foot from Dyche Stadium after football games.

department, the institute invited 125 choir directors and organists from through-out the country to work with guest lecturers — all recognized church music authorities. Lecturers from Northwestern included Horace Whitehouse, associate professor of organ and church music; Walter Allen Stults, associate professor of voice; and Frank M. McKibben, professor of religious education. The institutes spawned a series of pamphlets, written or compiled by the best church musicians of the day, that dealt with nearly every aspect of the field. From evaluations of hymn collections to tips on working with difficult ministers, these booklets helped students learn how to succeed as church musicians.

Graduate study flourished during Beattie's tenure, as colleges and universities began to prefer job candidates with master's degrees. When Beattie became dean,

graduate enrollment stood at 22, an increase over the 9 enrolled at the beginning of Beecher's tenure. By 1939, 85 students were enrolled in the graduate program.

In 1931 the graduate division required that applicants to the master's program hold a bachelor of music, bachelor of music education, or bachelor of arts, fine arts, or science degree with a major in music. By 1938 the list was simplified to bachelor of music, bachelor of music education, or equivalent. Majors in Northwestern's master's program expanded to include church and choral music, public school music, and musicology — renamed music history and literature in the 1940s — in addition to the original graduate program in theory and composition. The School of Music did not offer the doctor of music degree until 1953.

JULIAETTE H. JONES (G41) I have never forgotten the excite-ment among the piano students when word circu-lated that Percy Grainger had broken a string on the piano in Kurt Wanieck's studio, where he was warm-ing up for his evening performance on campus. Everyone was already ex-cited over the opportunity to hear Percy Grainger in concert, but to know that he had the muscle to break a piano string was super thrilling.

HARRY HOLMBERG (39, G40) As an instrumental major, I spent a great deal of time working with Glenn Cliffe Bainum and the band as well as playing trombone and percussion in the symphony under George Dasch. I also sang in the men's chorus. The band rehearsed in Fisk Hall, which was quite a distance from the rest of the music classes. We used what had been the auditorium for a rehearsal room — a large, spacious area on the second floor.

I was the band librarian my sophomore year, and the next two years I was the band manager, which included conducting duties. I was band president in 1938–39. For four years I was on the National Youth Administration with the band at a monthly stipend of $15. I remember the satin-lined capes we wore — flashy and fairly good at keeping out the cold.

Rehearsals for Waa-Mu Shows were in the North Shore Hotel, and performances were at the National College of Education Auditorium (we gave our band concerts there also). Summer school was always interesting, with Bainum bringing in many guest conductors for a week or so: Percy Grainger, Ray Dvorak, Frank Simon, Edwin Franko Goldman, to name a few. We played a lot of Bainum's new transcriptions. Concerts were held on the lawn in front of Deering Library. I also played in Bainum's summer professional band for Grant Park concerts in Chicago. Olive Arthur, Bainum's secretary, was often the vocal soloist.

I remember helping Bainum organize a band for the *Chicago Tribune* all-star football game at Soldier Field. The teams were college senior all-stars and the recent professional champion. The band was made up of around 200 college students from the Chicago area. The *Chicago Tribune* furnished electricians to put lights on sousaphones, percussion, trombones, etc. It was quite a show! This was in the 1930s, so battery packs were large and heavy and not always reliable.

Being in school in prewar years did not preclude political activity. I remember the demonstrations against going to war unless the country was invaded. We had a band participate in what I believe was the Oxford protest rally. I'm not sure how sincere we were, because I am sure we all went when we were called.

Bands

BETTY BRIDGE GREENE (41) The subject of band uniforms came up one day. Back then the girls all wore skirts, but they began to want to wear trousers. Some band directors objected. But Dean Beattie said we'd have to admit that trousers were more modest than skirts for high-stepping marchers. We all had a good laugh.

ABOVE, TOP
The University Band of 1903–04
ABOVE, BOTTOM
The Tau Kappa Phi mandolin club in 1893

OPPOSITE, TOP
Alumni Day on June 9, 1951
OPPOSITE, CENTER
John P. Paynter presents his teacher, mentor, and predecessor Glenn Cliffe Bainum with a citation of merit in February 1965.
OPPOSITE, BOTTOM
A Bainum knot, one of the elaborate sailor's knots Bainum enjoyed tying

Despite the popularity of bands in post–Civil War America, bands at Northwestern got a later start. According to the 1889 *Syllabus,* Conservatory of Music professor C. Montgomery Hutchins led the first band — a cornet band — in 1887. The first marching band began as a 17-member mandolin club organized to support varsity sports. In 1898 it evolved into a student-run brass band with a budget of $100; the group met on the mornings of games to vote on what to play. In 1904 the group gave its first annual concert, and the trustees authorized $700 to pay a director and buy instruments for the 20 members.

While those small, loosely organized student-run bands with no official affiliation arose from time to time, the first University-sanctioned band was established in 1911, thanks to Dr. Milton Cruse of the Dental School. Having organized an orchestra of dental students, he was approached by the University about starting a band to "add a little pep and ginger during the games." Cruse rounded up music and posted flyers on the Evanston campus asking anyone who could play an instrument to report to practice. His efforts yielded about 20 men, who suited up in new University-provided uniforms to perform at the season's first game. This was the band's first appearance on the athletic field; it went on to play at basketball games.

The next year the group reassembled, still short of instruments and music. A 1916 report by the Special Committee on the Band detailed a process for choosing the band director, limited the number of band members to 30, set the pay for members, and listed the practice schedule for both the football season and the rest of the year. But the band didn't come into its own until 1920, when the trustees voted to provide funds to maintain it as a permanent ensemble. (At that time Northwestern was the only Big Ten school without an official band.) The money paid for instruments, accessories, and uniforms. School of Music professor Osborne McConathy was appointed to chair the Band Committee, but students were still largely responsible for running the group.

By the following year McConathy had increased the band's membership to 80, and the *Alumni News* took note of his efforts:

"Northwestern finally has a band. Professor McConathy of the School of Music has developed a bunch that can stir a crowd of semi-petrified fossils. The way it aroused the crowd at the games this fall was good to see and feel. As far as our band is concerned, it has trimmed every team that we have been up against this season."

In the early 1920s a student committee elected by members managed the group and oversaw its musical direction. Under student director Edward Meltzer, appointed in 1922, the band accompanied the football team on out-of-town trips and appeared at Indianapolis Speedway races. During Meltzer's second year as director, the band — now numbering nearly 100 — gave concerts throughout the year in addition to its gridiron performances.

It wasn't until 1926 that, on Lutkin's recommendation, the University band became part of the School of Music. Glenn Cliffe Bainum was hired as Northwestern's first full-time band director.

Previously director of music for the public school system in Grand Rapids, Michigan, Bainum arrived in Evanston to find that only 17 men were enrolled in the band. By the first football game of 1927, that number was up to 80, and the band spelled out "hello" on the field during its first appearance. This was just the beginning of a tradition of entertaining half-time performances under Bainum, an innovator in marching band formations. He served as director of bands until 1953.

During this era the same ensemble served as both a marching and concert band. Concerts were often held in Patten Gymnasium, and members were drawn from both within and outside the School of Music.

Initially the band's programs consisted largely of school songs and crowd-pleasing marches and overtures. Any large-scale composition performed was usually a band arrangement of an orchestral work. By the 1940s original works for band were heard with greater frequency, though old favorites remained popular; as one program stated, "Few band conductors would consider a program complete without at least one or two Sousa marches."

John P. Paynter succeeded Bainum in 1953 and furthered the program begun by his mentor. By then the school had two bands — marching and concert — though their personnel often overlapped. In 1954 Paynter organized the elite Chamber Band, later renamed the Band Ensemble and eventually the Symphonic Wind Ensemble. By 1959 the Varsity Band was established to give music education majors an opportunity to perform on secondary instruments.

Four bands emerged from the department's 1960 reorganization: the Symphonic Wind Ensemble, the Marching Band, the Symphonic Band (formerly the school's original concert band), and the Concert Band, formerly the Varsity Band. Later in the 1960s the department grew to include the Stage Band, eventually renamed the Jazz Ensemble, and other jazz groups. The Contemporary Music Ensemble, begun in the composition department under M. William Karlins in the '60s, became part of the band program in 1983, with Don Owens as director and Karlins as associate conductor.

1950
DRUM MAJOR COAT

1995
DRUM MAJOR COAT

1950
MARCHING BAND HAT

1995
MARCHING BAND HAT

DELORES WHEELER DICKINSON (48) Did you know that Northwestern's Marching Band did not have baton twirlers until during World War II? When I got there in 1944 they decided to try twirlers. I was one of four.

OPPOSITE, TOP
Drum line with the Marching Band in 1972
OPPOSITE, OVERLAY
A pinwheel marching band formation devised by Bainum
OPPOSITE, BOTTOM
Paynter (far left) with the Symphonic Band
ABOVE, TOP
A Marching Band pregame show in 1976
ABOVE, BOTTOM
Paynter in uniform in the late 1970s
FOLLOWING PAGES
The Northwestern University Band performing at the 1951 Commencement

Bands

JULIA CALDWELL MITCHELL (41) I will never forget Kurt Wanieck's words to me at my first piano lesson with him, when I was told to purchase the Schirmer edition of Chopin's Impromptus and bring the one in A-flat to my lesson three days later. I must have had a quizzical look on my face, because he added, "Memorized, of course!" I all but lived in a practice room, but I did it. That was his method, I soon learned: Memorize first, then work out the details.

Students in the School of Music were frequently given complimentary seats to the opera or concerts in Chicago. I recall going with others in formal attire on the el to hear Grace Moore in *La Bohème* and to a performance of *Madama Butterfly,* where we were excited to be sitting in a box next to Walter Damrosch.

On the lighter side, I have always been grateful to have been in college during the big band era. We could dance to Dick Jurgens at the Aragon, Bob Crosby at the Blackhawk, Orrin Tucker's Orchestra at College Night at the Edgewater Beach Hotel, Jimmy Dorsey at the Junior Prom in 1940, Russ Morgan at the Navy Ball, and yes, even Benny Goodman.

Our graduating class of nearly 2,000 was to be the largest in the University's 90-year history, and all was prepared on the lush green of Deering Meadow. One detail was overlooked: rain! So I received my degree in the First Presbyterian Church, where the music, speech, engineering, and journalism schools held their graduation exercises.

This did not dampen my pride in my Northwestern degree. It has meant more to me with each passing year.

ABOVE
Albert Noelte conducting an orchestra
OPPOSITE, TOP
Beattie instructing children in 1933
OPPOSITE, BOTTOM
Bainum with the Marching Band

Faculty

A number of influential teachers joined the School of Music faculty during the Beecher and Beattie eras. Among these were David Van Vactor (G34), a composer and Chicago Symphony Orchestra flutist, and Arcule Guilmette Sheasby, director of the string instruments department, who taught from 1928 to 1954. George McClay graduated from the school in 1928 and immediately joined the faculty, eventually becoming associate dean. Violinist and violist George Dasch was hired the same year, and under his leadership the orchestra grew to more than 100 students, faculty, and local amateurs. Pianist Emily Boettcher taught briefly at Northwestern before embarking on a successful concert career. Max T. Krone led the A Cappella Choir from 1935 to 1939, winning national recognition for the group on its 11-concert East Coast tour and a nationally broadcast performance at Carnegie Hall.

Other longtime faculty members who came to the school during this period were organist Theodore Lams in 1930; clarinetist Domenico de Caprio, flutist Emil Eck, cellist Dudley Powers, and physics of music professor Ruth Fox Wyatt in 1931; low brass instructor Jaroslav Cimera, musicologist Felix Borowski, and future *Instrumentalist* founder and publisher Traughott Rohner in 1933; pianists Kurt Wanieck in 1935, Pauline Manchester Lindsey in 1937, and Harold Van Horne in

No Skirting the Issue

LEONA EDIDIN SWIRSKY (44) In the early 1940s it was unusual for female students to wear slacks. They were rarely worn, especially to school.

To say that Dean Beattie was adamant about women students in the School of Music not dressing this way was putting it mildly. So when, on one below-zero day, a few of us came to school wearing pants under our skirts, Dean Beattie lashed out at us. To him it was unladylike and unacceptable, and he let us know in no uncertain terms. How attire has changed!

My first experience at practice teaching was in the second grade of Noyes School in Evanston in the fall of 1943. Each morning for 20 to 25 minutes there was a music lesson. One morning the door opened and in walked Dean Beattie. I panicked! I had no idea that he would appear. I stood there unable to speak, let alone conduct the class.

Of course, the dean was experienced at no-notice visits. He came to the front of the classroom, talked to the children, had them sing for him, and in his own inimitable way took over. That was great for me because I could not have conducted a class. I was in shock.

I hasten to add that after that, no matter who came into my classroom, either as a student teacher or a classroom teacher, it never fazed me.

1938; future theory chairs Earl Bigelow in 1938 and Frank Cookson in 1939; future dean George Howerton in 1939; pianist Louis Crowder and voice professor Hermanus Baer in 1941; percussionists Edward Metzenger and Clair Omar Musser and voice teacher Mary Ann Kaufman in 1944; orchestra conductor Herman Felber and future theory-composition head and assistant dean P. Arrand Parsons in 1946; and organ chair Barrett Spach and composer Anthony Donato in 1947.

Faculty members hired by Lutkin continued to exercise widespread influence within the school and beyond. Director of bands Glenn Cliffe Bainum, famous for his innovations in marching band formations, led the school's band program to national renown. Eugene Dressler was a much-beloved voice teacher and briefly directed the opera workshop; Lura Bailey taught generations of piano students. Walter Allen Stults continued to bring recognition to Northwestern through Pi Kappa Lambda, of which he was president for many years.

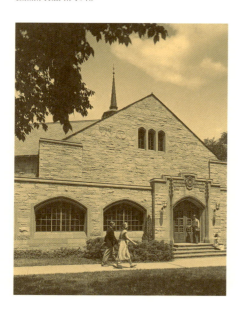

Campus Expansion

"I couldn't believe that the vaunted Northwestern music school was stuck in an old
building such as Willard Hall. I still can't," wrote Loren McDonald (G42), who
added that "Lutkin Hall — new when I was there — somewhat made up for it."
While alumni have fond memories of the present Music Administration Building,
the building's age and space limitations proved restrictive for the school's flourishing ensembles and programs.

Music Hall had barely opened in 1897 before Lutkin began an annual plea
for additional accommodations in his reports to the president. But it wasn't until
April 1930 that a solution seemed imminent. The Presser Foundation of Philadelphia
agreed to donate $250,000 toward a new music building if Northwestern raised a
matching amount. University administrators agreed, and by the end of June the
school was only $25,000 short of its goal. Designs for the city-block-long music com-
plex included a 1,200-seat auditorium dedicated to Peter Christian Lutkin plus a
library, classrooms, private studios, practice rooms, and a smaller auditorium.

The campaign continued into the fall, but with completion of architectural
plans in 1931 the building's estimated cost rose to $600,000. Groundbreaking was
thus postponed until budget adjustments could be made. The final estimate later
that year came in around $630,000; at that time $550,000 had been raised, with an
additional $50,000 pledged by an anonymous source. The Board of Trustees
approved construction of Presser Hall pending verification of the anonymous pledge.
But when President Walter Dill Scott reported in January 1932 that the anonymous
donor could not give the money at that time because of business difficulties, the
Board of Trustees voted to postpone construction of Presser Hall indefinitely.

During the Depression, the original Presser Hall donors canceled their
pledges. Then in the late 1930s discussion resumed about erecting a music building, though considerably downscaled. Administrators chose to build a small auditorium in memory of Peter Christian Lutkin; it was completed in 1941 at a total cost
of $500,000.

Around the time of Lutkin Hall's construction, the music school was granted
almost exclusive use of the newly renovated Willard Hall. In the summer of 1940,
the school moved its offices, library, classrooms, and some studios there from their
previous location at 1822 Sherman.

Lutkin Hall

ABOVE
Lutkin Hall's organ pipes in the late 1940s

RIGHT
Students in the Lutkin Hall lobby

BELOW, TOP
A 1941 sketch of Lutkin Hall

BELOW, BOTTOM
The one that got away: an architectural drawing of Presser Hall, planned in the early 1930s but never built

Lutkin Hall was almost an auditorium in the Presser Hall of Music. The small chapel-like hall next to the Music Administration Building was originally planned as part of a major music complex, but the Depression put those ambitious plans to rest. Lutkin Hall was built as an independent structure in 1941.

University architect James Gamble Rogers, also designer of the Deering Library, designed Lutkin Hall in modern-Gothic style; it was built in Lannon stone with limestone trim. The cornerstone was laid on June 12, 1941, and the 409-seat hall was completed later that year. President Franklyn Bliss Snyder, Dean John W. Beattie, and Chicago Symphony Orchestra conductor Frederick Stock spoke at the dedication service, and the A Cappella Choir, founded by Lutkin in 1906, sang his Choral Blessing.

The Lutkin Hall organ had been built by Cassavant Frères in 1909 as a gift from a group of College of Liberal Arts alumni. Originally housed in Fisk Hall, the instrument was furnished with a new console, electrification, and two new stops (for a total of 33) before its move to the new auditorium.

In its early years, Lutkin Hall served as a recital hall, classroom, chapel, and home to the A Cappella Choir. Today the School of Music continues to use it year-round for classes, recitals, and concerts.

Lutkin Hall

OPPOSITE

Another tradition: a class meeting outside Lutkin Hall on a warm day in 1957

ABOVE

Rev. Ralph G. Dunlop and the Chapel Choir at a Sunday University Chapel Service in Lutkin Hall in 1956

RIGHT

A late-1960s scene in the Lutkin lobby

Years in Harmony

DONALD BRYCE THOMPSON (46) Harmony with Frank Barton Cookson was a major influence in my life. He introduced us to the then-striking dissonances of Vaughan Williams's Fourth Symphony, explored all manner of new and novel processes, and, best of all, convened a small group of interested students in the evening at his home, where we discussed music, brought sketches of compositions, and shared ideas and interests. In short, it was magical and was the prime reason why after completion of my military service I continued studies toward degrees in music composition.

Some of my fondest memories of Northwestern are things that happened at the various dance jobs that Connie Wedberg's big band played. As I remember, we had four saxes, two trumpets, two trombones, Connie on piano, Max on double bass, and a female vocalist. I played lead alto. We worked the North Shore, playing for all manner of dances and once at the Evanston Woman's Club. That latter was a real challenge since our book didn't exactly have that much in the way of discreet salon music, but they liked us anyway.

I have never forgotten trying to find a piano in the Beehive, classes on the beach, wondering why we were permitted to use a building (Willard Hall) that had a condemned top floor, inspiring and dedicated instructors, Cahn Auditorium, Waa-Mu as influenced by the V-12 unit, writing for the *Purple Parrot,* White Castle hamburgers, studying in Scott Hall, and "Northwestern for her pretty girls!" (words from a popular fraternity song of the period).

HAROLD A. HEDLUND (48) *Fresh out of the U.S. Air Force, newly married, and determined to break into show business, I wrote to Dean Beattie to see if I could come to Northwestern. He wrote back to tell me that the school had more students than it could handle and that I should stay in Kansas.*

So in early December of 1946, I caught a train to Chicago to see if I could talk my way into Northwestern. I took my transcript to George McClay, the registrar. He told me that if I received written acceptance, I should show up on January 7, 1947, with my letter in hand to enroll. Of course, I did not receive the letter of admittance. I had about a D-minus average at Emporia State. But on January 7 I went to the School of Music to try to talk my way in.

Wall to wall people. George McClay told me I had to talk to Dean Beattie. I waited and waited and finally got up to his door and was taken inside his office. He looked at the name on the transcript and said, "Hedlund . . . Hedlund . . . I wrote to you. What did I tell you?" I admitted that I was there to try to talk my way in. He took one look at my transcript and blew his stack! If you knew him, you know what I mean.

He told me there was no way I could get into Northwestern. At that point, I put on my best act. I told him not to blame me for something that happened in my teens. I had been through the war and served my country, and I knew exactly what I wanted to do.

He thought for a minute or so, looked up at me, and said, "Get your butt in there and enroll." As I got to his door, he added, "And if you don't have a B average at the end of every quarter, out you go!"

I was in! I made it, but not without help. By the time I graduated, I had two Waa-Mu Shows under my belt, and my harmony professor, Vern Chalkely, had given me a background in harmony that has stayed in my mind and heart all these years. I also remember my wonderful voice teacher and friend, Cliff Toren; one of my best friends ever, Joe Miller; and Winifred Ward in the School of Speech, who opened up the world of poetry for me.

OPPOSITE
Students cross Sheridan Road in the 1940s.

ABOVE
Joe Miller coaches dancers for the 1930 Waa-Mu Show, Whoa There. *It was later produced by Universal Pictures as* Life Begins at College.

60TH. ANNUAL
TOURNAMENT
OF
ROSES

Rose Bowl

Rose Bowl

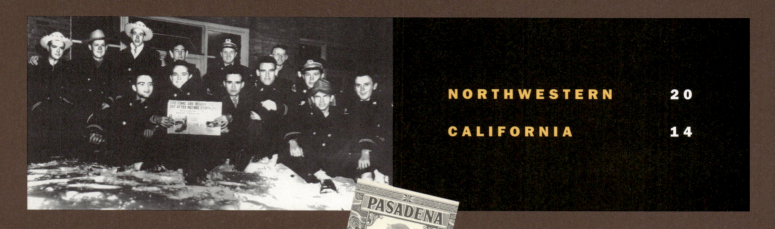

NORTHWESTERN   20

CALIFORNIA   14

By the late 1940s, Glenn Cliffe Bainum had built up a marching band program that ranked with the best in the country. In 1949 it was rewarded with a trip to the Rose Bowl. The 1948 Northwestern football team lost to Notre Dame and Big Ten champion Michigan, but victories over Purdue, Minnesota, Ohio State, Wisconsin, and Illinois gave the Wildcats second place in the Big Ten. Conference rules prohibited Michigan from going to the Rose Bowl two years in a row, so the purple was on its way to Pasadena.

After the Rose Bowl appearance was announced, Marching Band members led students in mass demonstrations and class cutting. The group — at that time still limited to males — traveled to California by train as guests of the Chicago and North Western Railroad. After winning raves for its performance in Pasadena, the band was snowbound for several days in Cheyenne, Wyoming, on the return trip to Evanston.

OPPOSITE
The beginning of the 1949 Rose Bowl Parade

ABOVE
On the train trip back from the Rose Bowl, snow held up the band and the cheerleaders in Cheyenne, Wyoming for several days. (The football team had taken a more southerly route.) Future director of bands John Paynter was one of those stranded, much to the disappointment of his future wife, Marietta. "I was home (in Wisconsin) baking cookies for John. We were supposed to attend a big formal, but I got a telegraph that said, 'Snowbound in Cheyenne. Wish you were here. Sorry I won't be able to make it to the formal.'" The cookies she sent to Evanston were stale by the time he got home. The football team gathered at the Davis Street train station to greet the band's belated arrival.

ABOVE
A parade celebrating the Wildcats' Rose Bowl invitation on November 22, 1948

RIGHT
A pre–Rose Bowl rally

OPPOSITE
The Rose Bowl–bound Marching Band performing on campus

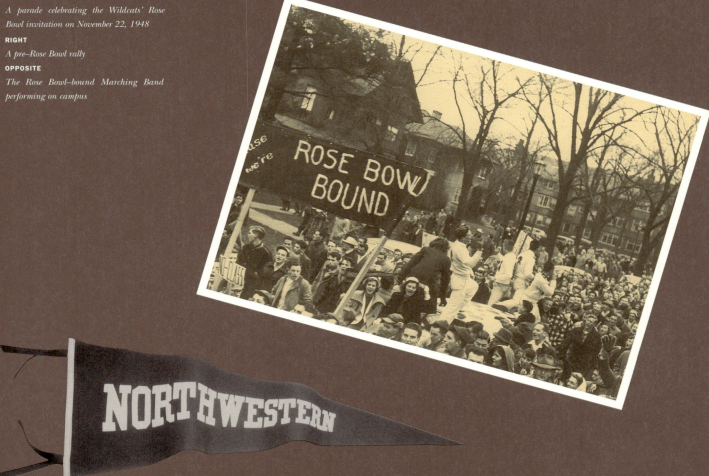

Rose Bowl

Rose Bowl

Bainum Prepares the Band

After rehearsing every other day starting December 1, the Rose Bowl–bound Marching Band met in Evanston on December 27, 1948, and left for Los Angeles by train on December 28, arriving on December 30. Once there the band drilled every possible minute except in the evening. Unable to afford hotel accommodations, band members used their Pullman train berths as hotel rooms. "Get your baths at the town barbershop," advised band director Glenn Cliffe Bainum, "or take a G.I. bath in your helmet."

The following admonitions are excerpted from Bainum's three-page letter of November 29, 1948, to the Marching Band.

"The entire football Marching Band goes. As you can readily understand, we ALL go, or NONE. . . . If I start to run into personnel problems, the deal is off.

"Start the trip wearing full uniform, including overcoat. We play for a big send-off in the station before entraining. . . . Change on the train and hang up uniform to keep it in press during trip. Probably stopovers and parades en route, so uniform must be available and in condition. . . . Before entraining there will be a rigid and thorough inspection of uniform and equipment — with special attention to black shoes and sox, and such details that we sometimes get careless about. Let's see to it that every element of sloppiness and untidiness is eliminated, and SHINE UP YOUR INSTRUMENT until you can't look at it without eyestrain.

"I have assured . . . our sponsors . . . that we will pay strict attention to the important matter of making a good impression at all times, by cleanness and neatness of personal appearance, and by orderliness and dignity of deportment. This is a university band, not a prep-school band.

"The band will be divided and organized into squads or sections, and a section leader appointed in charge of each. Squads will be billeted in adjoining sections of the cars, with their section leader. He isn't there to wipe your noses or button you up, but he sure will catch hell if any noses are unwiped or flaps open in his squad. And you can cuddle on his shoulder if you get homesick."

Bainum listed the itinerary for January 1 as follows:
"Morning: Participate in Parade of Roses (not entire route of march, however).
"Afternoon: Can't think of anything just now, but there's sure to be something going on in a big city like that.
"Evening: Possibly an alumni dinner; otherwise free. Quite probable — a Marche Joyeuse et Triomphal *partout* and some playing on street corners in downtown L.A.

"It is important that we get our show in top shape before exams week, and above all, that we leave nothing to finish up after arriving in L.A. The drills there should be for polishing up the performance, and I want them to be brief and not leave you all tired out for your sightseeing and shindow wopping. (That does it! I'd quetter bit.)"

OPPOSITE
A float in the 1949 Rose Bowl Parade
LEFT
The Northwestern University Marching Band in its first Rose Bowl Parade in 1949

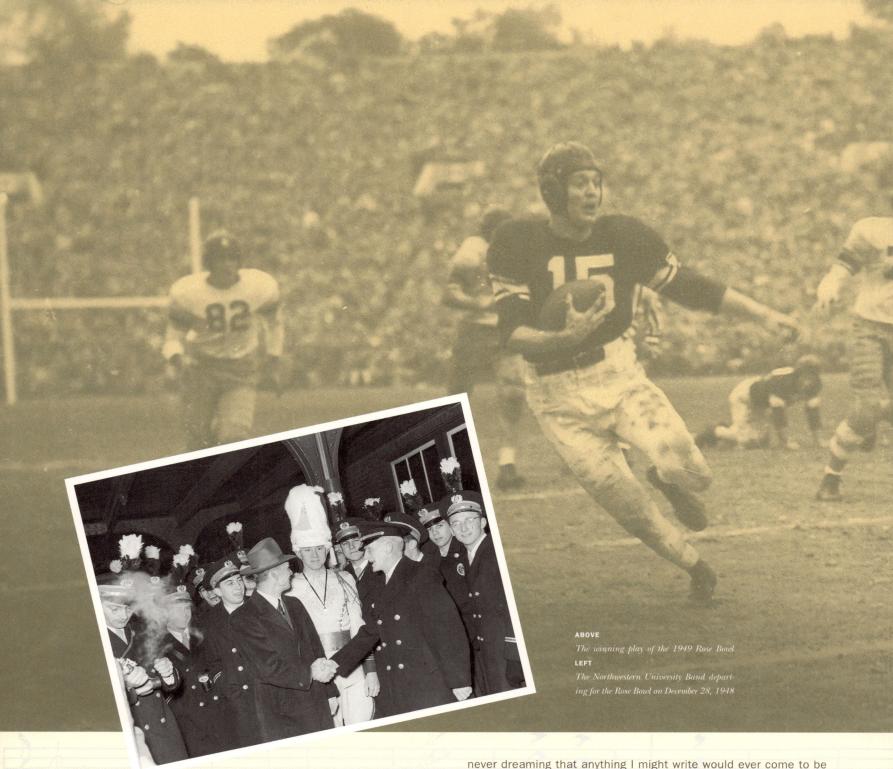

ABOVE
The winning play of the 1949 Rose Bowl
LEFT
The Northwestern University Band departing for the Rose Bowl on December 28, 1948

How I Came to Write "Go-U-Northwestern"

by Theo C. Van Etten (Phar. 13)
From the *Alumni News*, 1929

Of the thousands who have thrilled to the tune of "Go-U-Northwestern," few know the composer or the story of how the song came to be written. Here is the story as told by the composer himself, Theo C. Van Etten . . . as he was when he wrote the famous Northwestern song, both words and music, without assistance 17 years ago.

Back in 1912, at the Northwestern-Indiana game at Bloomington, the Northwestern Band, of which I was a member, marched around the field just before the game, playing the song of another college. This "went against the grain," for I thought Northwestern should have a real song of her own. There were songs, I guess, but none seemed to stand out, none seemed to be recognized as the Northwestern song. So upon returning home — Northwestern having won the game — and still filled with the spirit of the occasion, I decided to write a song,

never dreaming that anything I might write would ever come to be known as "the Northwestern song."

I worked on the song, and worked on it — words and music — and put in a Northwestern "yell" for good measure. Finally completing it, I had it arranged for the band, and took it out to Evanston for rehearsal.

The following day the last game of the year, I believe, was played with Illinois. During the "half" a cheerleader announced that the band would play a new Northwestern song.

The composition was played. It went over with a bang. The crowd wanted to hear it again, and it was repeated. It was then announced that the song would be rehearsed the following Friday in Chapel. There it was that the song was played and sung and taught to the students, from one manuscript I had sent to Evanston.

I lived then as I do yet on the South Side, attending the Pharmacy School at Clark and Lake Streets, and I don't believe that I was in Evanston again after that Illinois game.

The thing that has thrilled me most during the last 17 years has been to attend a football game and hear the crowd sing "Go-U-Northwestern."

You now have the story of how "Go-U-Northwestern" came to be written, a story that I have told to but very few.

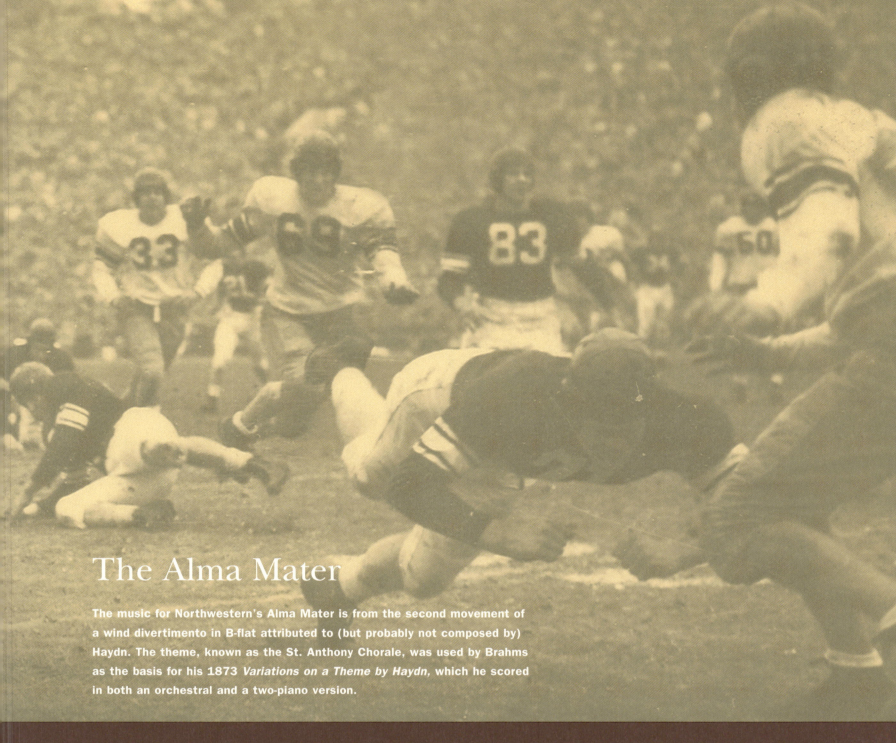

The Alma Mater

The music for Northwestern's Alma Mater is from the second movement of a wind divertimento in B-flat attributed to (but probably not composed by) Haydn. The theme, known as the St. Anthony Chorale, was used by Brahms as the basis for his 1873 *Variations on a Theme by Haydn,* which he scored in both an orchestral and a two-piano version.

The Alma Mater text has evolved considerably over the years. The Latin words were written around 1905 by Northwestern English professor J. Scott Clark, assisted by former Latin department chair Daniel Bonbright and former Latin professor James Hatfield. The words are based on the Northwestern motto, which is drawn from Paul's epistle to the Philippians (chapter 4, verse 8): "Finally, brethren, whatsoever things are true, whatsoever things are honest, whatsoever things are just, whatsoever things are pure, whatsoever things are lovely, whatsoever things are of good report; if there be any virtue, and if there be any praise, think on these things."

Peter Christian Lutkin arranged the St. Anthony Chorale for use as Northwestern's school hymn in 1907, and his version is still performed today. It was first heard at the 1912 Commencement ceremony, with Clark's Latin words; both text and music were printed in the program. Previously Northwestern had used "America" at the close of graduation ceremonies.

Harvey Reeves Calkins, an 1888 graduate, later wrote an English translation that fit the rhythm of the music, and it was printed in the 1922 alumni newsletter. But the Glee Club continued to sing the song in Latin at games through the early 1950s, while "America" replaced the Alma

Mater at Commencement after 1945. Observing that no one could sing along with the Latin version, director of bands John P. Paynter assigned student band manager Thomas Tyra (54), then a junior, to write an English version. He wrote new words rather than a translation of the Latin text. First printed in the 1958 Commencement program, his version is still used today.

Hail to Alma Mater!
 We will sing thy praise forever.
All thy sons and daughters
 Pledge thee victory and honor.
Alma Mater, praise be thine.
 May thy name forever shine.
Hail to Purple! Hail to White!
 Hail to thee, Northwestern.

CHAPTER 4

The Howerton Years

1951–71

CHAPTER 4

The Howerton Years

1951–71

When George Howerton assumed the dean-ship in 1951, the School of Music was growing in both reputation and size. John Beattie had made the school a leader in undergraduate and graduate music educa-tion, and the GI Bill had brought postwar attendance to a new high. Enrollment reached an all-time record of 744 full-time students in 1949–50. Facilities were overcrowded, and despite new faculty hirings, professors' schedules were packed.

The University as a whole had 10,400 students — 8,200 in Evanston and 2,200 in Chicago — enrolled in 13 schools, with land and buildings valued at $31 million. Housing for both faculty and students was difficult to find.

Nationally, a new era was beginning as World War II veterans flocked home to resume civilian life. The country was poised to maintain its seat of world economic power; at that time the United States held 6 percent of the world's population but produced 50 percent of its manufactured goods, 57 percent of its steel, 62 percent of its oil, and more than 80 percent of its automobiles. During the war, America's scientists had developed two momentous technological innovations: the computer and the atomic bomb.

But the end of the war did not necessarily mean peace. The Cold War nurtured suspicions and distrust. The Korean War, the Cuban missile crisis, and the Vietnam War further strained international relations. Socially, a rising suburbia was creating division in America's urban areas. Population began to skyrocket with the postwar baby boom. Race relations simmered, reaching a boiling point during the 1960s. Dress, attitudes, music, and other social norms began to change drastically. Through it all, the School of Music moved with the times.

PREVIOUS PAGES
An Easter service at Alice Millar Chapel
ABOVE LEFT
George Howerton in 1951
LEFT
Visiting Suzuki expert John Kendall (right) conducting a workshop for Suzuki teachers

George Howerton

A choral director on the School of Music faculty since 1939, Howerton came to the deanship determined to make Northwestern's School of Music competitive with Eastman and other top American music schools. Aided by one of the school's largest bequests — the $3.5 million Elsie S. and Louis Eckstein Northwestern University Musical Endowment Fund — the new dean set about achieving his goal as he helped build up the faculty, the opera program, the performance major, and the overall curriculum. Also during Howerton's two-decade tenure as dean, the doctoral program was established, a series of renowned performers visited campus, the Music Library grew, and Alice Millar Chapel was erected.

BELOW
A drawing of the Northwestern campus

A Surprise Bequest

Fundraising wasn't always part of the School of Music dean's job description. In fact, the first major private donation to the school came as a complete surprise.

In 1951 the School of Music received an unexpected bequest of $3.5 million, which greatly aided Dean George Howerton's efforts to expand the school's programs. The gift from the estate of Elsie S. Eckstein, a Chicago arts patron who had died on April 27, 1950, made Northwestern's School of Music one of the country's most generously endowed music schools at the time. The resulting Elsie S. and Louis Eckstein Northwestern University Musical Endowment Fund was set up

to provide scholarships, improve equipment and facilities, expand the library, and build up programs by hiring more faculty members.

Louis Eckstein achieved great success in the pharmaceutical business and then invested much of his fortune in Chicago Loop real estate. A director of the Metropolitan Opera from 1932 until his death in 1935, he had founded the Ravinia Opera in 1911, and the Eckstein family continued to own Ravinia Park until donating the land to the Ravinia Festival in the 1940s. His widow, Elsie Eckstein, was named honorary chair of the festival on its founding in 1936.

As late as 1973 the Eckstein family still ranked among the six largest individual contributors to Northwestern. The fund continues to be a major source of the nearly $1.6 million in scholarships and assistantships awarded annually to graduate students.

In 1973, still honoring the bequest, the Eckstein String Quartet was formed as a faculty quartet in residence. It consisted of three Chicago Symphony Orchestra members — co-concertmaster Samuel Magad, violinist Edgar Muenzer, and violist Robert Swan — and former CSO solo cellist Dudley Powers, chair of the School of Music's string department.

Favorite Hangouts in the 1940s and '50s

Cooley's Cupboard, for its great baked goods, coffee, and chocolate waffles

White Castle on Emerson Street

Hoos Drug Store, which then had a lunch counter

Mrs. McGovern's on Davis

Robin Hood's Barn at 1623 Chicago Avenue

Evanston's four movie theaters: the **Varsity** and **Valencia** downtown, the **Evanston** on Central Street, and the **Coronet** on Chicago Avenue

Irv's and Harriet's (a music and speech hangout) on Clark, where J. K. Sweets is now

West Campus (east Skokie)

South Campus (Howard Street)

ABOVE

Dancing at the Military Ball with the Eddy Howard Band at Sherman House, seen in a photo from the 1954 Syllabus

BELOW

A student teacher leading a class at Evanston's Lincolnwood School in 1952

OPPOSITE

Willard Hall in the summer of 1953

The Postwar Boom

For the school, as for other colleges around the country, the postwar years were a period of readjustment. When peace returned in 1945, the music school continued with business as usual but with almost twice as many students. Classes and offices were housed in the Music Administration Building, Music Hall, Practice Hall (Beehive), and Lutkin Hall. The recently constructed Cahn Auditorium provided space for large concerts. Returning veterans rejuvenated the large ensembles — the A Cappella Choir, band, symphony orchestra, and glee clubs.

Bursting attendance records limited space, and everyone had to make do. Thomas Willis (49, G66), a student at the time who went on to serve in the administration, commented that "the place was really overflowing." Marietta Paynter, wife of director of bands John P. Paynter, recalled that finding housing was next to impossible. The University tried to keep up with the demand for space by setting up Quonset huts, some next to the Music Administration Building, but private housing remained tight. "People would line up at the *Evanston Review* to get the [housing] ads," said Mrs. Paynter, who worked for the paper in the early 1950s. "They would try to bribe people to get the ads before they came out."

As a freshman, organ major Thomas Schaettle (53, G54) was assigned housing in one of the Quonset huts in front of the Music Administration Building. He admitted that "I was lazy a couple of times when I was in that music hut — I rolled out of bed, tossed on clothes, and just made it simultaneously with the arrival of [Professor] Ewald Nolte for freshman theory and sight-singing." With enrollment soaring, he found it difficult to get adequate practice time on the school's organs. "In my first year we were assigned only nine hours of organ practice time a week — a joke for an organ major. I was glad about my third year, when seemingly many GI students had gone and things were less congested." Schaettle began restoring the large organ in the Varsity Theatre to gain access to an instrument and also made a pact with the Lutkin Hall janitor to practice there on Friday nights.

Finding a Home Away from Home

IZOLA E. COLLINS (G53) My story is a little different from most others for two reasons: I was only able to attend Northwestern during the summer sessions, because I financed my education there by teaching in a small town in Texas (Bay City); and I entered Northwestern during the summer of 1949, before the dormitories became integrated. So I did not have the experience of feeling like a genuine "Wildcat."

I arrived at the Registrar's Office, and then the Dean's Office, with a large trunk and a small suitcase filled with my belongings, only to discover that no living accommodations had been made for me. The dean of women gave me a list of homes of African American residents of Evanston with their telephone numbers, and I was on my own. My only alternative was the 'I' House, as they called a small, wooden-frame, two-story house on campus — the International House, for all foreign-born students. It was filled to capacity. I was forced to live this way for the remainder of my Northwestern career until 1953, when dormitories were declared integrated, and I chose to experience my last summer on campus.

One either chooses to live humiliated, as a second-class citizen, or as a person of color who understands the prejudiced mind and rises above it, becoming even stronger because of these experiences. I choose the latter.

Electa Gamron — my unyielding, unpitying piano instructor — brought me from my meager capability up to Northwestern's standard for my piano requirement for a master's degree in music education. I took Glenn Cliffe Bainum's Arranging for Band course with his protégé, John Paynter, who was about to take over his teacher's position the next fall. All Bainum talked about were the glory days of going to the Rose Bowl the previous football season.

MARIETTA PAYNTER (WIDOW OF JOHN P. PAYNTER, DIRECTOR OF BANDS 1953–96) The Northwestern Apartments on Orrington Avenue were built after the war for much-needed faculty housing. None of us had any money; rent was plenty high. But we were all in the same boat. It wasn't just music school people, it was people in every field — engineering, liberal arts, etc. A lot of them were grad students who had fellowships and maybe one child, or were expecting one. By the time

number two came along, you moved out because it wasn't big enough. It was a great place to live. Some people in downtown Evanston would look down their noses — oh, those people in the Northwestern Apartments. It was the low-rent district.

It had a wonderful restaurant on the first floor that was really for guests — great food. It was like the Allen Center today. There was no air conditioning, but other than that, it was great.

Happy Birthday, Northwestern!

In 1951 the entire Northwestern community celebrated the University's 100th anniversary. It was a century earlier — on January 28, 1851 — that a charter was granted establishing "the North Western University." Northwestern's centennial celebration included concerts, theater productions, conferences, convocations, and an art exhibit. At the Centennial Convocation on December 2, 1951, the University gave awards to 100 outstanding individuals from the six states of the original Northwest Territory. Among them were writers Carl Sandburg and Thornton Wilder, architect Frank Lloyd Wright, Senators Paul H. Douglas and Robert A. Taft, and Nobel Prize–winning chemist Harold C. Urey.

THOMAS WILLIS (49, G66) *accompanied for George Howerton as an undergraduate.*

George Howerton was extremely aware of time. We had A Cappella Choir rehearsal for a whole hour, but no more. So you zapped in, started, and when you were finished, you were finished. He had all sorts of aerobic exercises, and he insisted that his TA and I do them. And he always came into choir dressed in a short-sleeved T-shirt with stripes or something on it. He was a big husky guy and worked extremely hard. You knew everybody was going to work. The thing I liked about George, besides the fact that he was exceptionally intelligent, was that he had a large repertory, which helped the students a lot. And given his choice, he was going to proceed as fast as he could. I liked to work at that level and at that pace. He was going to build a repertory quickly. He wanted a choir that could sight-read. As a consequence, we did concerts that had a more interesting combination of repertory than any of the rest.

Degrees

The Howerton years brought much curricular change to the School of Music. In the postwar era the school began offering two new degrees. A PhD in music had already been available through Northwestern's Graduate School, but it was not until 1953 that the School of Music began offering its own doctor of music degree in performance (organ, piano, violin, and voice), composition, and church music. The basic requirements included three years of advanced study (two in residence at Northwestern), a reading knowledge of French and German, recitals, research projects, and 108 hours of credit, all to be completed within seven years.

In 1961 a new master's degree appeared in the course catalog. Though graduate students had previously been able to concentrate in organ or church music, they now could pursue the subject in depth through the master of sacred music degree. Students in the new program still took lessons in either organ or voice and focused on church choir repertoire, liturgics, and choral conducting. But the new degree — offered jointly by the School of Music and Garrett Biblical Institute (renamed Garrett Theological Seminary in 1962) — also encompassed religion and religious education courses. Degree candidates served an internship in church music or religious education. Despite the program's practicality, only one person completed it. John R. Heidinger (G65), who enrolled in 1962, recalled it as "a wonderful experience" but added that perhaps "the problem with the degree and the reason for its ultimate withdrawal seemed to be that applicants came in with a fine music background but without the theological background that would have aided them in courses at Garrett."

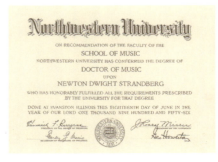

TOP

Piano professor Gui Mombaerts leading a chamber music class in 1952

BOTTOM

The first doctoral diploma bestowed by the School of Music

124

Music Theory and History

While remaining true to founding dean Peter Lutkin's vision of producing well-rounded musicians, the school added courses and faculty members to equip students for new demands of the profession. Scholarship was on the rise, and performance opportunities were multiplying. As the 1964–65 catalog stated, "The School of Music unites the conservatory approach — with its development of fine technique, beautiful tone, and expressive style — and the academic approach," using research as a tool "by which performance becomes a more meaningful experience for both listener and participant."

When Howerton became dean, the school offered bachelor of music and music education and master of music degrees with majors in applied music, theory and composition, music history and literature, church and choral music, and public school music. Students received two applied lessons per week and were required to practice at least three hours per day. If they wanted to perform outside the University, they needed permission from their advisers.

Howerton added faculty and courses to the theory and history departments to strengthen the school's level of music scholarship. Among new theory and composition courses was Band Arranging, taught by Glenn Cliffe Bainum. The mid-1950s brought opera history to the curriculum, and in the 1960s jazz finally appeared on the course roster. New music history courses in the postwar era included The Physical Basis of Music, Comparative Musicology, and Primitive Music, which taught music of the "native peoples from Africa, the Americas, the Pacific, and Asia." Several of these courses were taught by anthropology professor Richard Waterman.

Longtime faculty members who came on board early in the Howerton years included music historian John F. Ohl, who taught many graduate-level history courses during his tenure from 1951 to 1973. "John Ohl was a true character," said Kurt Hansen (G83), now a faculty member. "He was a real scholar who wore railroad engineer hats and whose speaking voice had all the charm of a chain saw. He could not talk quietly. His commentaries at recitals nearly cleared Lutkin Hall."

In the 1960s the school attracted composers Alan Stout and M. William Karlins. To assist with expanding music history course offerings in the 1960s, musicologist William Porter joined the faculty in 1961 and ethnomusicologist Klaus Wachsmann in 1968. Theory professor John Buccheri arrived in 1968.

Alumni of the period have fond memories of their theory teachers. Thomas Willis cited piano and theory professor Earl Bigelow as a special mentor, saying that "he did what would work for me and kept my head on straight." Thomas Schaettle recalled Ewald Nolte as "a sterling and exacting teacher." In Nolte's counterpoint classes, said Schaettle, "We tore music apart and charted it through all major periods and styles. Then we had to compose in precisely that style. *No* compromise, *no* imperfection. An

example: One day I turned in something composed in the style of Hindemith (I thought). Nolte's eagle eye went over it in class; then he said, 'Schaettle, this *isn't* in the style of Hindemith' — *rip* — and into file 13. I had to do it all over." Yet Schaettle also remembered Nolte's personal kindness. "One year Freeman Orr and I decided to stay at school over Thanksgiving recess. That Saturday, Nolte came through the former Music Hall, where most practice organs were. He heard the two of us practicing, opened the doors, and asked why we had not gone home. Then he invited us over to his house for lunch."

VIDA CHENOWITH (51) Frank Cookson taught with an informal ease that belongs to one highly gifted; his aim was always to engage his students. The man possessed not an ounce of vanity.

In his seminars extra chairs were brought into his office, and the sessions were conducted with wit and informality, though they never lacked in dignity or content. In composition class he preferred that students pull their chairs up to the piano as he sight-read their compositions. Everything about his teaching seemed effortless. Seated casually at the piano, with his legs crossed, he delivered whatever was set before him. Whether

dealing with multiple clefs, atonal harmonies, or messy, handwritten scores, he coped with ease. As a mentor he was unhurried and kind.

In demeanor he possessed the rare ability to combine genuine warmth with a prevailing dignity. His image in the halls of the music school is vividly remembered, his jacket unbuttoned and flapping to his quick gait. His trademark in dress was the bow tie, white shirt, horn-rimmed glasses, and tweed sports coat. His slender physique was crowned with a shock of prematurely gray hair. Always unassuming, always receptive; students loved him.

128

ABOVE
William Ballard conducts the Men's Glee Club.
RIGHT
Retiring associate dean George McClay (center) accepts a portrait of himself presented by Dean George Howerton (left).

DON LOOSER (G63) George McClay was responsible for my admission and matriculation. Kind and encouraging, he was the consummate counselor to a stranger in the city. Whether a student needed a place to bank, a place to live, a ticket to the symphony, or a church job, Dean McClay somehow made things all come together. And in spite of the fact that he always seemed in a dither, he always had time for students.

Clifton Burmeister and Hazel Morgan headed my chief area of study. Burmeister always seemed confidently above it all as he escaped for his daily swim at the Y, while Morgan obstinately edited the prose of her graduate students while chain-smoking her way toward her next book. Both knew each of us well, however, and managed to direct our professional paths along higher roads than seemed previously possible. They were futurists before the name was coined.

It was my great fortune to study piano with Louis Crowder. His studio, across the stairs from Mr. McClay's office, would ceremoniously swing open at the end of a lesson to announce his readiness for your time together. It was as if he were making a stage entrance into the hallway each time. He was a physical person, robust and passionate. I can still sense the range of his persona as illustrated by his scarf, fur hat, and dark, Cossack winter overcoat in contrast to the tiny demitasse from which he drank coffee all day long. He was a great friend and guide.

As one whose life has been centered in accompanying, I found enormous gain in the studio of Hermanus Baer. The model of gentility, he viewed the singer and pianist as a musical duo. I can still hear his wonderful laugh. My mental image of his studio is of order, discipline, and enlightened realization.

Grigg Fountain's humor is legendary; his musical performance was astounding; his choral experience was a gold mine; and his friendship was providential. My years under his tutelage were at Lutkin Hall, pre–Millar Chapel. It certainly was a more intimate environment and challenging for worship. I remember when Jack Fischer fainted and fell over on me during the "Lutkin Amen."

ABOVE

A chorus rehearsing in Lutkin Hall

Church and Choral Music

During this time the church and choral music program introduced courses in improvisation and organ literature. Eventually the department grew so large that it divided into two separate entities, with church music adding such courses as Performance of Thorough Bass, Hymnology, Liturgics, and Service Playing and the Chant. In the 1950s students began doing internships as assistants to music directors in local churches. The curriculum also added courses in organ history and design; Schaettle said he knew of only one other school — the University of Michigan — that offered such a course in the 1950s. "Thus 'Cousin' George McClay's class in that subject was truly a shining beacon," he recalled. "McClay's memory of European organs — like his memory of students' class schedules — was fantastic. The class was held in late afternoon, so we weren't bound by the clock. He brought notes along but didn't use them much. Mostly he just lectured 60 miles an hour, those baby blue eyes gazing off out the window. We wrote furiously trying to take it all down, always getting writer's cramp."

Another highlight was Barrett Spach's class in organ literature. Spach sang in professional choirs and was reportedly an exacting perfectionist. Richard Ditewig (G63) reported that "'Papa' Spach, as he was affectionately called, always pulled out his pocket watch before every class and solemnly placed it on a small desk on the Lutkin stage. He carefully timed his lectures, which illumined the organ literature from the Renaissance through late baroque periods." Schaettle recounted that one day he was "called to the organ just to play a hymn. I flubbed — the fireworks began, and Spach went right through the roof of Lutkin Hall several times in an ever-increasing crescendo. We were all quaking in our shoes."

DONALD KINGTON (51) I had more contact with George Howerton than most A Cappella Choir members because he selected me as one of two tenors in the eight-voice choir for Lutkin Hall's Sunday morning service, where he played the organ and directed the choir. We made five dollars each Sunday, and because of this employment I had to sign up for Social Security; before that, I had never had a job that required a number.

The choir would do a new (to us) anthem each Sunday, with the only rehearsal being an hour (or maybe two) before the service. I never let this activity interfere with my Saturday night activities, much to my great discomfort on many Sunday mornings. Somehow I lived through it, and Howerton never called my hand on my obviously poor state.

One of my lingering memories of the music school main building is of the University's art department, then located on the first floor of the west side. I always felt it to be alien territory as I dodged tripods, palettes, and canvases on my way in and out of the building. I had the impression that the art students weren't particularly fond of music students either.

When I returned to Evanston in the fall of 1953, I was impressed with the progress the school had made. The old Victorian relic had been remodeled with new lighting, lowered ceilings, and hi-fi sound equipment (with bass-reflex speakers) in many classrooms. Also, the fledgling opera program was beginning, with acting classes — taught by School of Speech faculty members — offered on our part of the campus. I was in a tiny class with Ardis Krainik, later of Lyric Opera of Chicago fame. Ardis and I were partners in several two-character scenes in that class.

By the 1960s organ was the required instrument for all church music majors; concentration in voice or piano was no longer accepted. Organists could still take religion courses at Garrett. The school's organ inventory included instruments by Holtkamp, Möller, and Schantz; the Möller and Schantz practice organs were housed in Music Hall. Alice Millar Chapel opened in 1963, complete with a 75-stop Aeolian-Skinner organ.

Longtime organ faculty members from the period included Richard Enright (church music and organ department chair from 1962 to 1989), Grigg Fountain, and Karel Paukert. Many followed Lutkin's example in serving as organists in Chicago-area churches, including Enright at the First Presbyterian Churches of Evanston and Lake Forest and Paukert at St. Luke's Episcopal Church in Evanston. Organ and church music professor Thomas Matthews began Evanston's Bach Choir.

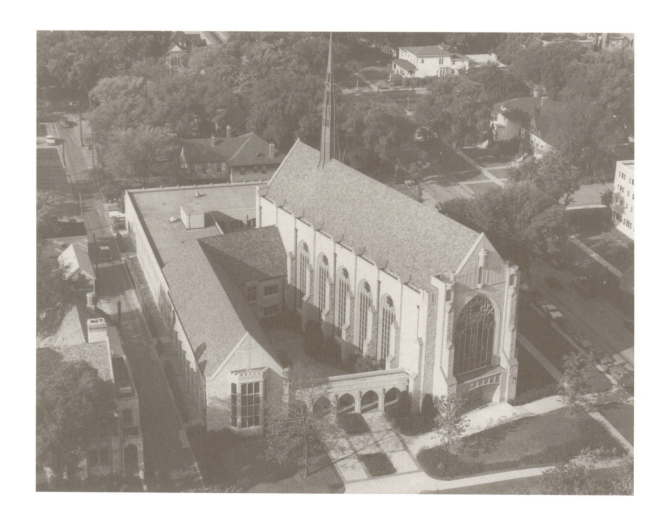

Alice Millar Chapel

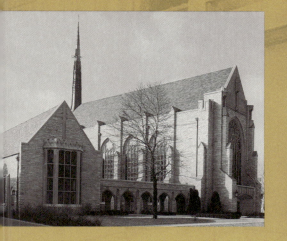

The opening of Alice Millar Chapel gave School of Music students another performance and practice venue. Made possible by a gift from Mr. and Mrs. Foster McGaw, the Alice Millar Chapel and Religious Center was dedicated in the fall of 1963. The main chapel was named for Mr. McGaw's mother, Alice Millar, and the smaller Jeanne Vail Meditation Chapel for a daughter of Mrs. McGaw. The third building in the complex, Parkes Hall, was named for William Parkes, who in 1952 donated the land where the buildings stand. The complex was designed by the architectural firm of Jensen and Halstead.

The 12 stained glass windows in the main chapel depict themes proposed by a faculty committee appointed by Chaplain Ralph Dunlop. Alumni Charles W. Spofford and his wife donated the chapel's 75-stop Aeolian-Skinner organ.

Once the chapel was completed, weekly worship services with the Chapel Choir moved from Lutkin Hall to Millar Chapel. Millar and Vail Chapels continue to host organ recitals, church services, chamber concerts, weddings, and celebrations.

THOMAS SCHAETTLE (53, G54) When Jean Langlais came to play a recital in Lutkin, I sneaked into the hall to see how the blind organist got to know the instrument. His daughter came with him, and his fingers went like tentacles on each stop jamb at the top. His fingers came over each knob as she read its name once, and he had it. She sat down, and he was on his own.

Music Education and Placement

The music education program maintained its reputation as one of the strongest anywhere, and keyboard was the emphasized instrument. Like the theory and history departments, the program introduced more specialized courses. Among these was Instrumental Administration, which focused on methods, contests, and problems of intonation, tone quality, balance, and interpretation. Other new courses dealt with primary school teaching. Whether for elementary or secondary schools, the vocal and instrumental music education programs emphasized student teaching. The curriculum expanded to include courses for doctoral music education students, and the department began to address the subject of college-level teaching. Longtime professors in the program during Howerton's time included Clifton Burmeister, Alice Magnusson Clark, Hazel N. Morgan, Sadie Rafferty, Josephine Wolverton, Earlene Burgett, John Paynter, Traugott Rohner, and Jack Pernecky.

The Placement Bureau, directed by Burmeister, also continued to emphasize music education. Noting that it frequently received "inquiries for well-equipped teachers," the bureau placed an announcement in the catalog stating that "as a rule, either highly gifted and trained specialists are in demand, or candidates who are able to teach two or more branches, such as piano and voice, piano and theory, voice and violin, or music education courses and theory. As a result, the more broadly educated and advanced a student is, the more chance he has of obtaining a good position."

Instrumental Performance and Applied Music

In the early decades of the school, the primary applied areas were piano, organ, and voice. These programs maintained their strength during the Howerton era with such keyboard professors as Gui Mombaerts, Louis Crowder, Pauline Lindsey, Wanda Paul, Barrett Spach, Richard Enright, and Karel Paukert and voice professors Elizabeth Wysor, Norman Gulbrandsen, Gerald Smith, Irene Jordan, E. Clifford Toren, and Walter Carringer.

In the 1950s, with the advent of television, the proliferation of bands, and Howerton's goal of competing with the nation's top music schools, demand grew for instruction in other instruments. This led Northwestern to expand its offerings in instrumental lessons and courses.

At first instrumental instruction was relegated to a sidebar in the catalogs, and students could not always pursue their first choices. Harry E. Holmberg (39, G40) said that "when I enrolled in the fall of 1935, I was told that I could continue to study percussion instruments but that they were not considered a qualified performance area so I would have to choose some 'musical instrument.'" Through

the efforts of faculty member Clair Omar Musser, percussion was one of several areas that began coming into its own at Northwestern during the 1950s, with marimba as a particular specialty.

Howerton hired flutist Emil Eck, French hornist Philip Farkas, oboist Robert Mayer, percussionist Edward Metzenger, violinist Robert Quick, cellist Dudley Powers (previously part-time), bassoonist Wilbur Simpson, trumpeters Vincent Neff and Renold Schilke, tubist Arnold Jacobs, and trombonist Frank Crisafulli, who also taught baritone and euphonium. Initially, those taking lessons in tuba, baritone, euphonium, and saxophone

ABOVE

Gordon Peters (second from right), a teaching associate in percussion, performing with members of the Northwestern University Percussion-Marimba Ensemble

BELOW

Harpsichord professor Dorothy Lane

FOLLOWING PAGES

Piano professor and preparatory department chair Guy Duckworth conducting a workshop on his group piano instruction methods in the late 1960s

were required to study an additional related instrument. Jim Bestman (58, G59) blazed a new trail to become the first student to receive a master's degree in saxophone, and Frederick Hemke joined the faculty to teach the instrument. By 1965 the faculty included two instructors each for tuba, bassoon, French horn, and flute. Trumpeter Vincent Cichowicz, flutist Walfrid Kujala, and oboist Ray Still, all of the CSO, came to teach in the program; they were joined by trumpeter Luther Didrickson and violinist Samuel Thaviu from the Pittsburgh Symphony. Reflecting the new status of applied music at the school, 1960s course catalogs listed each major applied instrument as its own department.

In 1953 Northwestern became one of the first universities in the Midwest to offer a major and a master's program in harpsichord. Harpsichordist Dorothy Lane joined the faculty, and the instrument was given departmental status, on par with piano and organ. In addition to fulfilling the requirements of a typical performance major, harpsichordists were expected to perform in ensembles and learn continuo playing. By the end of the decade the school owned two harpsichords, both constructed by John Challis.

By the 1960s Northwestern had acquired several rare violins and cellos, which were made available to seniors and graduate students for recitals or solo appearances with the Symphony Orchestra or Chamber Orchestra. Accumulated over many years, the collection included a 1724 Stradivarius violin (donated by Mr. and Mrs. C. P. Dubbs); the Ferdinand Gagliano violin and two bows, made by Stradivari (given by Francis Knight); and a violin made by Giovanni Battista Guadagnini (presented by Hans D. Isenberg).

Ensembles

In the 1950s a chamber music program emerged at the school. Its goals were twofold: to give the public a chance to hear chamber music, and to give students the experience of playing in various chamber music ensembles. Faculty member Anthony Donato taught the Chamber Music Ensemble course, leading a group of approximately 35 players in studying and performing classic and modern works for smaller instrumental combinations. The course had been required for piano and string majors but increasingly emphasized wind instruments as well. A group of faculty members formed the Northwestern University Chamber Music Society to perform music for strings in combination with piano, woodwinds, and brass. During 1952–53 the Fine Arts Quartet of Chicago (violinists Leonard Sorkin and Joseph Stepansky, violist Sheppard Lehnhoff, and cellist George Sopkin), known for its frequent concert and radio performances in the area, set up residence at Northwestern. Students in the Chamber Music Ensemble course received at least one hour of coaching each week with a member of the Fine Arts Quartet or Chamber Music Society. By the mid-1950s the school had two chamber music courses and a chamber orchestra, and by 1960 students could perform in vocal chamber and madrigal groups.

After the war the school's bands were better than ever. Many returning veterans had benefited from band experiences abroad, sometimes under Northwestern's Glenn Cliffe Bainum, who had served the country as head of bands in Europe. When Bainum suffered a serious heart attack in September 1950, 22-year-old John P. Paynter, slated to begin graduate work that year, was asked to fill in as act-

ing director of bands and teach the very courses he was to take. In 1953 he became the actual director. At that time the band department consisted of two bands, marching and concert, though the concert band did not meet until winter and spring quarters.

Paynter took the Marching Band to other Big Ten campuses and to Pittsburgh, Cleveland, Toledo, Rockford, and other cities. In 1955 he founded Band Day, inviting high school bands from all over Illinois to participate in a Northwestern football game halftime show. In 1954, following the lead of Eastman's Frederick Fennell, Paynter founded the University's wind ensemble; in 1960 he established an additional concert band, the Symphonic Band. Frederick Miller joined the faculty in

ABOVE
The Fine Arts Quartet rehearsing in 1952
LEFT
The Northwestern Saxophone Quartet in 1963

Same to You

According to John P. Paynter, Glenn Cliffe Bainum was always too busy preparing for concerts to answer his mail. "He ignored his unanswered mail, often dictating replies to an immense stack in one day, or sweeping it all from his desk to the wastebasket while he picked up the phone instead," recalled

Paynter. "His procedure for handling Christmas mail was slightly more original and a great deal more efficient. He would simply turn over the greeting card and write the words 'same to you' before mailing it back to the sender. Somehow, from Glenn Cliffe Bainum, it made a very personal message."

1965 as assistant director of bands. In 1966 the American Bandmasters Association convention was held at Northwestern, with Ferde Grofe, Morton Gould, and Leroy Anderson participating. By the end of the decade, students could perform in jazz ensembles and take a course on writing for stage band.

One new Northwestern ensemble focused on the old, another on the new. The Collegium Musicum, directed by music history and literature department chair John F. Ohl, studied and performed unfamiliar music of all periods, particularly works for small vocal-instrumental combinations. Membership was open to all students. Composition professor M. William Karlins founded the Contemporary Music Ensemble in the 1960s to perform 20th-century music, particularly electronic and avant-garde works and pieces using new notation systems.

Howerton handed over the leadership of the A Cappella Choir to William Ballard in 1954. Ewald Nolte took over the Chapel Choir, which sang for Sunday services at Lutkin Hall; he was succeeded in 1961 by Grigg Fountain, who further developed the group after its 1963 move to the newly opened Alice Millar Chapel.

TOP
Sousaphonists in the Marching Band in 1953

BOTTOM
The Marching Band in action

A Royal Visit

Princess Irene of Greece made a stop at North-western's School of Music during her winter 1967 visit to the Chicago area. The purpose of her trip was to observe American practices in music education. At Northwestern she chatted with students and attended Opera Workshop rehearsals. According to a Northwestern photographer, she laughed out loud during a scene from The Barber of Seville, *which pleased students.*

142

Visitors and Exposure

Under Howerton the Northwestern campus attracted many prominent visitors, including concert violinist Joseph Szigeti, who in 1954–55 gave a series of lecture-demonstrations on violin literature. Soprano Lotte Lehmann graced the school's halls frequently throughout the 1950s and '60s, working individually with students and giving lecture-demonstrations. The piano duo of Vitya Vronsky and Victor Babin gave concerts and worked with students. Organist André Marchal gave master classes in performance and technique, presented recitals, and coached students privately. Other visitors included conductor Robert Shaw, singer Pierre Bernac, pianist and composer Dave Brubeck, sitarist Nikhil Banerjee, tabla player Kanai Dutta, and composers Francis Poulenc, Zoltan Kodaly, Roger Sessions, Vittorio Giannini, Robert Russell Bennett, and Wallingford Riegger.

Composer Kristof Penderecki visited Northwestern during his first trip to the United States in the 1960s. "It was pure chance," said composition professor Alan Stout. "When the Minnesota Orchestra gave the premiere of his *St. Luke's Passion,* he stopped in Chicago for a couple of days, and I met with him. I asked, 'What are you doing tomorrow morning? Would you like to come to Northwestern to talk with students?' He said certainly. He came, talked, and played some of his tapes."

The Opera Workshop drew national and international attention to Northwestern through television broadcasts and visits by prominent composers. Among these was Aaron Copland, who in 1958 came to Evanston to direct his opera *The Tender Land,* give a lecture, and meet with students and faculty.

With the exploding popularity of television in the 1950s, network appearances by student soloists and ensembles brought Northwestern valuable exposure. Visits to Chicago's NBC, ABC, and CBS stations gave students experience in performing for radio and television.

In 1966 Frederick Hemke took the Northwestern Saxophone Quartet on a tour of the Far East. Under the auspices of the Cultural Presentations Program of the U.S. State Department, the three-month tour visited 11 countries.

From Iron Curtain to Stage Curtain

Known for presenting infrequently performed works, the Opera Workshop gave American audiences a rare opportunity to see Dargomyzski's *The Stone Guest* when its production of the opera was telecast on Chicago's WTTW in 1968. First produced in 1872 but never previously translated into English, *The Stone Guest* is considered a key work in the development of Russian opera.

Opera Workshop director Robert Gay obtained a microfilm copy of the Russian score through the efforts of Irwin Weil, then an associate professor in Northwestern's Slavic department. During a trip to the Soviet Union, Weil searched music stores for the opera without success before eventually finding the score in Moscow's Lenin Library through a friend's assistance. The librarian there was very cooperative and charged nothing for making a microfilm copy to mail to the United States. He asked only that he be sent original-language recordings of operas, since foreign recordings were not available in the Soviet Union. Several albums were immediately sent to him.

Xenia Youhn, an assistant professor in the Slavic department, made a literal translation of the libretto, and Gay, with doctoral voice student Ronald Combs (G69), then wrote the sung translation.

Opera Workshop

A Scene from
"RIDERS TO THE SEA"
by Ralph Vaughan Williams
Performed January 22, 1952

ABOVE
An Opera Workshop dressing room

LEFT
A scene from the 1952 production of Ralph Vaughan Williams's Riders to the Sea

BELOW
A scene from the 1958 production of Aaron Copland's The Tender Land

Operatic literature had always been a component of vocal training at the School of Music, but opera study took a major step forward in 1946 with the founding of the Opera Workshop by Ruth Heiser. A noted singing teacher, she began the workshop in collaboration with Northwestern's theater department to give students opportunities to learn and perform standard operatic roles. She was succeeded by voice teacher Eugene Dressler, who directed the program from 1954 to 1957.

The new program coincided with two contemporary movements in opera: expanding audiences by performing standard operas in English translations, and encouraging the writing of new operas in English. Northwestern was among the first universities to respond to these trends, and the Opera Workshop quickly became an integral activity at the school. Annual presentations included scenes and acts from the larger operas as well as complete chamber operas such as Puccini's *Gianni Schicchi,* Menotti's *The Telephone,* and Vaughan Williams's *Riders to the Sea.* In 1954 the program staged Britten's *Prima Donna* and Puccini's *Suor Angelica.* Students also performed short chamber works "al fresco," using only basic scenery and costumes.

The workshop brought in high-profile guest directors, among them Aaron Copland and Lotte Lehmann. In 1957 Boris Goldovsky arrived to stage *The Marriage of Figaro,* bringing Robert Gay as his assistant. In an *Opera News* article, Gay said he had done "most of the legwork" for the production, and he must have done it well; the following year Northwestern hired him as Opera Workshop director. Because there was no opera department, Gay held a dual appointment in the Schools of Music and Speech. A leading baritone with the Philadelphia Opera Company, Goldovsky Opera Theatre, and New England Opera Theater, he had taught and studied at Boston University and the Berkshire Music Center before coming to Northwestern.

Under Gay's leadership the Opera Workshop gained a national reputation. Each year he presented both full-scale and studio productions, drawing on both standard and contemporary repertoire but with particular emphasis on 20th-century chamber operas. In keeping with the current trend, all productions were sung in English; Gay felt that the singing actor's native language was

ABOVE
The pit orchestra for the February 1977 production of Kurt Weill's The Rise and Fall of the City of Mahagonny
LEFT
Composer Aaron Copland coaches students for the 1958 production of his opera The Tender Land

ABOVE
Robert Gay directing Sir Michael Tippett's
The Knot Garden *in 1974*

BELOW
Program for the Opera Workshop's 1966
world premiere of The Number of Fools

the most effective vehicle for bringing greater understanding and appreciation of opera to students and audiences. His program also offered classes in stage technique, opera production, directing, and acting. Students were urged to repeat the courses because new material was studied each year. According to Kurt Hansen (G83), Gay "really knew how to excite students."

Operas were selected six months to a year in advance of production, and auditions (open to all Northwestern students) were held early so that principal performers could learn their roles over the summer. Workshop students who were not in the cast focused on technical work, striving to produce uncomplicated yet exciting sets and costumes while keeping production costs low. The operas were staged in Cahn Auditorium.

During Gay's first year as director, the workshop's production of Bernstein's *Trouble in Tahiti* was broadcast on Chicago educational television station WTTW. Other productions that year were Donizetti's *Don Pasquale* and Handel's *Semele,* the opening event of the School of Music's three-day Handel Commemoration Festival. Subsequent years saw productions of works by Roger Sessions, Francis Poulenc, Leonard Bernstein, Samuel Barber, Georges Bizet, Robert Ward, Ralph Vaughan Williams, and Benjamin Britten. World premieres included *The Number of Fools* by Robert Beadell (49,

G50) and *Walker-Through-Walls* by faculty member Anthony Donato; among the U.S. premieres were Hans Werner Henze's *A Country Doctor,* Luciano Berio's *Passaggio,* and Isang Yun's *Butterfly Widow,* which was presented (with Gyorgy Ligeti's *Requiem)* at Chicago's Civic Opera House for a Music Educators National Conference convention.

In 1974 the workshop presented what was arguably its most highly touted production, the U.S. premiere of Sir Michael Tippett's *The Knot Garden.* The idea originated with music librarian Don Roberts, who had

heard that Tippett was seeking an American production of the work; the event coincided with the Music Library's acquisition of the manuscript of the opera. Music critics, agents, and VIPs from around the country attended the production, which sold out weeks in advance. Tippett spent five days on campus, talking frequently with students and the press. The reviews were very favorable for the production and its student performers, who had spent nine months preparing for their roles. Roberts was concerned about Tippett's reaction to the all-student cast, but less than a minute into the dress rehearsal he was relieved to see the composer wipe a tear off his cheek.

Northwestern's opera program returned to television with an hourlong version of *Falstaff*, broadcast on WTTW in January 1968 and later distributed throughout the United States by the Educational Television Service. The workshop went on to present a series of short operas especially chosen and prepared for the small screen — *Country Doctor*, Mozart's *Impresario*, and Monteverdi's *Battle of Tancredi and Clorinda* — as well as telecasts of Mozart's *Don Giovanni* and Dargomyzski's *The Stone Guest*.

Gay retired in 1983 and was succeeded by Richard Alderson, who expanded the workshop's offerings to two or three main-stage productions each year "to give more people an opportunity to perform and give the orchestras a chance to learn new repertory," he said. Under his direction the Opera Workshop gave the Chicago-area premieres of Barber's *Vanessa* and Mecham's *Tartuffe*, the U.S. premiere of Merikanto's *Juha*, and the world premiere of *The Aspern Papers* by 1954 School of Music graduate Philip Hagemann, all with all-student casts and production crews. For *Vanessa*, librettist Gian-Carlo Menotti gave lectures and seminars and observed rehearsals and performances; Hagemann visited campus for rehearsals and performances of *The Aspern Papers*. For *Juha*, a Finnish opera, the Finnish ambassador to the United States and the consul general from Chicago hosted an opening night reception.

The year Alderson became workshop director, the School of Music received a large endowment from William E. Ragland in honor of his wife, operatic soprano Edith Mason, to fund the opera program. Consequently the workshop was named the Edith Mason and William E. Ragland Opera Theater.

Professor of opera Rhoda Levine directed the program from 1993 to 1996. Michael Ehrman served from 1996 to 2000 as resident opera director and head of the Opera Workshop; a graduate of Northwestern's Department of Theatre, he was a former student of Robert Gay.

Courses offered have included Techniques for the Singing Actor under Gay; Opera Scene Recital, Opera Performance, and Opera Workshop under Alderson; and Opera Laboratory, Acting Techniques for the Opera Singer, Opera Performance, and Techniques for the Singing Actor under Ehrman. In 1998 the school instituted a new master's degree program in opera production.

Music Library

The Music Library, which had begun as a few books in the campus's main library —
the Charles Deering Library — grew substantially during the 1950s. Howerton felt
that a good school needed a good library. The 1945 course catalog had described
a "special" library, housed in a room in the Music Administration Building, with a
collection consisting of valuable reference works and ensemble scores as well as full
orchestra scores and parts for symphonies, oratorios, overtures, and concertos. A
library of anthems, part songs, cantatas, and oratorios was also available for sight-
singing and choral classes. By 1951 holdings had grown to include 4,000 records.
In 1960 the Music Library contained approximately 13,600 books on music, more
than 10,000 scores, and 6,300 records; five years later it had almost 18,000 books,
15,000 scores, and 9,000 recordings. It occupied a whole wing of the building, with
its microfilm reader and some collections stored in a blocked-off stairwell.

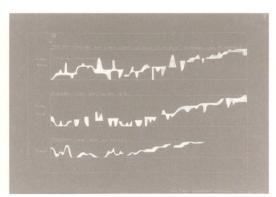

FAR LEFT
Manuscript of John Lennon's "The Word"
LEFT
Score of Gyorgy Ligeti's Volumina

Northwestern's Changing

Describing his first look at what became Northwestern's Evanston campus, University founder Orrington Lunt wrote, "Going to the lakeshore and looking north, I saw the high, sandy bluff. . . . It continued in my dreams of that night and I could not rid myself of the fairy visions constantly presenting themselves in fanciful beauties — of the gentle waving lake — its pebbly shore."

From the beginning, the Lake Michigan shoreline has been a defining aspect of the University's Evanston campus. Over the decades the beach has hosted concerts, games, and countless parties.

Shoreline

OPPOSITE AND ABOVE

Left to right: an evening gathering in the 1940s; sunbathing on the pier in 1943; the pier in 1955; lifeguards on duty at the beach

BELOW

The campus shoreline in the 1950s, before construction of the lakefill

In 1962 the University began the lakefill project that would change the shoreline and eventually lead to construction of two new School of Music buildings. But filling in the lake to expand Northwestern's Evanston campus was scarcely a new idea.

After Northwestern founder John Evans and his fellow trustees purchased some 700 acres of land for a campus 12 miles north of Chicago, they had no money left for building on it. So they divided the land into city lots, named the community Evanston, and proceeded to sell and rent the lots for material, money, and labor to start their first building.

As early as 1893 Northwestern officials began to realize that selling the land surrounding the campus might have left the University with inadequate room to grow. So a drastic plan was conceived: to fill in a segment of Lake Michigan. The general plan resembled the one undertaken seven decades later, complete with a lagoon (with a course laid out for crew races). Other features included an 800-seat grandstand for football and sheds to protect horses from bitter winds during football games. The idea, though, was soon abandoned in favor of acquiring still-available, fairly inexpensive land around the campus.

A similar plan emerged in the early 1930s but was shelved because of the Depression. In 1959, however, after two difficult land acquisitions for dormitories, administrators began seriously researching the possibility of extending the school into the lake.

After some study they discovered that pushing the campus eastward would cost about a third as much as attempting to spread westward.

The expansion plan was publicly announced on October 14, 1960. After approvals from the Evanston City Council, the Cook County board, the Illinois legislature and governor, and the U.S. Army Corps of Engineers, construction began on July 11, 1962.

Almost immediately an unexpected controversy arose. Mary-Missouri Company, which Northwestern had contracted to fill the lake, had contracted with the Bethlehem Steel Company to obtain sand from a harbor that the steel company was dredging in Porter County, Indiana. Letters and calls flooded President J. Roscoe Miller's office, accusing Northwestern of conspiring with both companies to ruin the Indiana sand dunes. Northwestern had known nothing of Mary-Missouri's contract with Bethlehem Steel but had no choice but to honor its agreement. Attempts to assuage the enraged public were initially unsuccessful, but a *Chicago Sun-Times* editorial on April 24, 1963, pointed out that "directing abuse at Northwestern University . . . is like abusing a home builder because his contractor obtained his lumber from a forest preserve."

The new campus was dedicated as the J. Roscoe Miller Campus on October 7, 1964. It became the site of the new library, Norris University Center, the Frances Searle Building, and two new music buildings — Pick-Staiger Concert Hall and Regenstein Hall of Music.

OPPOSITE, TOP
The first bargeload of stone for the lakefill arrives on July 11, 1962.

OPPOSITE, BOTTOM
Reviewing plans for the lakefill

ABOVE AND RIGHT
Lakefill construction in progress

BELOW
The lakefill dedication on October 7, 1964, with John P. Paynter leading the band

ABOVE
The South Quadrangles in spring 1969.
Many undergraduate social activities in the
1960s revolved around the University's 27
fraternities and 18 sororities.
BELOW
Studying at the beach
OPPOSITE, BACKGROUND
Aerial view of the Marching Band in Dyche
Stadium
OPPOSITE, INSET
Cheerleaders at the 1962 Homecoming game

Student Life

The postwar influx of veterans brought a new seriousness and maturity to student life. As Thomas Willis recalled, 18-year-old freshmen were scarce. Many students were newlyweds starting a new life after surviving the war. But students in the late 1940s and '50s still knew how to have fun. In addition to enjoying fraternity and sorority parties, they took advantage of symphony concerts, operas, plays, and other arts events in Chicago. Evanston's movie theaters were a popular draw. Going to Chicago on the el was relatively cheap and safe, so much of the city was accessible from Evanston.

University activities drew crowds as well. According to Elva Waldon Nibbelink (50, G51), during home football games the only students on the south campus were she and a few like-minded music students who remained to practice. The annual Waa-Mu Show attracted much energy and attention, and student contributors included Sheldon Harnick (49), later the lyricist of *Fiddler on the Roof*. Bands and orchestras each presented one concert per quarter. In the summer, concerts were held on Deering Meadow every Wednesday night, a tradition initiated by director of bands Glenn Cliffe Bainum.

NORTHWESTERN vs IOWA

LEFT
A break between classes
OPPOSITE, TOP
An Opera Workshop dressing room in 1977
OPPOSITE, BOTTOM
A bonfire on the beach for the 1967 Homecoming

RICHARD DITEWIG (G63) Friday evenings found me, along with several other students from the University and Seabury-Western Theological Seminary, in choir rehearsal at St. Luke's Episcopal Church at Hinman and Lee Streets. How I loved the quiet walk on Hinman Avenue from Sheridan Road down to Lee Street and back. I had no car at the time, nor did very many other students. Evanston was one of the most beautiful, orderly cities I had ever seen.

If liquor was a lure, Evanston was not the place to find it. Students interested in drinking went to bars or clubs on the south side of Howard Street (the Chicago-Evanston border), which also offered pizza places, jazz, and a bowling alley. For students with a car, "west campus" — otherwise known as Skokie — was the place to go.

Going out was no problem for men; reportedly they could stay out all night if they wished. For women, however, it was another story. They were subject to curfews, plus regulations governing when men could be entertained in dorm or sorority-house lounges and just how long a female could "say goodnight" to her date in the lobby. Women had to sign in and out and when going to downtown Chicago were required to leave a phone number where they could be reached. Female students who overstepped their boundaries were "campused" for specified periods. Such rules remained in place for women through the late 1960s, although rumor has it that some found ways to work around them; friends knew how to sign in their roommates.

In the '60s student life began to change with the times. Students still dressed for dinner, and women still signed in and out of dorms, but unrest was brewing. Students for a Democratic Society was founded in Michigan in 1962, and chapters of this activist group spread quickly to college campuses throughout the country. In 1965, after several antiwar demonstrations elsewhere in the United States, a chapter of SDS was organized at Northwestern. The first massive antiwar event on campus was a Vietnam teach-in in 1967. More demonstrations, sit-ins, and discord followed in 1968. The unrest peaked with a student strike in response to the U.S. invasion of Cambodia and the killing of four Kent State University students in May 1970.

In Search of Hair

Before the late-1960s obsession with abundant hair, Northwestern's School of Music needed lengthy locks — seven feet long, to be exact. The 1963 Opera Workshop planned to present Debussy's *Pelléas et Melisande*, and Melisande required golden tresses to let loose at the tower window as Pelléas stood below.

Sarajane Levy, costume designer for the production, checked every wigmaker in Chicago — more than 30 in all — and found nothing. Evidently horsehair weighed too much and human hair cost too much.

Even a Melisande wig stored at the Metropolitan Opera cost too much, although it hadn't been used in 50 years. Then a New York wigmaker suggested something called Dynel, and Levy tracked down its source — Union Carbide's synthetic textile division. Later described by Opera Workshop director Robert Gay as "another big business that loved operas," Union Carbide provided the needed material. Levy was thrilled with Dynel, noting that "you can curl it, braid it, wash it, and it's nonflammable."

Protests

While student unrest at Northwestern did not lead to tragedy as it did at Kent State University, students were much involved with the issues of the time. Organized student activism began with the founding of the Student Association for Liberal Action in 1961 and the Northwestern Students for Civil Rights in 1964.

Northwestern's first student protests of the 1960s were "gentle Thursdays" or love demonstrations, held next to military drill fields by the University's chapter of Students for a Democratic Society (SDS). Members also passed out leaflets and participated in parades, teach-ins, antiwar rallies, and sit-ins.

Like activists on other campuses, SDS members protested University collaboration with war-aiding corporations. In 1967–68 students objected to on-campus recruiting by Dow Chemical, a manufacturer of napalm for the war in Vietnam. In May 1968, a month after the assassination of Martin Luther King Jr., 100 black students locked themselves inside the Bursar's Office at 619 Clark, demanding changes in Northwestern's "racist structure." A rally advocated an African American studies program and increases in recruitment, financial assistance, and housing units for African American students. This led to increased recruitment of African American students and faculty, the establishment of the Department of African American Studies, and changes in the Student Affairs department.

With the U.S. invasion of Cambodia and the killing of four students at Kent State University on May 4, 1970, Northwestern — like many other schools across the country — went on strike. SDS members and followers barricaded Sheridan Road near Scott Hall. More than 5,000 people assembled at Deering Meadow and demanded that the administration agree to five conditions, including removal of all credit from the ROTC program, publication of the University's stock portfolio, sell-off of any stocks invested in war-related agencies, and stripping campus security guards of firearms. The strike drew overwhelming campuswide support.

"Kent State hit Northwestern so hard," recalled Thomas Willis, then of the musicology faculty. "My kids decided they would boycott classes. They asked me if I would come and just simply talk with them. Then we had the whole discussion about grades. If they boycotted classes, how were they going to get grades? If they didn't

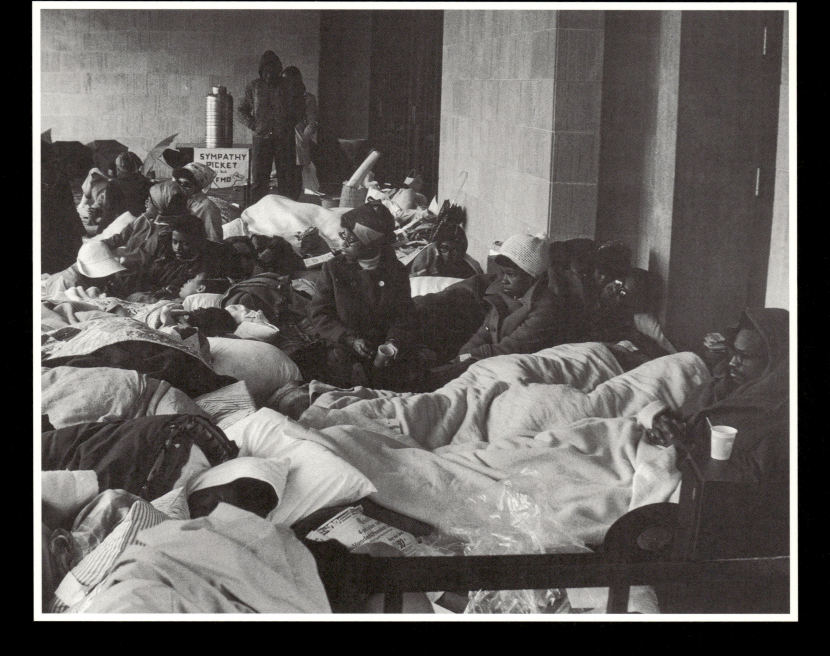

get grades, how were they going to graduate? If they didn't want to graduate, why did they want to stay in class?"

Frances Larimer, another faculty member at the time, recalled that "the Music Administration Building was locked during the strike, but a few dedicated music students climbed the fire escapes, then surrounding the second through fourth floors, to go in through unlocked windows to practice. This was a turbulent time for students and faculty alike."

Kurt Hansen, then a student and now a member of the voice faculty, described the period as "a very exciting and scary time, a time of real questioning. But it wasn't all serious." Jim Moore, then head of the music school's admissions office, insisted that the situation was "relatively tame at Northwestern. The University was closed for three days and students threw a barricade across Sheridan Road, but it was really nothing. I happened to go to Ohio State for a conference during that time and was actually afraid to be outside on the campus."

On May 12, after two previous attempts, students and faculty voted to establish the "New University." This allowed students to participate in the antiwar effort while still going to class, where they received a "T" as a grade. Some of the courses offered in the New University were Noon Peace Workshop, Peace Commencement, The War at a Feeling Level, Draft Resistance Seminar, Examinations of Myths and Symbols of Peace and War, and Northwestern Whither Goest Thou? The strike ended on May 13, and the following fall the New University curriculum was dropped for lack of funding.

"I taught a course called the Aesthetics of Rock, which was more a student-run seminar," said Willis. "They had to bring their own tapes and discuss them. I said if they wanted to smoke, we'd have to find someplace off campus. So they did."

Clifton Burmeister, then chair of the music education department, thought the University handled the situation well. He also believed that the crisis proved educational for administrators. "It made us take a hard look at why these students could raise support," he said. "It gave us a whole new look at ourselves."

CHAPTER 5

The Miller Years

1971–89

CHAPTER 5

The Miller Years

1971–89

In 1970 the School of Music catalog declared that "music in America is coming of age." Fifty years earlier the country could boast fewer than 100 symphony orchestras, with the four major ones made up almost entirely of European-trained musicians. According to the American Symphony Orchestra League, by the early 1970s U.S. orchestras numbered more than 1,200. Many of these new orchestras were in cities with populations of less than 50,000; most of their members and many of their conductors were products of American music schools. The number of bands had multiplied as well, ranging from community bands to school bands at all levels, from grade school to college. Many universities and high schools had started wind ensembles. Marching bands now presented elaborate halftime shows, stepping ever higher and faster. In the choral arena, school and church ensembles were joined by professional touring groups such as Fred Waring's Pennsylvanians and the Robert Shaw Chorale. Opera companies around the country were growing as well, performing for larger audiences created in part by television exposure, improved fundraising, and community outreach.

When Thomas W. Miller arrived as dean of the School of Music in 1971, he immediately set out to ensure that the school was staying abreast of the times in doing the best possible job of educating students. Under his leadership the school undertook a sweeping revision of the curriculum and launched a more intensive recruiting program.

During the 1970s and '80s the school hosted an increasing number of renowned guest artists and major conferences. Composer-conductors John Cage

Do you remember . . . Marshall Field's, Elizabeth Parsons at your recital, Swenson's ice cream parlor? Buffalo Joe's, the Keg, the first NUSO performance under Victor Yampolsky? The Hut, bitterly cold Chicago winters, mud piles on the unfinished landfill, camping out to claim the Rock?

and Pierre Boulez visited several times; Dmitri Shostakovich and Witold Lutoslawski received honorary doctorates. Northwestern offered summer programs in cooperation with the Ravinia Festival. With the diversification of music careers came more degrees and certificate programs. Technology came to the school as a sideline in the 1970s and quickly grew. The Music Library moved from the Music Administration Building to 1810 Hinman Avenue to the Deering Library, each time growing in stature and size. Electronic and computer music studios were built, and the Music Administration Building was renovated. Music Hall became home to the Department of Human Resources as Pick-Staiger Concert Hall and Regenstein Hall of Music opened their doors.

Thomas Miller

While new to Northwestern in 1971, Thomas Miller was well acquainted with administration. Before coming to Evanston, he was dean of the School of Music at East Carolina University in Greenville, North Carolina, where he had served as trumpet instructor, varsity band director, and first assistant dean. He had also held visiting professorships at Boston University, the University of Northern Colorado, and the University of Hawaii.

Once at Northwestern, Miller seemed eager to test fresh ideas and spread new perspectives. An article by Peter Gorner in the *Chicago Tribune* of February 14, 1971, quoted Miller as saying, "Hey now, promise you won't portray me as some wild-eyed radical Mister Music about to descend upon Northwestern and throw traditions up for grabs."

Miller believed that Northwestern existed to develop excellence and therefore reward its students and faculty for that excellence. Gorner's story went on to quote Miller's plans for the school: "Insofar as education is concerned, as a private school freed from the strictures of state agencies, perhaps we ought to be in the forefront of innovations I see being made across the country. . . . The faculty and I must sit down together and discuss projects we all have in mind. Only when they feel a rapport and strong support from the administration will they feel free and willing to experiment. I think freedom is vital, the freedom to try new ideas."

PREVIOUS PAGES
The lobby of Pick-Staiger Concert Hall

OPPOSITE, TOP
Dean Thomas Miller in 1982

OPPOSITE, BOTTOM
A typical scene on the Music Administration Building's first floor in 1979

ABOVE
Students hang out at Michellini's Restaurant, a popular 1976–77 destination. Located at the northeast corner of Foster and Maple, it burned down in December 1978.

BELOW
The Lunchbag Opera, a performance piece by guest composer-lecturer Robert Moran, on November 18, 1977

Favorite Hangouts

In the early 1970s Evanston offered little in the way of fast food, according to Richard Alderson, who joined the Northwestern voice faculty in 1970. Until Burger King opened across from the Music Administration Building in 1976, the closest fast food outlets were in Skokie. Alderson listed hangouts of the time as Yesterdays, the Sherman Snack Shop, and Norris University Center.

The Grill at Scott Hall, Deering Library, and the beach were also popular hangouts, recalled Kurt Hansen (G83). "There were two distinct groups of partiers: You either partied in Skokie or on Howard Street," he added. "Evanston was dry. Getting a 'usable' ID was always a problem if you weren't 21. There were two movie theaters in downtown Evanston, the Varsity and the Coronet. People also went down to the Loop, and Rush Street and Old Town were popular."

Other favorite hangouts included the Hut, the Huddle, Hoos Drug Store, and, by the 1980s, J. K. Sweets, Swenson's Ice Cream Parlor, and Buffalo Joe's.

And exercise that freedom they did, spurred by Miller's aspirations to foster excellence and to revitalize Northwestern's School of Music as a leader in higher music education. Acting on his own convictions as well as the urgings of several faculty members, Miller challenged the entire staff to review the school's course offerings, which in 1972 led to the implementation of a new curriculum. He also strengthened the school's performance departments by naming Chicago Symphony Orchestra members to the faculty and bringing in renowned guest artists for lectures, demonstrations, and master classes. He sought to further develop what he perceived as the underdeveloped departments of music history and theory as well as the Music Library and the orchestra.

During Miller's tenure the school hosted an increasing number of international and national conventions. He started *Fanfare* magazine, forged a partnership with the Ravinia Festival, oversaw

ABOVE
A 1973 Summer Band concert on the steps
of the Rebecca Crown Center
BELOW
Practicing in a piano lab in 1979
OPPOSITE
A 1980 Chamber Orchestra rehearsal

the construction of Regenstein Hall and Pick-Staiger Concert Hall, and helped inaugurate new undergraduate and graduate degree programs. The Northwestern University Music Society was established to support the school's concert activities. The faculty expanded and music technology grew.

A New Curriculum

The curriculum ranked highest on Miller's agenda. "The first of my challenges to the faculty," he said at the opening faculty meeting in September 1971, "is to devise a progressive, innovative curriculum at the graduate and undergraduate levels." He appointed a faculty committee — chaired by associate dean Frederick Miller — to formulate a plan, and within a year the school implemented one of the most extensive curricular revisions in its history.

The call for change was not entirely unexpected. According to theory professor John Buccheri, who joined the faculty in 1967, the times were rife not only with political turbulence but also with challenges to all phases of musical training and teacher preparation. In an article describing the 1972 revision, he wrote that "there were strong convictions emerging: Every musician should experience the perspective that composition brings to the understanding of music; the elementary school teacher should share some of the same experiences with the Machaut Mass as the musicologist training as a medievalist; the performer needs some of the same analytical tools as the budding music theorist. All young musicians . . . must engage the music of the day to integrate contemporary practice and thought with the past. And finally, the Earth as a global village made imperative the study of 'musics' of other cultures."

Animal Farm

Voice professor Richard Alderson recalled that in the 1960s and early '70s there was a cote of racing pigeons in the Music Administration Building's attic. "A man visited them regularly to feed and race them from a dormer window," said Alderson.

Dorothy Wyandt, director of placement services and a member of the school's staff since 1975, remembered animals at the other end of the building. "There is a sub-basement in the Music Administration Building, and a full-sized person cannot fit down there," she recalled. "Years ago, cats and raccoons lived there. A woman fed them, and they just kept reproducing. It always smelled. Cats would sit around the edges of the window-sills and just look in and talk to us. But finally when the dean's secretary got fleas and the music theory secretary was wearing a flea collar around her ankle, the school got serious and boarded up the holes. The cats were taken out. After they were gone, there were mice. And for years, people who had to go down there would find animal skeletons."

Questioning the ways music schools taught, educators of the time asked themselves: Are the fundamentals of music no more than the rudiments of notation? Does learning the history of music consist of accumulating and memorizing names, dates, and themes in Western art music? Does instruction in basic music theory simply mean instruction in harmony and voice leading? Miller offered another reason for change by describing his own experience: "I have studied four different major systems or theories of understanding music. Every school I went to had a different system. It was maddening. There were so many competing systems for understanding music, there wasn't an overall cohesiveness nationally."

Seeking answers to these questions were the musicians involved in Comprehensive Musicianship, an approach to music education that originated with the Ford Foundation–funded Contemporary Music Project (CMP). At first the project emphasized putting young composers in public schools to write music for school groups, but when the composers got there, the schools' teachers had difficulty with the new music. As Miller explained, "They didn't know how to rehearse it, they didn't know how to explain it, and they very often couldn't even satisfactorily analyze it for themselves."

Northwestern was involved with CMP from the beginning. George Howerton, Miller's predecessor as dean and a member of the project's policy committee, organized a seminar on comprehensive musicianship in 1965 that established the CMP agenda. Participating in the seminar were such prominent historians and theorists as Alan Forte, Leonard Ratner, and Arthur Bergner. A year later, schools throughout the country ran experimental courses under the auspices of the Institutes for Music in Contemporary Education (IMCE). Arrand Parsons, then chair of the theory and composition department, played a vital role in Northwestern's 1965 seminar and served as Midwestern regional director of IMCE. As program head, Alan Stout designed and taught an experimental class at Northwestern from 1967 to 1969, assisted by Joseph Schwantner (G66, G68), then a doctoral student.

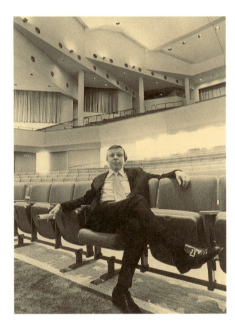

OPPOSITE
Deering Library on a rainy day in 1977
ABOVE
Dean Miller takes a seat in Pick-Staiger Concert Hall in 1976, shortly after its completion.
BELOW
Professor Arrand Parsons (center) and his wife chat with a colleague.

The committee that Miller appointed to evaluate the curriculum came up with recommendations reflecting the comprehensive musicianship philosophy outlined by the Contemporary Music Project. According to committee member Frances Larimer, CMP suggested that music course work and applied studies for each undergraduate year be given a mutual context and connected to a historical period so students could better understand the holistic relationship among their various music studies. "The position we took at Northwestern," said Miller, "was that it doesn't matter whether you're going to be a performer, a music educator, or any other kind of musician. There was a base of musical understanding and knowledge that every musician should possess." So the school identified courses that were basic to every musician's education and made them required courses.

A committee chaired by Richard Alderson (a member of Frederick Miller's curriculum committee) developed the new sequence. Formally approved in the spring of 1972 and first implemented with the freshman class the following fall, the new curriculum divided course offerings into two years of basic studies and two years of specialized study. Previously Northwestern had offered the traditional two years of music theory (writing and analysis), two years of ear training separate from theory, and one year of music history in the sophomore year. The new system offered students a two-year Musicianship sequence that met daily for an hour; history professors lectured two days a week, while theory professors took the other three. Basic studies also included applied lessons, ensemble study, and basic skills (sight-singing, ear training, and keyboard).

The six quarters of Musicianship covered the traditional periods of Western music history — medieval and Renaissance, baroque, classical, romantic, and 20th century — as well as world music, including music of Africa, South America, India, Indonesia, the Middle East, Europe, North America, and Asia. Ethnomusicologist Klaus Wachsmann, who held joint appointments in the School of Music and the linguistics department, helped create the world music course, given in the first quarter of the freshman year to provide the broadest possible context for music studied in later quarters. This in itself was revolutionary; a relatively new discipline in the 1970s, ethnomusicology was then almost exclusively a graduate-level field. When ethnomusicology scholar and performer Paul Berliner joined the faculty in 1977, the world music class began delving more deeply into Indian classical music, African music (especially the mbira music of Zimbabwe), and jazz.

Theory courses mirrored the music of the era being studied. The first quarter focused on involving students in a variety of musical activities. Recalls Buccheri, "While we were still using pieces of music to teach the facts and principles of music theory, we were, much sooner, able to use music theory to teach pieces of music. Students were motivated by the realization that music theory offered them tools (aural and visual, analytical and conceptual) to learn any piece of music, in much the same way that fingering, pedaling, and interpretive skills were necessary to learn a Beethoven piano sonata."

After this sweeping curricular change, smaller adjustments followed. When he arrived at Northwestern, Miller considered band, performance, music education, and organ and church music the school's strongest programs. So while striving to keep these top-notch, he sought to develop the school's other programs.

To bolster the music history department, which then included composer Alan Stout, Miller brought in medieval music scholar Theodore Karp. William Porter covered the baroque era, and Judith Schwartz was later hired to teach classical music. Romantic music specialist Richard Green joined the staff in 1977. Music history was dropped as an undergraduate major but was reinstated in the fall of 1992.

Bennett Reimer joined the music education faculty in 1978, and in 1984 he founded the Center for the Study of Education and the Musical Experience. Work by faculty members and graduate students in the center resulted in numerous publications.

Orchestras

Early Northwestern "orchestras" scarcely fit the term as we now understand it; in the late 1800s the word denoted both large and small instrumental ensembles. An 1879 issue of *Tripod* mentions an orchestra consisting of fewer than a dozen players, and a six-member chamber ensemble listed in the 1886 *Syllabus* was called the "Beta Theta Pi Orchestra." The Conservatory of Music offered a program of study for "performers on orchestral instruments," and a course catalog stated that students received experience in ensemble playing. But a true Northwestern orchestra was still a decade away.

In 1895 Peter Lutkin and a small group of violinists organized the first University orchestra, which gave its first concert on May 2, 1896. The group performed shorter works and movements from symphonies. Almost immediately the orchestra opened its membership to amateur players from the Evanston area, beginning a long-standing relationship between the orchestra and the community. With the ensemble's membership and performance opportunities increasing, the 1897 course catalog listed Symphony Orchestra as a class that met once a week to rehearse.

In 1912 violin faculty member Harold E. Knapp took charge of the orchestra with the objective of performing the "great" composers and enhancing music appreciation. The group's first concert that fall was actually an open rehearsal in Fisk Hall that included works by Haydn, Beethoven, Saint-Saëns, Mendelssohn, and Strauss. During the year the group not only performed the usual concerts for the school and community but also played for nonmusic majors in Lutkin's new course Appreciation for Music. In the spring the orchestra provided musical entertainment and accompaniment for the University-wide graduation for the first time and dedicated a

concert to concertos performed by graduating seniors.

Finding the necessary instrumentation presented challenges. "In the early endeavors . . . wind parts were supplied on the piano and organ, but each year some forward step has been taken in the addition of instruments," stated a 1913 news article. By that year, "with the help of gifts, the school owned a more varied collection of instruments."

When Knapp assumed the orchestra's leadership, only a third of the players were students; but by 1915, when the membership rose to 80 musicians, students occupied all but six chairs. The orchestra expanded to new performance venues that year, giving three concerts rather than two — at New Trier High School and Patten Gymnasium in addition to Fisk Hall. Concerts were well received, and capacity audiences became the norm. Before concerts, Lutkin visited local schools to teach children about instruments of the "modern" orchestra and to preview major themes from the pieces on the programs.

The orchestra, however, was suffering growing pains. Earlier concerts had been presented in the stageless Fisk Hall, but with the group's expanded size the hall lost half its seats. Difficult setup procedures and conflicts with athletic events made Patten Gymnasium an inconvenient option, so the orchestra was without a permanent home. Financial difficulties mounted as the orchestra continued to pay professional players while charging no admission for community concerts. In 1920 Chancellor L. Jenks, president of the Evanston Township High School Board, pleaded with townspeople for monetary support. "During the war we were told to give until it hurt," he wrote in the *Evanston News Index*. "Our orchestra has done even more than that. It has given to Evanston until it is bankrupt. It must

have financial aid or perish." The community came through in 1923 by merging the orchestra with the Evanston Musical Club to form the "Evanston Symphony Orchestra under the Auspices of Northwestern University."

Knapp retired in 1928 and was succeeded by George Dasch. By 1936 the orchestra — renamed the Northwestern University Symphony Orchestra — drew a third of its ranks from students outside the School of Music and maintained a waiting list for new members. With World War II, however, orchestra concerts ceased because so many students enlisted in the armed forces. Herman Felber resumed rehearsals in 1946, conducting the group's first postwar concert on February 14.

Felber sparked controversy by programming new works by Howard Hanson, Albert Noelte, Arne Oldberg, and other contemporary composers. After Felber stepped down (he continued to teach orchestral and conducting techniques), Thor Johnson accepted the school's new full-time position as director of orchestras in 1957. He introduced the orchestra to such new American composers as Richard Cummings, Wallace Berry, Benjamin Lees, Arthur Foote, and Wallingford Riegger and began to involve the ensemble in the Opera Workshop. Johnson's farewell to the school was a performance of Mahler's Symphony no. 5 at the Commencement convocation.

Hugo Vianello expanded the 80-member orchestra's instrumentation to include Pyrex bowls and auto brake drums in performances of new music. Bernard Rubenstein introduced still more contemporary music. Fearing that concert halls were in danger of becoming cemeteries where only old music was played, he insisted in a 1970 *Milwaukee Journal* article that audiences must be educated in new music before they can render judgment on it.

Succeeding Rubenstein was Robert Marcellus, originally brought to Northwestern as a member of the clarinet faculty in 1974. Formerly principal clarinetist of the Cleveland Orchestra under George Szell, he drew on his experience as conductor of the Cleveland Civic Orchestra, Peninsula Music Festival, Interlochen Arts Academy Orchestra, and Scotia Chamber Players.

Victor Yampolsky assumed the podium as director of orchestras in 1984. Trained as a violinist under the rigorous Soviet system,

he won a scholarship to Tanglewood after auditioning for Leonard Bernstein in Rome; this led to a position in the Boston Symphony Orchestra. In 1993 he was named the first chairholder of the Carol F. and Arthur L. Rice Jr. University Professorship in Music Performance. In addition to conducting NUSO, Yampolsky is music director of the Omaha Symphony and the Peninsula Music Festival.

The University Chamber Orchestra was founded by Knapp in 1915 as a 35-member junior orchestra composed entirely of music students. It began to flourish in its own right under Anthony Donato, who joined the School of Music faculty in 1947.

A third Northwestern orchestra was established in 1992. Conducted by Stephen Alltop (G96), the 90-member Philharmonia provides orchestral playing opportunities for students from outside the School of Music.

OPPOSITE
Hugo Vianello and NUSO recording Verdi's
Falstaff
ABOVE
The 1952 WNUR Orchestra
RIGHT
Taping for the Music Cable Series in 1980

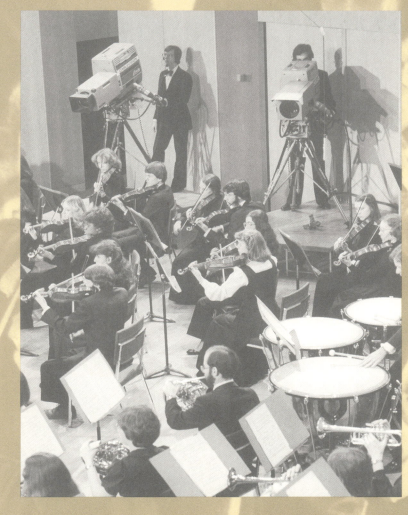

Lutkin Hall Named a Landmark Site

In 1976, the year of the U.S. bicentennial, Lutkin Hall was recognized as a landmark site of American music. At the Commencement convocation in June of that year, music education professor Clifton Burmeister — representing the Illinois Music Educators Association — presented a plaque commemorating Peter Christian Lutkin to Dean Thomas Miller. The award was conferred by the Exxon Corporation in conjunction with a joint Bicentennial Commission composed of members of the National Music Council and the Music Educators National Conference. The plaque hangs in Lutkin Hall.

ABOVE

Cliff Colnot assisting members of the Jazz Ensemble in 1975–76

Degree Programs

The number of degrees offered by the School of Music rose dramatically during this era. In 1970 the school had four degree programs — bachelor of music, bachelor of music education, master of music, and doctor of music — with majors in the various instruments, voice, organ and church music, and composition. PhDs in music theory, music history, and composition required course work in the School of Music but were conferred by the Graduate School.

In 1975 the bachelor of arts in music degree made its debut. Described as a "nonprofessional degree program," it allowed students to explore more courses in liberal arts by requiring fewer music credits. According to the course catalog, it was "intended for the student who has a strong ability in music but who is not necessarily interested in a musical vocation." As of June 2000, 140 students had received the BA in music degree.

As graduate enrollment increased during the 1970s and '80s, graduate degree programs expanded as well. In 1975 Paynter developed a master's degree in conducting under the umbrella of the new conducting and performing organizations program; the program eventually added a doctorate in conducting. Piano professor Frances Larimer developed a doctoral program in piano performance and pedagogy in 1977; students divided their performance studies among solo work, accompanying, and chamber music.

In 1978 a grant from the Fund for the Improvement of Postsecondary Education (FIPSE) helped revolutionize Northwestern's graduate programs. Under associate dean Jack Pernecky's supervision, the school developed competency tests in music history and theory for incoming students; those who passed could take more advanced courses as part of their degree programs. Other results of the FIPSE grant included graduate internships and assistantships and courses in string pedagogy and chamber music.

The school began offering a certificate in performance in 1984. As Miller explained, "For the performer, the master's degree is usually the terminal degree," but many performance majors wishing to continue their applied study "would enter the doctoral program with absolutely no intention of ever finishing." He said that the certificate program offered graduates one year of study before they "hit the audition circuit."

Joint degree programs with the College of Arts and Sciences (as the College of Liberal Arts had been renamed in 1963) and the Technological Institute were devised in the early 1980s. The joint bachelor of music and bachelor of arts program with the College of Arts and Sciences, established in 1980, enabled a student to obtain two degrees in five years. The five-year bachelor of music and bachelor of science in electrical engineering or computer science was established in 1982. As of June 2000, 130 students had completed the BM-BA program with the Judd A. and Marjorie Weinberg College of Arts and Sciences, and 13 had completed the BM-BS program with the Robert R. McCormick School of Engineering and Applied Science.

BELOW
Piano professor Frances Larimer supervising students in the first piano lab in 1971

RIGHT
Student cellist Stefan Kartman (87) in a master class with Harvey Shapiro

Pulitzer Prize Winners

In the 1970s two School of Music alumni joined Howard Hanson (16) and Sheldon Harnick (49) as winners of the coveted Pulitzer Prize. (Hanson won the music Pulitzer in 1944 for his Symphony no. 4, Harnick the drama Pulitzer in 1960 for the musical *Fiorello.)*

Composer Ned Rorem (44) was awarded the 1976 Pulitzer Prize in music for *Air Music,* subtitled "Ten Variations for Orchestra." Described as a "showpiece for a virtuoso orchestra," the work was premiered on December 5, 1975, by the Cincinnati Symphony Orchestra, which had commissioned it as part of its U.S. bicentennial observance.

Joseph Schwantner (G66, G68) captured a Pulitzer in 1979 for *Afternoons of Infinity,* commissioned by the American Composers Orchestra and premiered on January 29, 1979, in New York City's Alice Tully Hall.

Performance

Miller's first course of action in the performance area was to elevate the status of 11 Chicago Symphony Orchestra members who were teaching lessons at Northwestern. Accorded full faculty status with benefits were string bassist Warren Benfield, hornist Frank Brouk, trumpeter Vincent Cichowicz, trombonist Frank Crisafulli, harpist Edward Druzinsky, flutist Richard Graef, tubist Arnold Jacobs, flutist Walfrid Kujala, violinist Edgar Muenzer, bassoonist Wilbur Simpson, oboist Ray Still, and clarinetist Jerome Stowell. Announcing the promotions on January 11, 1972, Miller noted that the professorships were "awarded not only in recognition of the musicians' individual achievements, but also in appreciation of their collective efforts as members of the Chicago Symphony Orchestra."

The voice department instituted studio classes for all performance majors. Based on the master class approach, these group sessions complemented the students' private lessons.

Another change came with auditions for ensembles. "Auditioning internally for orchestra and band changed around 1974," said flute professor Walfrid Kujala,

who had begun teaching at Northwestern in 1962. "Until that time, the procedure each year was that when students entered the school during New Student Week, they would audition individually for the orchestra director and band director. That audition was your only audition for the year. If you did poorly, it set you back. We began to feel that this was not a fair way to handle student placements." With the approval of director of bands John Paynter and director of orchestras Bernard Rubenstein, the performance faculty instituted pooled auditions, with students playing from behind a screen. "It's not a perfect system," said Kujala, "but we do it often enough — three times a year — so that if you have a bad time, there's always a chance to recoup and do better. It also gives students a better idea of how professional auditions might be run and allows them to cover a large chunk of repertoire."

Available majors expanded as well with the addition of guitar and lute in 1980. Margaret Mistak was the school's first guitar teacher; guitarist Anne Waller joined the faculty in 1987, and eventually guitar courses were added and a guitar ensemble was formed, reflecting increasing American interest in the instrument.

More aggressive national recruitment also began during the Miller era. Under James Moore, then director of field services, the school's admissions, placement, and alumni services became more assertive and service oriented. Moore traveled to as many as 30 cities each year for auditions to recruit top students, and he developed the School of Music's recruitment brochure into a more appealing, detailed viewbook. He also used new technology by writing computer programs to assist in the admissions and placement operations. Placement director Dorothy Wyandt observed that "Jim was an innovator not only in developing press materials but in being aware of the competition's focus and what the admission requirements were. He knew how to reach out to more and more people."

Ensembles

During the 1972–73 academic year University Chorus was created to perform large-scale choral works. Made up of singers from the Men's and Women's Glee Clubs, other students, faculty, staff, and members of the community, the chorus still thrives today. Margaret Hillis, director of the Chicago Symphony Chorus, headed the school's choral program until 1977, when she was succeeded by Robert A. Harris. The University Chorale and the University Singers were established in 1978.

The Chapel Choir continued under its director, Grigg Fountain. Students loved singing in the choir; one trombonist enjoyed it so much that he took Chapel Choir as his major ensemble instead of band. Kurt Hansen (G83), Fountain's assistant for many years, recalled that "there was never a week where we sat in the same place: We had sectionals, quartets, ensembles, circles, squares, facing the front, facing the back. He wanted everyone involved to know that they were important to the sound."

The orchestra program was expanding at this time as well. Robert Marcellus, principal clarinetist of the Cleveland Orchestra under George Szell, led the Symphony Orchestra until 1984, when Soviet-trained conductor Victor Yampolsky came to Northwestern as director of orchestras. Under Yampolsky's leadership the orchestra's reputation grew dramatically.

The schools' bands thrived under director of bands John Paynter, a consummate musician and teacher who challenged students to strive for excellence. High School Band Day remained a popular draw in the Chicago area. The Marching Band continued to flourish, with players drawn from throughout the University; women were admitted to regular membership for the first time (other than during wartime) in 1972. That same year, Paynter invited Marching Band alumni back

for Homecoming, launching a growing annual tradition. Nicknamed the NUMBalums (Northwestern University Marching Band alumni), the group draws former Marching Band members from all over the country to attend reunion events and to march in the football pregame and halftime shows and the Homecoming parade.

The Symphonic Wind Ensemble continued to grow in reputation, and in 1983 the group toured the East Coast, making stops in Washington, New York, and Boston. By that time its repertoire included both new and standard works, and concerts were often long. Paynter's widow, Marietta,

ABOVE
Director of bands John P. Paynter letting loose at the 1974 Indiana game
RIGHT
NUMBalums marching around the track at the football stadium
BELOW
The 1975 Homecoming game

reported his having suggested that his epitaph should read, "Here lies John Paynter. His concerts were long, but damn, they were good."

Under the auspices of the band program, the Jazz Workshop entered the school's offerings in the early 1970s with various directors, including Cliff Colnot and Bill Hochkeppel. In 1979 Don Owens took over the jazz program when he was named assistant director of bands and associate professor of conducting (he also directed the Marching Band and the Symphonic Band). With only an ad hoc major in jazz then available to interested students, Owens set out to develop a more extensive program. In 1981 he started Northwestern's Jazz Festival, an annual event that brings in a guest artist to perform with the school's jazz ensembles and give master classes and clinics.

Around 1983, with three big bands (Jazz Ensemble, Jazz Band, and Jazz Lab Band) and no combos at the school, Owens decided to experiment with reorganizing the jazz ensembles. He created two jazz "pools," one for Jazz Ensemble and one for Jazz Lab Band; each pool comprised enough players to create a big band plus several drummers, bassists, pianists, and extra horns for combos. Subsequently the jazz program continued with those two bands and a few combos. Among Owens's other innovations was what he termed a "jazz studies module for nonjazz players, so interested kids could get coaching in the phrasing of jazz, especially kids who played 'wrong' instruments — flute only, double reeds, clarinetists who didn't double on saxophone, and strings." Owens continued to add jazz to the curriculum through a concentration in jazz studies by introducing such courses as Advanced Jazz Writing and by bringing in guest instructors to help teach courses and seminars in jazz theory and jazz improvisation. The Vocal Jazz Ensemble was formed in 1985. In 1988 the Jazz Ensemble toured the East Coast, performing in New York, Philadelphia, Baltimore, and Washington.

TERESA COWIN MUIR (79) The wind faculty used to listen to juries on the top floor of Music Hall (now Human Resources), and during hot weather it was unbelievable in there. Another flute player and I sent ice cream in right before we were scheduled to perform. They of course were not bribed that easily — but I remember being a lot less nervous for that jury!

TOP LEFT
The Symphonic Wind Ensemble performing in 1980

TOP RIGHT
The Symphonic Wind Ensemble rehearses under Paynter in 1979. Remember that eagle eye and ear?

BOTTOM
The Jazz Ensemble in rehearsal

FOLLOWING PAGES
Paynter rehearses the Symphonic Band in Music Hall in the 1970s

Music Technology

The technological revolution at the School of Music began in the 1970s with the arrival of a Moog synthesizer. From there, as in society worldwide, technology moved into all aspects of the school. First came the Electronic Music Studio, then the Computer Music Studio, and still later the Mac Lab.

At the beginning of the 1970s theory professors John Buccheri and Donald Fisher visited the Moog Music Company in Trumansburg, New York, and with their recommendation, theory and composition department chair Lynden DeYoung arranged the purchase of a Moog I synthesizer, two two-channel reel-to-reel tape decks, a stereo power amplifier, and two column speakers. In the fall of 1971 Stephen Syverud, a composer specializing in electronic media, joined the faculty and immediately used this equipment to put together the Electronic Music Studio and create courses with two interested students. He viewed the equipment not as an end in itself but as a means of fostering creativity and individual expression.

The new studio gave its debut concert that April in Lutkin Hall, the first in an ongoing quarterly series. In addition to presenting students' taped pieces, the event featured lights by Gary Gand — who later founded his own company, Gand Music

ABOVE

Early work in the Electronic Music Studio

and Sound. That spring Syverud taught the school's first electronic music course, and technology soon spread from the composition program into other areas. In 1975 the Contemporary Music Ensemble explored the avant-garde in a concert using synthesizers, generators, and tape. The Electronic Music Studio continued to expand, often with the help of both music and non-music students. Eventually three courses were developed, an introductory course and two advanced courses; later, independent-study curricular options were offered. The studio grew to include samplers, synthesizers, computers, tape recorders, a production mixer, modifying devices, a four-channel monitor system, MIDI equipment, and patch panels for interconnecting the equipment.

Computer music specialists Gary Kendall and Peter Gena joined the faculty in 1976 and immediately set up the Computer Music Studio — originally at the Frances Searle Building and since 1992 at the Music Administration Building. To equip the studio, the school purchased its first computer, a DEC PDP 11/34, in 1977; it was intended for projects in "sound synthesis and psycho-acoustic research." Kendall and Gena fashioned a sound synthesis program, a music composition language, and a music score outputting program. The curriculum added courses in computers and music.

In 1978 Northwestern furthered its commitment to music technology by hosting the International Computer Music Conference. More than 400 musicians and audio-technology engineers from the United States and Europe attended concerts, lectures, seminars, demonstrations, and displays exploring the many areas of computer applications in music. Discussion topics included software synthesis techniques, digital recording, signal processing and music input languages, interactive music systems, and compositional processes.

Increased enrollment and the need for more equipment led to the opening of a second, smaller electronic music studio in 1980. Syverud described it as a less threatening environment for introducing students to electronic music's basic concepts. Housed on the fourth floor of the Music Administration Building, both studios were designed for individual use and equipped with top-notch sound-producing, modifying, and recording equipment. The smaller studio included an ARP 2600 synthesizer, two two-channel tape decks, one four-channel tape deck, one cassette tape deck, one eight-channel mixer, additional modifying equipment, a four-channel monitor system, and a patch panel.

3-D Sound in *Twilight Zone*

The Computer Music Studio and Gary Kendall had their time in the limelight in 1985 when executive producer Philip DeGuere hired Kendall and then–doctoral student William Martens to create 3-D sound for a remake of Rod Serling's television show *The Twilight Zone*. To help sound "come alive," Kendall and Martens had developed a spatial reverberator (a patented process) that allowed a recorded sound to be processed by a computer using software they had written. Similar to "surround sound," the process allowed for the proper static positioning so that the auditory image corresponded with the visual image on the screen. DeGuere liked the idea and hired them to enhance the CBS show's opening theme, composed and performed by the Grateful Dead.

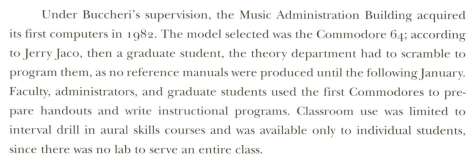

ABOVE
Gary Kendall (right) working on sound for
The Twilight Zone *in 1985*

Under Buccheri's supervision, the Music Administration Building acquired its first computers in 1982. The model selected was the Commodore 64; according to Jerry Jaco, then a graduate student, the theory department had to scramble to program them, as no reference manuals were produced until the following January. Faculty, administrators, and graduate students used the first Commodores to prepare handouts and write instructional programs. Classroom use was limited to interval drill in aural skills courses and was available only to individual students, since there was no lab to serve an entire class.

Also in 1982 the Computer Music Studio, still headed by Gary Kendall, received a $1.6 million grant from the System Development Foundation to support his research on computer-localized sound. The result, a 3-D sound project patented in 1984, was used on the revival of the *Twilight Zone* television series in 1985.

By 1985 students could pursue a master of science program in "computer studies in music" and could take advantage of greatly expanded course offerings in music technology. In 1987 computers made their way into regular classrooms; freshmen entering that fall took classes in the new Macintosh lab in Andersen Hall. Kendall and Gary Greenberg taught theory on Macintoshes. Students in Greenberg's class did most of their homework on the computer, using a music notation program and compositional tools in LOGO, a programming language used by educators to teach structural concepts and programming skills. Kendall used computer simulations to map music and illustrate structural connections. Many students who emerged from music technology courses in these formative years found jobs writing jingles, creating video games, and working in recording studios.

Administratively, computers began infiltrating the school's offices. Kay Price, now department assistant in the undergraduate studies office, credited James Moore as "one of the key people in technology advancement in the School of Music. He was always first in line for us to get the most efficient computer equipment and classes to learn everything about it. We were one of the first offices to have the CPT word processor, which was a predecessor to computers, and it certainly helped with the repetitious jobs of printing personalized letters." Added Dorothy Wyandt, "Jim was on the absolute edge in writing computer programs. The programs he wrote for admissions were great, and he wrote a marvelous program for me for placement."

All Downhill

When the Music Library was located in the Music Administration Building, the weight of the collections caused the floors to slant downward. Reportedly a pencil could roll from one side of the hall to the other without being pushed.

Music Library

Miller saw the Music Library as an integral partner with the school. To foster a closer relationship between the two, he invited the library staff to faculty meetings. As he put it, "How else can a library respond to the needs of the student body unless they know what the music school is up to?"

Don Roberts came to Northwestern as head music librarian in January 1969, and in the coming years the library began its evolution from a collection on the second floor and stairwells of the Music Administration Building to a full-fledged library on the second floor of the Charles Deering Library. When he arrived, Roberts found that "the University librarian wanted the Music Library to develop a collection of distinction in an area of music that was appropriate for the School of Music." Because no other music library was focusing on the 20th century, and because the accessibility of contemporary materials made acquiring them a cost-efficient strategy, Roberts began to emphasize the acquisition of 20th-century music, particularly printed music, recordings, and autograph materials. A major milestone was reached in December 1969 when arrangements were completed for Chicago Symphony Orchestra music director Fritz Reiner's scores, books, recordings, and other memorabilia to come to Northwestern upon Carlotta Reiner's death. In 1971 the acquisition of a portion of the Moldenhauer Archive furthered the library's goal of creating a strong collection of primary sources.

In 1972 lack of space and a fast-growing collection forced the library to move from the third floor of the Music Administration Building to its own facility at 1810 Hinman Avenue, previously home of the transportation center library and today occupied by the anthropology department. This was considered a permanent move, but when the second level of Deering Library became available, Roberts and his colleagues decided that the Deering space would better serve the Music Library's needs. The move was completed in September 1976, and Deering has been the Music Library's home ever since.

At the time of the move to 1810 Hinman, the library contained 55,000 books, printed music, and recordings. "From 1971 on, we have basically been receiving every piece of newly published, serious contemporary music issued in the world, and we are the only academic music library to accomplish this goal," said Roberts. With the 1976 move to Deering came a new music listening center incorporating state-of-the-art technology; the equipment has since been upgraded several times.

Library Collection on Tour

It was probably the longest tour in Northwestern's history. After appearing from November 7, 1979, to January 25, 1980, at New York's Drawing Center Art Gallery as part of an exhibit tracing the development of notation, Northwestern's *Notations* collection traveled the United States for two years under the auspices of the Smithsonian Institution Traveling Exhibition Service. The tour concluded at Northwestern's Mary and Leigh Block Gallery. The exhibit

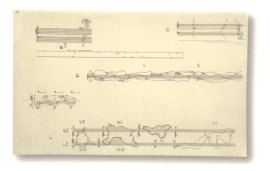

was sponsored by the National Endowment for the Arts and the Council on the Arts.

Northwestern's *Notations* collection contains more than 400 manuscripts by 278 composers. Compiled by composer John Cage for the benefit of the Foundation for Contemporary Performance Arts, it includes completed works as well as preliminary sketches. Several were written specifically for Cage and the *Notations* collection.

TOP
John Cage with students during a 1976 campus visit

BOTTOM
A Cage manuscript from the Notations *collection*

Shostakovich Visit

*Given the Cold War attitudes prevailing in 1973,
a visit from Soviet composer Dmitri Shostakovich
surprised even Dean Thomas Miller. "The restriction
[for traveling] was somehow lifted," he
said. "I was told to give an invitation, but no one thought it would
be accepted. The University invited him, and when I heard he
was coming, I couldn't believe it.
The Soviets did send people along to
watch him, though."*

*"Shostakovich was an incredibly courageous per-
son," recalled composition professor Alan Stout. "He
spoke only Russian; fortunately, Irwin Weil (professor of Slavic languages) was around. Shostakovich
was extremely frail. You could tell that he had had a
stroke. He would hold a pen in his right hand and
guide his right hand with his left hand. He was
almost blind and died the year after [he visited]."*

*"His wife did speak English except when the
Soviets were around," added Miller. "She was in my
home having a conversation in English with my wife
when the secretary from the Soviet embassy
walked into the room. She immediately
stopped speaking English and
switched to Russian. This happened
several times during the weekend,
so we knew she understood what was
being said. In addition to the embassy
secretary, the entourage included an official
translator from the Soviet Union and two lower-level
people I was told were KGB officials. The Northwestern administration was worried that there would
be some kind of demonstration embarrassing to the
University, so the whole weekend Shostakovich was
here, people from public safety and security were in
my front and back yards and at the Orrington Hotel.
It was an interesting experience but very stressful.
But Shostakovich was a very good guest, very genial."*

Northwestern and the Greater Musical Community

Visits by renowned guest artists and conventions of professional societies became increasingly frequent on campus, coinciding with the Music Library's acquisitions of notable manuscripts and with Miller's desire that the school be a leader on the national music scene.

Among the Moldenhauer Archive manuscripts was Martinu's Violin Concerto no. 1, long considered unfinished and lost. Its arrival at Northwestern resulted in the work's world premiere with soloist Josef Suk and the Chicago Symphony Orchestra, conducted by Sir Georg Solti. After Northwestern acquired the manuscript of Sir Michael Tippett's *The Knot Garden*, the composer came to campus twice, once to attend the opera's American premiere in a production that drew international press coverage. Other library-instigated visitors included composer John Cage, whose donations to the library included his correspondence files as well as his files relating to performance arts.

During Miller's deanship, Northwestern presented conductor James Levine, musicologist Gustave Reese, lexicographer Nicolas Slonimsky, and composers Milton Babbitt, Witold Lutoslawski, and Dmitri Shostakovich with honorary doctorates and hosted such visitors as Sir Georg Solti, Madame Serge Prokofiev, Gian-Carlo Menotti, Sir Neville Marriner, Ned Rorem, Phyllis Curtin, and Elliott Carter. Olivier Messiaen came to Evanston in 1978 for a series of events honoring his 70th birthday. Conductors Erich Leinsdorf, Carlo Maria Giulini, and Pierre Boulez spoke with students during multiple visits. Vocalists Lucia Popp, Sherill Milnes, Tito Gobbi, Carlo Cossuto, and Judith Raskin gave master classes. Beverly Sills told students how she prepared for her roles as Elizabethan queens in the Donizetti operas. The Cleveland and Chicago Symphony Orchestras and many others, from both this country and abroad, performed at Pick-Staiger. Pianist John Browning and wind conductor Frederick Fennell spent time at the school as visiting instructors. Jazz artists Maynard Ferguson and Wynton Marsalis performed with student groups. Other visitors included pianist-conductor-composer André Previn, pianist Ralph Votapek (60), guitarist Christopher Parkening, the Empire Brass, Philip Jones and his brass ensemble, conductors Sir David Willcocks and Sir Charles Mackerras, and composers Philip Glass, Gunther Schuller, John Rutter,

ABOVE

Madame Serge Prokofiev on campus in 1977

BELOW

Composer Sir Michael Tippett (second from left) with Dean Thomas Miller (second from right) and music librarian Don Roberts (right)

FOLLOWING PAGES

The Marching Band parading through downtown Evanston in 1982

The Knot Garden

The 1974 American premiere of Sir Michael Tippett's *The Knot Garden* attracted critics and audiences from around the world. The summer 1974 *Fanfare* quoted Tippett as saying, "I was deeply moved . . . It was a memorable experience. Because the singers are so young, they were willing and able to do things that would be very difficult to **obtain from any singer over the age of 30. I felt in no sense that it [the Northwestern production] was being done by students." The opera was directed by Robert Gay and conducted by Bernard Rubenstein, with sets designed by theater professor Samuel Ball and coaching by Frederick Ockwell.**

Mauricio Kagel, Gerhard Stäbler, and Marta Ptaszynska. And visits were not restricted to Western artists. Ugandan musicians presented a performance and demonstration as early as 1971, and the first Soviet jazz group to perform in the United States appeared at Pick-Staiger in 1986.

For professional societies, the University's lakeshore campus in Evanston proved an attractive site for conferences and conventions. In 1973 Northwestern welcomed deans and department chairs from across the country to a national forum — sponsored by the Contemporary Music Project — on the graduate education of the college music teacher. The Society for Music Theory held its first meeting at Pick-Staiger in 1977. A World Music Festival and International Computer

Conference were held in 1978, and the following year the Sixth World Saxophone Congress met at Northwestern. In 1984 bassists descended on campus to attend the International Bass Convention, organized by then–faculty member Jeff Bradetich. In 1986 the International Conference on Music Bibliography came to Evanston.

Northwestern's reputation drew a delegation from the People's Republic of China. In 1980 five Chinese music education experts spent several days observing classes, talking with faculty, and touring the campus.

Seeking to forge better ties with the North Shore community, Dean Miller formed a partnership with the Ravinia Festival in 1972. The program augmented the School of Music's summer schedule with classes, seminars, lectures, and workshops by internationally renowned artists and scholars at the festival site in Highland Park on Chicago's North Shore. The program was open to graduate students, performers, educators, and the general

public. Practice facilities, living quarters, transportation, and regular classes were available to those who enrolled. The first program offered study in chamber music, violin, cello, and piano with such artists as Itzhak Perlman, Janos Starker, and the La Salle String Quartet. Ensuing workshops featured Roberta Peters, Lynn Harrell, Alexis Weissenberg, Jean-Bernard Pommier, Benita Valente, Rudolph Firkusny, the Bach Aria Group, Beverly Sills, William Bolcom, Joan Morris, and Chicago Symphony Orchestra musicians Adolph Herseth, Ray Still, Dale Clevenger, Walfrid Kujala, and Arnold Jacobs.

The School of Music also solidified ties to its own alumni with the birth of *Fanfare* magazine in 1972. Explained Miller, "During the first year I was here, the alumni had one great complaint: that we never hear from the University except when they want money." The solution was an alumni magazine, for which he credited James Moore "because he put it together on a shoestring." Moore edited *Fanfare* until 1985, when he was succeeded by Thomas Willis.

New Construction

Miller felt the music school should contribute to the well-being of the entire University through an active cultural life and curricular participation in musical activities. While classes and courses of study for nonmusic majors increased, the campus concert scene suffered from space constraints.

"We didn't have any decent concert halls," said Miller. "Lutkin was a charming recital hall, but you couldn't hold a full symphony orchestra on its stage. So we played in gymnasiums when we could get there. We shared Cahn Auditorium with many other constituencies. It was a three-ring circus. We were renting Evanston Township High School and trucking all of our gear out there. Here we were, a major music school aspiring to be the best in the country, and we had no decent hall in which to perform.

"When I came here in 1971, there was this gigantic blueprint for new construction on the lakefill, and part of that was a huge music complex that had a concert hall, recital hall, music library, and new music building. It was an integrative facility that had originally been designed to cost in the neighborhood of $4 million to $5 million. As a result of inflation, costs had risen to $20-something million. Of course during the interview process I was presented with this wonderful plan that we're going to build on the lakefront, and everyone really expected it to happen. When I got here, the reality of it came that there is no way you can fund $20 million."

The consensus at the school was that a new performing facility was the top priority, and Miller began seeking potential donors for a concert hall, hoping that later the remaining money could be raised for the rest of the lakefront music complex. "We did get the concert facility — thank goodness," said Miller. "With the way the

gift was given and the fact that we had that money, we needed to move on it. We couldn't sit around for 15 years waiting to raise the rest of the $20 million."

So with a $4 million gift from Albert Pick and his brother-in-law, Charles Staiger, the school built Pick-Staiger Concert Hall. "It was a wonderful experience," said Miller. "We had a great team — the faculty who worked on the project, the architect, the acoustician, and all the consultants. We got interesting ideas from lots of places. We went up to Ottawa to see the new performing arts facility for the Canadian performing arts; we were most interested in the use of glass. The architect wanted to use glass, and the faculty did not want a fishbowl. We were all thinking about the nice box shape of the Concertgebouw in Amsterdam because acoustically that was a known entity. We were determined that we would have something that worked acoustically."

After plans for Pick-Staiger forged ahead, the Regenstein Foundation offered a donation toward a new music building. By this time Music Hall, home of the band and instrumental departments, was in such poor repair that replacing it became the school's next major priority. Regenstein Hall of Music was completed in 1977, and Music Hall passed to the Department of Human Resources.

"The idea was that the next building was going to be for piano and voice departments and the last one for the whole academic department, but those plans got put on hold," said Miller. "I don't know that I would have agreed to the construction of Regenstein out on the lakefill had I known then that the school was never going to finish the building program and we were forever going to have a divided campus, which I feel is poor both educationally and philosophically. It is bad because it separates the faculty and students and exacerbates an already deep division between the so-called academic and performance areas. Hopefully someday that will change."

Pick-Staiger and Regenstein

A dream of the school's faculty and staff for years, Pick-Staiger Concert Hall was the fifth building to rise on the lakefill campus and Northwestern's first concert hall. The $4 million edifice was funded by gifts from Albert Pick Jr. and Charles G. Staiger and named in honor of Pick's wife, Corinne Frada Pick — marking their golden wedding anniversary — and in memory of Pauline Pick Staiger, Pick's sister and Staiger's late wife.

Pick-Staiger was designed by Edward D. Dart of Loebl, Schlossman, Dart, and Hackl, creator of Chicago's Water Tower Place, and built by Pepper Construction Company, which also erected Norris University Center. Acoustician Lawrence Kirkegaard, then with Bolt, Beranek, and Newman, created the hall's flexible acoustics, using an adjustable overhead "cloud" canopy, a stage shell with 12 movable panels, and retractable curtains. The hall boasts a 1,003-seat auditorium, recording and lighting control booths, an orchestral music library, three office studios, and a rehearsal room dedicated to the memory of Arne Oldberg, piano teacher and conductor at the University from 1897 to 1941. The building was dedicated on October 26, 1975, in a performance featuring pianist Ralph Votapek (60), the first recipient of the school's Corinne Frada Pick Music Scholarship.

Built to replace Music Hall, Regenstein Hall of Music was funded by Chicago's Joseph and Helen Regenstein Foundation and

ABOVE
Pick-Staiger Concert Hall
LEFT
Breaking ground for Pick-Staiger with (from left) Chancellor J. Roscoe Miller, Albert Pick Jr., Corinne Frada Pick, and Charles Staiger

199

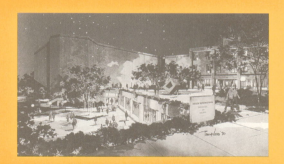

TOP
Regenstein Hall under construction

CENTER LEFT
Original plans for the music school's lake-front music complex

CENTER RIGHT
L. Walter Netsch, Helen Regenstein, Richard Pepper, and President and Mrs. Robert Strotz at the Regenstein groundbreaking in February 1976

BOTTOM
A student filing music in the band library, housed in the basement of Regenstein Hall

named in honor of Mrs. Regenstein, who was fond of art and music. The $4 million building was dedicated on November 6, 1977, with performances by the Eckstein String Quartet and pianist John Browning.

Regenstein houses the school's string, wind and percussion, and conducting and ensembles departments. Clad in serrated limestone, the three-level building was designed by Walter Netsch of Skidmore, Owings, and Merrill and acoustically designed by Kirkegaard for the teaching, rehearsal, practice, and performance of instrumental music. It includes departmental offices, 20 teaching studios for small classes and individual lessons, 35 practice rooms, 6 small rehearsal rooms, the band library, a resource center for the ensemble-music collection, a 3,000-square-foot rehearsal hall, and a 200-seat master class recital hall (with an adjoining recording studio) that accommodates both formal concerts and informal presentations. A spacious lounge offers views of the lakefill campus and the Chicago skyline.

CHAPTER 6

The Dobroski Years

1990 *to present*

CHAPTER 6

The Dobroski Years

1990 *to present*

When Thomas Miller stepped down as dean of the School of Music, he relinquished a choice spot in the music school world. Beginning in the 1980s Northwestern had consistently made the top 10 in prestigious national rankings of music schools. The institution continued to compete with other top schools for the country's best music students, offering such advantages as Chicago Symphony Orchestra players on the faculty, a strong curriculum, a university setting, frequent visits by well-known artists, and a location rich in culture. Many Northwestern music students spent their summers at the Aspen Music Festival, Los Angeles Philharmonic's Summer Institute, Berkshire Music Festival, or other major festivals in the United States and abroad. School of Music graduates continued to win choice playing and teaching jobs around the world.

Yet while the school's reputation and outlook remained strong, the world of music was continuing to change and grow, presenting new challenges to music administrators in higher education. Nationally, the number of applicants to music schools was declining, as were audiences for performers and jobs for teachers and orchestral musicians. Many music students now sought to pursue other disciplines as backup careers. Opportunities in music technology and music business were growing.

When Bernard J. Dobroski returned to his alma mater to assume the deanship, he immediately set out to boost fundraising, take advantage of the school's surrounding cultural opportunities, and engender more support for music and for Northwestern's music school. Under his direction the school has solidified ties with alumni, maintained its national ranking, and continued to reach out to the Chicago-area community. New faculty members have enhanced existing programs and helped create new ones. New programs such as jazz and music technology came into their own as full-fledged majors during the 1990s. Faculty members continued to win prestigious awards, enjoy widespread performance of their compositions, and present concerts all over the country. In 1995 the school celebrated its centennial and followed the Northwestern football team's Big Ten championship season to the Rose Bowl on New Year's Day of 1996.

PREVIOUS PAGES
The Marching Band in a Homecoming parade
ABOVE
Bernard J. Dobroski with a 1982 tuba class

There She Is . . . Miss America

In 1952, flutist Glenna Pohly (54) won national attention when she competed as Miss Illinois in the Miss America pageant. Years passed before the next School of Music contestant, but by the end of the century, watching Northwestern music students in the pageant had become an annual event.

First came voice major Sara Martin (95), a student of Sunny Joy Langton who appeared in the 1993 pageant. Singing "Hello, Young Lovers" from The King and I, she won the Bert Parks Award as one of the eight top talent-competition scorers not among the finalists.

Four years later Music Theatre Program student Kate Shindle (Speech 99) won the crown in Atlantic City. Coached by Kurt Hansen, her rendition of "Don't Rain on My Parade" from Funny Girl triumphed in the talent competition; she also won the swimsuit competition. Her year of cross-country travel as Miss America focused on AIDS prevention.

Piano major Jade Smalls (01) garnered the runner-up spot at the 1999 pageant. A student of Sylvia Wang, she performed Chopin's Etude in C-sharp Minor in the talent competition. A year later voice junior Jennifer Diane Powers — a student of Elizabeth Fischer and Kurt Hansen — won the talent competition singing "Quando M'en Vo" from Puccini's La Bohème.

Bernard J. Dobroski

According to the *Fanfare* article announcing Dobroski's appointment as dean, "When word first reached the statewide newspaper in Oregon that Bernard J. Dobroski would be leaving his post as dean of the University of Oregon School of Music in September 1990 to become the sixth dean of Northwestern's School of Music, it was not only news, it was the subject of a bittersweet editorial. 'In his four years at the University,' declared the publication, 'Dobroski has had an enormous impact on music education, and his influence on the cultural life of Oregon has been exceptional. Whether as cheerleader, participant, educator, or patron, he has indefatigably championed the arts. . . . When it comes time to go, he can leave knowing he has made a difference — a real difference — and that he will be missed.' It was one of a sheaf of testimonials from cultural leaders, public officials, and fellow administrators throughout the state."

Much of the Northwestern music community was already familiar with Dobroski and his energy. After earning an undergraduate degree at Carnegie Mellon University and a master's at Catholic University of America, he served at Northwestern for 12 years as a faculty member, assistant dean, and associate dean, meanwhile earning an interdisciplinary PhD in 1984. Among the subjects he pursued were performance, music history, instructional design, and conducting. His responsibilities as assistant and associate dean took him all over metropolitan Chicago. When Dobroski left Northwestern for Oregon, the Student Advisory Council gave him a scroll hailing him as a "compassionate administrator, demanding teacher, available adviser, diligent dissertation director, time-conscious appointment keeper, risk-taking entrepreneur, canny politician, fugal (sic)

ABOVE
Students at the Arch, erected in 1994
LEFT
Dean Dobroski with a student backstage at Pick-Staiger Concert Hall

ABOVE

Students performing Shakespeare at the Rock

BELOW

Sonja Kahler (G92) at the Alice Millar Chapel organ

gourmet, dedicated party planner, enthusiastic team player, loyal bandsman, accomplished tubist, encyclopedic Chordovoxer, and supportive friend to academics of all ages."

While at the University of Oregon, Dobroski also held the charter presidency of the College Music Society's Pacific Northwest chapter and the presidency of the Oregon Music Administrator's Association. He served as a contributing editor to the *Instrumentalist* magazine and as a frequent lecturer, conductor, adjudicator, consultant, clinician, and member of accreditation review committees.

On returning to the School of Music as dean, Dobroski reached out to the greater Northwestern community by greatly expanding opportunities for students outside the music school to take music courses and lessons, resulting in a major influx of nonmusic majors in the school's classrooms. He traveled throughout the world to generate support and funds for the School of Music, raising its profile internationally and inspiring a dramatic rise in gifts. He oversaw a reorganization of departments, the addition of interdisciplinary programs, and hirings of world-class musicians. He began an even more aggressive recruiting campaign to attract students, faculty, and staff members representing musical, intellectual, and cultural excellence and diversity. He worked to fortify existing programs with new courses and faculty members.

Whatever Dobroski's goals, he pursued them with enthusiasm. The 1990 *Fanfare* asked, "What is the source of all this energy? A missionary's zeal perhaps." Then it quoted the new dean: "Any institution can teach students to play louder or faster than any one else. It is the truly educated person who is able to really reach out and fulfill his potential as a human being. Music is a thread in the fabric of a comprehensive education. We can't just be an ivory tower on University Place. We need to touch the lives of all our students."

Strengthening the Community

One of Dobroski's major initial priorities was to strengthen the broader School of Music community. In his view, that community embraced music-loving friends of the school and former faculty and staff members as well as alumni, students, faculty, and staff. It was a community he sought to bring together through countless visits, more effective communication, and a proliferation of off-campus performances.

During his first year as dean, Dobroski resolved to meet every emeritus faculty member and many alumni to communicate a message of support from Northwestern, news about the school, and his goals for the future. After aggressively contacting countless alumni, he saw a need for even better communication, so he expanded *Fanfare,* the school's alumni magazine. He also poured money into the admissions office to upgrade student recruitment publications and launched quarterly and annual brochures to advertise performances at Pick-Staiger Concert Hall. As awareness of the school increased, more alumni began contacting the school for news and event information.

Another result of Dobroski's travels has been the dramatic growth in gifts to the school. Yearly donations grew from $509,637 in 1991–92 to a record of $2,825,479 in 1993–94 and a new record of $4,315,172 in 1998–99.

ABOVE
The 1991 choral picnic

A One-Woman Fan Club

BROOKE VON GILLERN FERMIN (99) I remember when I first saw Elizabeth Parsons (25). I was talking with my sister, Heather Von Gillern (92), and our mother after Heather's junior recital. As we stood outside Regenstein Recital Hall, Heather spotted someone she didn't recognize.

"Who's that?" she asked our mother, who had attended the music school in the late 1960s. "Mrs. Parsons," she replied. "She goes to all the recitals. She came to mine when I was here."

I had heard about the music school's "one-woman fan club," as Tom Willis described her, but never knew who she was. Later during the reception, she asked our mother why she was here. Even after 20 years, Mrs. Parsons still remembered her and what instrument she played!

But according to those who knew her better, that was typical of the woman whose life centered around Northwestern's School of Music. She had attended recitals and concerts several times a week since her college days, when she commuted to Evanston from Ravenswood to study theory with Peter Christian Lutkin and piano with Gail M. Haake. Over the years she kept track of her favorite students.

When Tom Willis asked her why she regularly attended Northwestern music events, she replied, "The students appreciate my coming, and I appreciate their talent. Music is my life and my world; I don't know what I'd do without it."

Mrs. Parsons always did and said what she wanted. University Chaplain Timothy Stevens's wife, Priscilla, described her at her memorial service: "She walked five miles a day, swam in Lake Michigan nearly every day from May to October, and regularly tuned into a popular TV fitness program for her morning exercises. Elizabeth's energy was phenomenal."

She ignored all warnings about the dangers of hitchhiking. Stevens's friend Janet Roth recalled driving south on Ridge Avenue when she saw Parsons on the opposite side of the street, trying to hitch a ride. Janet found a safe place to turn her car around and headed back north but only arrived in time to see Elizabeth climbing into a stranger's car.

After her death in 1991, Dean Dobroski spoke and the Northwestern Cello Ensemble and tenor Kurt Hansen performed at her memorial service. She is still remembered as the woman whose life revolved around the School of Music's concert halls.

Preparatory Program

Teaching precollege students at Northwestern dates back to before the dawn of the School of Music. Young students — both male and female — took music lessons at Northwestern Female College as part of their preparation for adulthood and college. The Conservatory of Music and then the School of Music offered lessons at the preparatory level, beginning in 1886 with free singing lessons. In 1901 the preparatory department was listed on its own in the music catalog for the first time; the 1903 catalog described its offerings as "excellent instruction" in piano, organ, voice, and theory. That year, newly graduated Louis Norton Dodge was appointed head of the preparatory department.

Turn-of-the-century preparatory students took lessons from School of Music graduates ("assistant instructors") and undergraduates ("student instructors"). A degree program that trained students to be piano teachers provided the preparatory program with many piano instructors as part of their pedagogy work. In the 1920s the school's catalogs classified precollege music students age 16 and older as "special students."

In the 1930s a team of Northwestern faculty members writing the Oxford Piano Course instituted a laboratory piano program, beginning with a new piano pedagogy course that was the first in the country. College students in the class observed the first children's group piano lessons, a model that is still used today. Although the pedagogy course was dropped from the curriculum in the early

1940s, Harriet Kisch — one of the student teachers from the early pedagogy classes — continued to teach, serving as director of the developing preparatory piano department for many years. She was succeeded by Guy Duckworth, who achieved nationwide renown as an exponent of group piano instruction. During the 1980s and early 1990s the program was directed by piano pedagogue and children's music composer Elvina Truman Pearce.

In the early 1960s the preparatory department and college-level pedagogy courses became more closely integrated. Frances Larimer, who had taught in the preparatory department for 10 years, helped develop college-level group piano and piano pedagogy programs. Larimer made group instruction a regular component of the pedagogy curriculum, a feature that continues to attract pedagogy students to Northwestern. With the addition of adult piano lessons and prepiano classes for young children, the name of the division was changed to Preparatory and Community Music Division to reflect the growing diversity of its student population. In addition to group instruction, other hallmarks of the preparatory piano program include creative work (composition and improvisation) and musicianship training. Piano students participate in yearly assessments sponsored by the Illinois State Music Teachers Association. Now directed by Mary Beth Molenaar, the program has undergone yet another name change to become the Music Academy of the School of Music.

The community string division flourished for many years under the leadership of former associate dean Jack Pernecky. With the establishment of a new School of Music string pedagogy program in the 1990s, the string division began to grow and became part of the Music Academy. Stacia Spencer now leads the division, which offers group instruction, chamber music, and private lessons taught in a modified Suzuki style. Like the piano program, the string division serves as a laboratory for observation and student teaching for Northwestern pedagogy students.

In 1993 Kindermusik — a program for children up to age seven — joined the Music Academy. Program coordinator Allison Ashley has been featured in documentaries, TV news programs, and magazine articles on music for the young child. The national Kindermusik curriculums were developed by a team of music educators based on the latest music education research.

In 1998 the National Guild of Community Schools of the Arts awarded full certification to the Music Academy. A scholarship program has been implemented to assist students who could not otherwise afford music lessons, and outreach music classes for families at risk are offered in partnership with Evanston Family Focus. At the end of the 20th century, Music Academy enrollment numbered almost 100 string students, 150 piano students, and 100 Kindermusik students, with many more on waiting lists.

Curricular Initiatives

Equally important to Dobroski was maintaining and elevating the school's reputation in its chosen areas of focus. New funds were used to expand existing programs and create new ones.

Part of Dobroski's vision for increasing the school's visibility and support included expanding course offerings for students not enrolled in the School of Music. Courses developed specifically for nonmajors (in addition to private lessons and ensembles) included Elements, Sounds, Gestures in Jazz; The Beatles: A Multidisciplinary Mystery Tour; History of the Symphony; Masterpieces of Opera; The Western Musical Tradition; Music Cognition; and Music and Mind, an introduction to the psychology of the musical experience. Dobroski enthusiastically supported the school's participation in the Integrated Arts Program, first offered in winter quarter of 1989 to provide opportunities for students of any major to take courses in art, theater, music, and dance. Classes use a hands-on approach to teach the basics of artistic disciplines. The program was developed under School of Speech professor Carol Simpson Stern in conjunction with composer Michael Pisaro, musicologist Faun Tannenbaum, assistant dean Mary Ann Rees, and Thomas Miller, who continued to serve on the music school faculty after stepping down as dean.

Dobroski also worked to allow music students to take greater advantage of Northwestern's educational opportunities by completing the development of interdisciplinary certificates, programs enabling interested students to pursue courses in areas where music intersects with another field. In 1989 the school began offering the first five of an eventual seven interdisciplinary certificates: commercial music, integrated arts, jazz studies, music business, music criticism, music technology, and music theater. Students pursuing these programs take classes in such subjects as radio/audio production, sociology of the arts, jazz history, finance, marketing, dance, magazine writing, and multimedia software development in the Judd A. and Marjorie Weinberg College of Arts and Sciences, Medill School of Journalism, School of Speech, and School of Continuing Studies. Jazz and music technology eventually were upgraded to majors.

ABOVE
The 1998 Percussion Ensemble
OPPOSITE, TOP
Students in Northwestern's preparatory program performing in Lutkin Hall
OPPOSITE, BOTTOM
Margaret Farish teaching preparatory string students

LEFT AND ABOVE
Scenes onstage and off at the May 1995 Jazz Festival, with Don Owens conducting the Jazz Lab Band

Music Theatre Program

*Musical theatre has flourished in various venues
at Northwestern for years, but only in the 1990s
did it become an academic program, offered
jointly by the Schools of Music and Speech.*

The Music Theatre Program's closest precursor was the
Opera Workshop under Robert Gay, who held a joint appointment
in the Schools of Music and Speech. But after Gay's retirement, the
workshop lost its official connection with the School of Speech and
became part of the voice and opera program.

In 1980 the theatre department hired Dominic Missimi to
teach acting and directing; the first production he directed at Northwestern was the musical *Pippin*. Under his leadership, and after
many years of discussion and planning, the Music Theatre Certificate Program was introduced in 1992. Still headed by Missimi, professor of theatre, the program has rapidly achieved widespread fame
and success, with many of its graduates appearing on Broadway, in
national tours, and in major theatrical venues nationwide.

The Opera Workshop is now part of the Music Theatre
Program, and Missimi works with its director to coordinate
repertoire and to vary eras and styles. Since 1994 the Music
Theatre Program has also produced the Waa-Mu Show, the
annual student-written revue first staged in 1929. As Waa-
Mu director, Missimi holds the Donald G. Robertson
Director of Music Theatre Chair.

By now as many as a dozen musical productions
are staged annually, including a traditional musical in
the fall, a full-scale opera in the winter, and Waa-Mu
in the spring. Casts are made up almost exclusively
of students, but faculty members, special guests,
and graduate assistants help with design, chore-
ography, and direction.

What made the program difficult to establish also makes it
unique. "This is the only university in the nation that offers a musical theatre program by two schools," explained Missimi. Auditions
for the program are open to freshmen and sophomores majoring in
voice in the School of Music or in theatre in the School of Speech.
The audition, also heard by the Opera Workshop director, consists
of a song, a monologue, and a dance selection.

After students are accepted into the program, they take
courses in a second area of specialization — actor training and other
theatre courses for voice majors, voice lessons and other music
courses for theatre majors. Required music theatre courses include
History of the Lyric Theatre, Music Theatre Technique, and

BACKGROUND
*The Music Theatre Program's 1998 produc-
tion of* A Chorus Line
ABOVE
*A dance rehearsal with choreographer Billy
Siegenfeld (center)*
OPPOSITE
*Dominic Missimi, head of the Music Theatre
Program, with students in 1993*

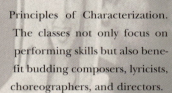

Principles of Characterization. The classes not only focus on performing skills but also benefit budding composers, lyricists, choreographers, and directors.

Kicking off the program was a 1992 production of Leonard Bernstein's *Mass*, featuring more than 200 performers (including 25 principal soloists, a marching band, and a rock band). Other offerings have included revues of songs by Gershwin, Rodgers, Bernstein, and Ellington; a 50th-anniversary production of *Oklahoma!* in 1993; the Chicago-area premiere of *A Wonderful Life* by *Fiddler on the Roof* lyricist Sheldon Harnick (49) in 1994; and the world premiere of *The Christmas Schooner* by John Reeger (Speech 72) and Julie Shannon in 1993.

The program has brought many special guests to campus. Mitzi Hamilton, a member of the original workshop for *A Chorus Line*, directed Northwestern's 1998 production of the show. Mark Hoebee (Speech 82), who staged the national tour of *Victor/Victoria* and the London premiere of *Dreamgirls,* has returned to his alma mater on several occasions, most recently in 1997 to direct *Sweet Charity.* The program has offered residencies with composers and lyricists, including Harnick and Larry Grossman (Speech 60). Other guests have included Stephen Sondheim, Tony Kushner, Donna Murphy, Desmond Heeley, Régine Crespin, and Jonathan Miller.

Former Music Theatre Program students have achieved noteworthy success. Heather Headley starred on Broadway as Nala in *The Lion King* and won a Tony Award for creating the title role in *Aida.* Kate Fischer (Speech 95) and Emily Kosloski (97) have played Cosette in the national tour of *Les Misérables,* and the show's Broadway company has featured Catherine Brunnel. Kim Varhola (Speech 98) has appeared on Broadway in *Rent.* National tours of *Phantom of the Opera* featured Jim Weitzer (Speech 96) as Raoul. Margaret Lloyd (95) appeared as Curly's wife in the Glimmerglass Opera's 1997 *Of Mice and Men,* directed by Rhoda Levine. Numerous other graduates have appeared in the national tours of such shows as *Les Miz, Show Boat,* and *Ragtime.*

Waa-Mu

Begun in 1929 as a joint effort by the Women's Athletic Association and Men's Union, the Waa-Mu Show quickly gained a reputation as "the greatest college show in America." Waa-Mu salutes all aspects of musical theatre with a variety of songs, sketches, and dance numbers. The material is all original, written primarily by University students. In 1951 the show gained its signature song — heard at the end of each show — when Lloyd B. Norlin (41, G42) wrote "To the Memories."

The production involves more than 200 people for its 10 performances each spring. Such stars as Ann-Margret, Warren Beatty, Nancy Dussault (Speech 57), Mary Frann (Speech 65), Heather Headley, Cloris Leachman (Speech 48), Shelley Long, Charlotte Rae (Speech 48), Tony Randall, Garry Marshall (Medill 56), and McLean Stevenson (Speech 52) got their start in Waa-Mu.

Only three directors have led the show over its 69-year history. Joe E. Miller staged Waa-Mu for its first four decades; he was succeeded by Tom Roland, director for the next 22 shows. Beginning in 1994, when Waa-Mu was first produced by the Music Theatre Program, the show has been directed by Dominic Missimi. In the pit, Mallory Thompson succeeded the late John P. Paynter as conductor in 1996.

"Waa-Mu really is a unique production," said Missimi. "There is no other show held on a college campus that is 100 percent original, orchestrated, choreographed, and produced at a Broadway level by students."

RIGHT
The Percussiuon Ensemble
BELOW
The Vocal Jazz Ensemble

Degrees

In 1993 music technology entered the curriculum as a bona fide major at both the bachelor's and master's levels. The school's first bachelor's degree in music technology was awarded to Matthew Moller in 1994, though earlier students had received ad hoc degrees in that field. A PhD was first offered in 1997.

A master's degree in jazz pedagogy joined the undergraduate certificate program in jazz studies (effectively a minor) in 1993. An ad hoc undergraduate major in jazz studies was also available to interested students, but by 1998 the faculty unanimously approved it as a new undergraduate major. The degree's curriculum combines ensemble participation and courses in jazz improvisation, composition, arranging, and history with electives in such areas as world musicianship, African American music, jazz in the public schools, the business of jazz, music technology, MIDI music systems, and multimedia software development. In addition to jazz lessons, students are required to take two years of applied lessons.

In 1998 a new master of music program in opera production made its debut. Voice and opera faculty members Karen Brunssen and Michael Ehrman devised the two-year program to combine the artistic and business aspects of opera. Degree candidates study set design, lighting, costuming, staging, musical preparation, repertoire, acting techniques, casting, and other elements of stage production. The program accepts one to three students each year.

Academic Studies

New faculty members and additional courses strengthened music theory, education, and history programs. In the music theory and composition program, Richard Ashley, John Buccheri, Alan Stout, Stephen Syverud, and Gary Kendall were joined by Candace Brower, Kevin Holm-Hudson, and Robert Gjerdingen. New computer programs made technology increasingly important in this area. Jay Alan Yim joined the composition faculty in 1989 and went on to win a grant from the John Simon Guggenheim Foundation, a commission from the Chicago Symphony Orchestra, and selection as one of four finalists for the Kennedy Center's 17th annual Friedheim Award for best new American orchestral work. Amnon Wolman, who arrived in 1991, attracted international attention with projects combining composition with the latest technology.

The academic and performance departments often joined forces to present integrated courses. In the 1991–92 school year, Buccheri and viola professor Peter Slowik jointly led a group of students through an analysis and performance of Bach's six *Brandenburg Concertos.* Wolman and tuba professor Rex Martin exchanged students to expose them to new perspectives.

The 1990s saw further expansion of the music education program. The arrival of Peter Webster in 1989 brought computers to the department. Nancy Whitaker came to the school in 1996 and began an outreach program to teach composition via computers to area elementary school children.

In November 1992 the school celebrated the University Press of Colorado's publication of *On the Nature of Musical Experience,* a collaborative research document written by members of Northwestern's Center for the Study of Education and the Musical Experience, a group of music education doctoral students and faculty members engaged in cooperative and individual research efforts. First in its field to be written through such a collaborative process, the book surveys the aesthetic views of 19 prominent philosophers, composers, theorists, composers, and educators to identify 14 common features of musical experience. The book was edited by center director Bennett Reimer, then the John W. Beattie Professor of Music Education, and Jeffrey Wright, then a lecturer in music education and assistant to the dean.

Music history as an undergraduate major was reintroduced in 1992, and opera specialist Thomas Bauman joined the department in 1996. In ethnomusicology, Virginia Gorlinski joined Paul Berliner, who won widespread recognition for his books *The Soul of Mbira* and *Thinking in Jazz* and received a grant from the John Simon Guggenheim Foundation for further study in Zimbabwe. Courses offered in ethnomusicology have included the African Mbira Class, Music of the World's Peoples, Improvisation and World Musicianship, and Jazz: Its Roots and Elements. Students in Berliner's mbira class construct an mbira, one of Africa's most popular and ancient melodic instruments, and develop basic playing skills.

ABOVE
Tabla drums from Paul Berliner's extensive ethnic instrument collection
BELOW
Berliner conducting a mbira class in his office, where a skeleton of a pilot whale hangs from the ceiling
FOLLOWING PAGES
The Symphony Orchestra on the Pick-Staiger stage in 1990

Music Technology

Under the leadership of music education professor Peter Webster, a computer lab (nicknamed the Mac Lab) was installed on the Music Administration Building's second floor, outfitted with Macintosh computers, keyboards, and a variety of programs. With in-depth CD-ROM studies and notation, scoring, and sequencing programs, the lab assists both aspiring composers and students struggling with homework.

In the last decade, technology has become increasingly integral to the school, with more and more professors incorporating it into their research and teaching. Composer Amnon Wolman espoused the idea that technology supplies composers with new instruments. Theory professor Richard Ashley created a computer program for designing and delivering analytical listening lessons with commercial CDs. With the help of music education doctoral students Maud Hickey (who joined the faculty in 1997) and Roland Telfeyan, John Buccheri created software programs that enable students to study scores and musical phrases and patterns more effectively.

Most recently, the school has established the Center for Music Technology, directed by Webster, to ensure that technology is accessible and understandable for all music students. An electronic classroom was constructed in 1995 with the center's assistance, and Webster helped link every studio, rehearsal hall, and classroom to the University's computer network. The school's Web page debuted in December 1996 and has since undergone periodic revisions.

The Electronic Music Studios now occupy two rooms on the top floor of the Music Administration Building and contain analog and digital recording equipment, synthesizers, samplers, effects processors, and sequencers. The basement of the building houses the Audio Media Laboratory, which supports Digi Design, Pro Tools System, Kurzweil 2500, SGI Indigo II, and Macintosh and PC computers and has the most current Macintosh sound processing software. It is used primarily by music technology and composition students.

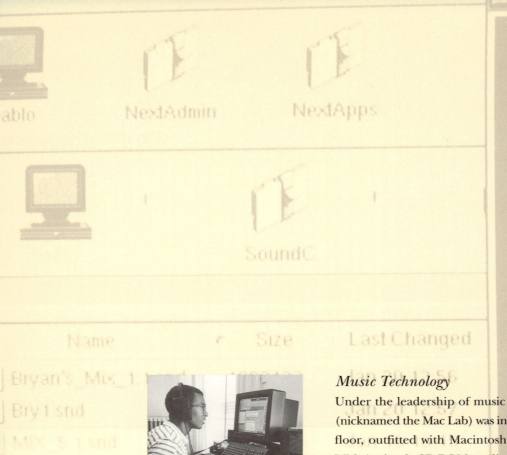

TOP
A student at work in the Mac Lab

BOTTOM
A Chicago Tribune (July 15, 1995) photo of Matthew Moller (left), who in 1994 earned the school's first bachelor's degree in music technology

Performance

The school has continued to take advantage of Chicago Symphony and Lyric Opera Orchestra members as private teachers. CSO associate principal hornist Gail Williams joined the faculty in 1989. When Ray Still retired as CSO principal oboist, he continued to teach at Northwestern; the school also hired his successor, Alex Klein. Among their CSO colleagues joining the faculty in the 1990s were clarinetist J. Lawrie Bloom and bassist Michael Hovnanian.

Michael Burritt joined the faculty as professor of percussion and led the Percussion Ensemble to national recognition. With the departures of trumpet teachers Vincent Cichowicz in 1997 and Luther Didrickson in 1998, the husband-and-wife duo of Barbara Butler and Charles Geyer, both alumni, arrived to fill their shoes. In the piano department, concert artist and contemporary music advocate Ursula Oppens joined the faculty in 1994; her performances in Chicago's Orchestra Hall and Carnegie Hall have won her national recognition.

The voice faculty scored major coups with the hirings of Grammy Award–winning bass-baritone William Warfield (famous for singing "Ol' Man River" in the 1951 film version of *Show Boat)* and Metropolitan Opera mezzo-soprano Mignon Dunn in 1994 and world-renowned baritone Sherrill Milnes in 2000. London and New York stage director and choreographer Rhoda Levine was named visiting professor of opera in 1993 and taught such courses as Improvisation in Opera and Principles of Characterization in addition to directing several school productions. Michael Ehrman, a School of Speech graduate, directed the opera program from 1996 to 2000. Other voice faculty members continued to perform throughout the community and the country. Elizabeth Fischer serves as artistic director of Italy's Bel Canto Opera Seminar each summer. In 1992 Bruce Hall and Sunny Joy Langton appeared in the world premiere of the opera *Under the Arbor,* presented by the state of Alabama and subsequently broadcast on public television more than 300 times.

TOP
Pick-Staiger Concert Hall at night
CENTER
Robert A. Harris with the Symphonic Wind Ensemble in 1996
BOTTOM
The NUSO string bass section

Bands and Orchestras

The number of School of Music ensembles grew in the 1990s, reflecting Dobroski's desire to accommodate all Northwestern students who wished to participate in an ensemble. In 1992 the Northwestern Philharmonia joined NUSO and NUCO as the University's third orchestra, directed by Stephen Alltop (G96), also director of music at Alice Millar Chapel. A new position, assistant director of orchestras, was added in 1996. In 1993 Victor Yampolsky, director of orchestras, was appointed to the Carol F. and Arthur L. Rice Jr. University Professorship in Music Performance.

Under Stephen Peterson's direction, the Marching Band won the Louis Sudler Award in 1992 and attracted national recognition for its performances at the 1996 Rose Bowl and the 1997 Citrus Bowl. Northwestern's Rose Bowl return was a dream come true for director of bands John P. Paynter, who as a student had played in the Marching Band for Northwestern's 1949 Rose Bowl appearance. Paynter suffered a stroke soon after returning from the 1996 Rose Bowl and died on February 4, 1996. One of his former students, Mallory Thompson, joined the faculty that fall as the school's third-ever director of bands.

TOP AND LEFT
The Marching Band on the field
RIGHT
Victor Yampolsky with orchestra students
OPPOSITE
The Chamber Orchestra rehearsing at Pick-Staiger in 1993

A Return to the Rose Bowl

In 1995 the unbelievable became a reality when Northwestern's football team went undefeated in the Big Ten and returned to the Rose Bowl for the first time since 1949. With the team's success came extensive exposure for the hard-core faithful: the Northwestern University Marching Band, then directed by Stephen Peterson and Matthew Ludwig. Game in and game out, band members had braved the blustery winds, snow, and sleet, supporting the team through its darkest days. For New Year's Day 1996 they reaped their just reward — new uniforms and a trip to sunny Southern California.

Fame came at a price, though. Marching Band members returned to campus December 26 for a week of early wake-up calls and a breakneck schedule in preparation for their role in the Rose Bowl.

A full day with lots of rehearsals was nothing new for players who had attended NUMB's annual band camp in Wisconsin. But few had experienced living in a Santa Monica hotel, dealing regularly with the media, and performing so frequently over a five-day period. Between departing on a chartered TWA flight at daybreak December 27 and landing in Chicago around 6 a.m. on January 2, the band played at the Rose Bowl, the Tournament of Roses Parade, a televised Main Street Parade at Disneyland, the Pasadena Civic Auditorium, Newport Beach's Pleasure Island shopping mall, and Universal Studios. In their free time, band members enjoyed Disneyland and a New Year's Eve party — celebrated on Chicago time (curfew was at 10 p.m. Pacific time).

NUMB received new paraphernalia for the occasion. Members sported new uniforms, made possible by hundreds

LEFT
John P. Paynter with alumni and students at the Rose Bowl

RIGHT
Merchandise celebrating the Wildcats' Big Ten championship

BELOW
Marching Band members enjoying a brief rest before the game

FOLLOWING PAGES
Graduate assistant Carolyn Barber (90, G95) and Paynter rehearsing with the Marching Band in California

of generous gifts, and the percussion section enjoyed new drumheads and cymbals. The drumheads were donated by Remo Company, the world's largest drumhead manufacturer; the company sent its own technician to the hotel to attach them. Percussion professor Michael Burritt's role as an endorser for the Zildjian Cymbal Company netted NUMB 10 new cymbals for the trip.

In addition to the 180 students traveling with the band, 25 School of Music faculty — among them Dean Dobroski, William Warfield, Sylvia Wang, and Frederick Hemke — went west to perform at other Rose Bowl–related events. And as director of bands, John P. Paynter made a last sentimental return to the Rose Bowl, where he had appeared with the band as a student in 1949. He died shortly after the trip, on February 4, 1996, but not before conducting the Marching Band in the Alma Mater one last time — at the Welsh-Ryan Arena rally honoring the returning Rose Bowl team.

The band enjoyed bountiful media coverage. NUMB was mentioned or covered in such newspapers as the *New York Times,* the *Los Angeles Times,* and *USA Today.* Band and faculty members appeared on numerous radio and television shows, including ABC's

Nightline and *Good Morning America* and CBS's *Sunday Morning.* Chicago reporters even met the exhausted band members at O'Hare when they returned. "It was weird — the media hovering over us," recalled Charles Hafner (Weinberg 98). "We were a news story."

Favorite Hangouts of the 1990s

Einstein Bros. Bagels (on the former site of Hoos Drug Store)

Yesterdays (which closed in 2000)

J. K. Sweets

Clarke's

Buffalo Joe's

Burger King

Oldberg Park (between Burger King and the Music Administration Building)

Norris University Center (especially the food court and game room)

The Lakefill

The lounge in Regenstein

The second floor lounge in the Music Administration Building

ABOVE

Bassist Rufus Reid (71) performing as guest artist in the May 1996 Jazz Festival

RIGHT

A Pick-Staiger performance by the Chicago Jazz Ensemble

Jazz

The jazz program grew to maturity in the 1990s under the leadership of Don Owens. A turning point came in 1990 when student Sam Struyk (93) approached Owens about his frustration with pursuing jazz piano at the school. A piano student for 12 years who had decided he did not want to be a concert artist, Struyk had already been signed by Atlantic Records to make several new age jazz recordings. He had come into contact with jazz pianist Michael Kocour and asked if he could study with him. David Kaiserman, then chair of the piano department, saw no reason why he couldn't; said Kaiserman, "We're a school, Sam is a good student, and if we can provide the instruction for him, why not?" Dean Dobroski supported the idea, so Kocour was "blended" into the school in 1991 to teach jazz courses for non-majors. The first class he offered attracted so many students that it had to be moved twice to larger locations. Other music majors heard of Struyk's lessons with Kocour and wanted to be able to do the same.

Shortly afterward, Owens had another chance to incorporate jazz into the music school, precipitated by a meeting with 1989 graduate Fred Hemke Jr., who hoped to begin work toward a master's degree. "I shared with him my dream of offering a graduate-level jazz pedagogy degree here," recalled Owens. "Within an hour I received a call from Dean Paul Aliapoulios, Dean Frederick Hemke, and Fred. Before I knew what was happening, Fred Jr. was accepted as an ad hoc major in jazz pedagogy." Percussion graduate student Hans Sturm heard about this development and petitioned to be a double major in percussion and jazz pedagogy. By the end of the year, the master of music in jazz pedagogy became an official degree. Successful alumni such as Fareed Haque (86), Matt Olson (94, G95), Loren Binford (58, G59, 62), John Parks (G94), and Rufus Reid (71) have come back to campus to perform and offer clinics for jazz studies students.

Fall 1993 saw an increased commitment to jazz as the school made Kocour's position full-time and hired Antonio García as associate professor of jazz studies, teaching jazz and Integrated Arts Program courses. García was instrumental in starting ComboFest the following year. Jazz courses for nonmajors drew heavy enrollment, and WNUR, Northwestern's student-run radio station, started jazz programming and a local infoline, eventually offered online. The National High School Music Institute, the school's summer high school program, began offering jazz studies in 1995 with improvisation study under García, master classes with Kocour, and big band rehearsal techniques with Owens. The undergraduate jazz studies degree was implemented in 1998.

In the mid-1990s the Jazz Invitational came to life. Each year Owens and his colleagues invite three outstanding high school jazz bands to participate in a full day of master classes, clinics, and performances, joined by a guest artist. The high school groups and the Northwestern Jazz Ensemble rehearse with the guest artist and faculty members, and the high schools' jazz directors are invited to conduct the ensemble. Jazz Invitational guests have included Bobby McFerrin, the American Jazz Philharmonic, the Lincoln Center Jazz Orchestra Sextet, Sonny Rollins, Phil Mattson, the Count Basie Orchestra, Chick Corea, Joshua Redman, Lennie Niehaus, Danilo Perez, Slide Hampton, James Moody, Max Roach, Marcus Roberts, and Eddie Palmieri.

ABOVE
Saxophonist James Moody visiting campus as headliner of the 1994 Jazz Festival

Now director of jazz studies, Owens says of the program's rapid expansion, "A great big thank you goes out to Dean Dobroski, who at the beginning of his tenure stated that he wanted to see our jazz program grow, and to Dean Hemke for making it happen."

A Surge in Donations

The Dobroski era has been noteworthy for a significant increase in donations to the School of Music. Major donors in the 1990s included J. Yule Bogue, Grace Fox Congdon, Dorothy Fox Johnson, Carol and Arthur Rice, Sanford and Jeanne Robertson, Charles and Beth Schroeder, and Richard L. and Helen Thomas. Ann Lurie hosted three musicales that raised $60,000 for the school. These funds have provided support for graduate students, visiting artists, and endowed faculty positions.

Reaching Out to the Greater Community

Reaching out to the Northwestern and Chicago-area communities was high on Dobroski's list of goals when he arrived as dean in 1990. Like Peter C. Lutkin before him, Dobroski wished to open the school's doors to students not majoring in music and to audiences in the community — partly as a way to build audiences for the future. The result was several new programs at the school.

While at the University of Oregon, Dobroski had taken his young children to music classes, only to find the sessions too "dumbed-down" or too long-winded for children to sit through. In 1991 he initiated Kids Fare, a series of participatory 45-minute programs for children aged three to eight to attend with their parents. Some Kids Fare favorites have included Powerful Pipes, an exploration of organ, brass, and voice; Brahms for Beginners; Boom Goes the Beat; Songs on Stage; and Strike up the Band, a chance for kids to march and play along with the Wildcat Marching Band. Dobroski loves his role of bringing music to youngsters. "We invite the kids to come onstage to touch the instruments," he explained. "We pass out chopsticks so that they can conduct."

The project expanded to offer several seasons of Family Concerts, bridging the gap between Kids Fare and formal concerts for children ages six and above. The programs included short works from standard repertoire with commentary by the conductor.

As part of the school's centennial celebration in 1995–96, the continuing education series Score Order was conceived. Dobroski had heard many concertgoers say they had loved a concert but wished they understood more about what they had heard. Launched in the winter quarter of 1996, Score Order offered Monday-night classes for people "who wish they knew something more about music." The series continued for four years, drawing on the volunteered time of faculty and students. The first year Score Order focused on the orchestral score and explored music from the performer's point of view. Other topics included "Demystifying Conducting and the Conductor" and "Is Music the Universal Language?"

A more mobile outreach program is Great Spaces, through which Dobroski took groups of three to four students to locales across the United States to perform for various groups. Over the course of a given year, he hosted more than 25 different programs in halls, senior centers, schools, malls, and even living rooms.

ABOVE
Dean Dobroski playing accordion for a class in the preparatory department
RIGHT
Children march with the band in a 1991 Kids Fare event
BELOW
Student performers at the University's "Family Day"

Cherubs

The National High School Music Institute flourished during the 1990s, growing in enrollment and programs. Traditionally called "cherubs," NHSMI students specialize in a specific area of music and take core courses in musicianship, composition, and conducting. Applied music — whether performance or composition — receives top priority, with special emphasis on chamber music. Students work with School of Music faculty one-on-one and in small group sessions.

Flutist Amy Lyons (96) attended NHSMI as a high school student. These recollections of her summer as a "cherub" originally appeared in the fall 1991 issue of the *Flutist Quarterly*.

The lump in my throat swelled as I walked into the Music Administration Building. While I stood in the registration line, my thoughts raced back to my initial audition for NHSMI with Don Owens. I could still remember my panic as I warmed up and heard a flutist in the next room, and the relief I felt when I discovered she was a college student, not another candidate for the camp. I knew that admission was competitive and only a limited number of musicians would be chosen. I was shaking as I entered Mr. Owens's office, but he soon set me at ease, and when I was accepted to NHSMI, a dream came true.

So there I was, being welcomed as a cherub by counselors and staff. Not every cherub planned to be a music major in college, but each had a deep interest and love for music. I soon felt like I was part of a big family, not just a kid at summer camp. We worked hard and received intense training. The camp itself is appropriately referred to as a college preparatory camp: We were treated like college students in most respects — the level of musical training, lessons, classes, etc.

As a member of the winds and percussion division, I attended daily rehearsals for Wind Ensemble and my chamber group, weekly flute lessons, and classes in music theory and conducting — and I still had practice time and free time. During the last two weeks when the strings arrived, I began attending orchestra rehearsals as well. All cherubs were given the privilege of attending any master classes conducted at Northwestern during our stay.

We attended concerts given by cherubs, faculty, and summer Northwestern ensembles. We took field trips, including a Chicago Symphony Orchestra concert at Ravinia, a Grant Park Symphony concert, a day at Orchestra Hall and the Lyric Opera, and a performance of Les Misérables. *Each cherub was encouraged, and each cherub improved. Everyone was given a chance to shine, whether through rotating chairs or playing with large chamber groups. It was exciting to be with people of diverse backgrounds from so many states and countries. One common event at mealtimes was the friendly camp battle dealing with accents and colloquialisms (such as "pop" versus "soda"). Everyone had fun with these wars, and I know that after five weeks I left with a bit of a Southern accent!*

The camp ended too soon for me. I was thrilled to be studying with Walfrid Kujala, and I loved making music with these people. I found it very difficult to leave the friends I had made and the aura of desire and dedication. The quality of instruction, selectivity of musicians, and friendliness of faculty made NHSMI the best music camp I have ever attended. I love music, and being a cherub was an experience I will remember for the rest of my life.

228

In addition to Nancy Whitaker's music education outreach program, public schools benefited from a project by voice faculty members Sunny Joy Langton and Bruce Hall, who in 1993 received a grant from the Evanston In-School Music Program to present opera in all 25 Evanston elementary and middle schools. Elementary students saw Northwestern voice students perform Pasatieri's *The Goose Girl*, and middle schools were treated to Langton and Hall performing Menotti's *The Telephone.*

Convocation

Begun in the 1950s as a required weekly solo class, convocation faded into history in the 1960s because applied departments felt students were overscheduled and that time could be better spent in departmental classes. But in 1990 it was re-instated in response to the divided campus created with the opening of the lake-front music facilities; faculty members felt that something needed to bridge the distance between the Music Administration Building and Regenstein Hall. Associate dean Frederick Hemke and piano professor Laurence Davis were especially instrumental in the program's revival.

Davis served as convocation's coordinator for the first few years and found it was no less valuable in the 1990s than it was in the '50s. "I felt we needed something to create a little more cohesion, to help students learn about other aspects of the school," he said in a 1994 *Fanfare* article. "At least to take a look, to see what's cooking."

Convocation developed into a vehicle for bringing faculty and students together to experience what was happening in various areas of the school. It offers 15 short concerts a year, scheduled in the school's three concert halls. Open to the public and advertised in the *Daily Northwestern* and elsewhere, the programs feature student and faculty performers, departmental presentations, and such guests as composer Ned Rorem (44) and *Chicago Tribune* music critic John von Rhein.

A Revised Curriculum

In the mid-1990s, Dobroski challenged the faculty to reevaluate the curriculum to keep ideas and courses current and fresh. In 1997 the faculty approved a revision that allowed expanded coverage of selected topics, giving history and theory professors greater autonomy. The new guide stated that "the faculty believe that each undergraduate should be given a comprehensive musical background, that the education should be centered on performance founded on scholarly studies in music theory and history, and that all musical training should be accompanied by a broad cultural background in the humanities. . . . The curriculum allows flexibility for students while providing an education that is basic for all musicians. Applicants in all areas who are accepted by the School of Music enter directly into a program of specialization that begins in the freshman year. The core studies, taken by all students, require the acquisition of minimum competencies and provide fundamental and essential experiences that complement the specialized studies in the declared major. Students are also required to complete studies in a number of allied subjects throughout the University and are given significant opportunities to explore other interests with free electives."

All freshmen take 100-level theory courses and move on to 200-level courses as sophomores. Music history begins during the sophomore year and continues into the junior year. The curriculum allows each program more autonomy in deciding what is appropriate for its majors. For example, the wind and percussion department requires only one year of keyboard skills, while the music education department requires two years and encourages majors to take a third. The increasingly popular musicology major requires a year of German. And all majors can fulfill their Area I distribution requirement (which consists of various science and math courses) with music technology courses.

Other changes included additions to the ear-training and sight-singing course Aural Skills. Students could still test out of the required two-year, six-level course but now have the option of continuing to study sight-singing and ear-training for a third year.

Visitors

The 1990s saw appearances by distinguished guests as well as major conventions. Chicago Symphony Orchestra music director Sir Georg Solti chatted with students in 1993, and conductor Pierre Boulez brought his Ensemble InterContemporain to campus the same year. Flutist James Galway gave a master class to a jam-packed Lutkin Hall in 1990; mezzo-soprano Marilyn Horne wowed audiences with her guest performance with the Symphony Orchestra in 1991. Soprano Anna Moffo visited in 1991; soprano Martina Arroyo surprised a voice solo class in 1994. An honorary degree was awarded to conductor James Levine in 1992. Visiting professors included ethnomusicologist Bruno Nettl and composers Anthony Davis, Mauricio Kagel, Gerhard Stäbler, and Marta Ptaszynska. Other visitors included violinist Pinchas Zukerman, voice alumna Grace Bumbry, future faculty member Sherrill Milnes, Chicago Symphony Orchestra music director Daniel Barenboim, the Chicago Symphony Orchestra Chamber Musicians, organist David Craighead, the United States Marine Band, the Summit Brass, composer-pianist Frederic Rzewski, Beatles associate Neil Aspinall, guitarist John Abercrombie, composer Yuri Falik, guitarist Oscar Ghiglia, lutenist Julian Bream, trumpeter Armando Ghitalla, jazz artist Wynton Marsalis, bassist Bertram Turetzky, and tubist Roger Bobo. In

229

ABOVE
Composer John Cage (left) with Dean Dobroski in 1992

BELOW
Jazz trumpeter Wynton Marsalis during a 1998 campus visit

1996, Bennett Reimer led the first of the Northwestern University Music Education Leadership Seminars (NUMELS) for leaders in music education.

Associations increasingly chose Northwestern as their convention sites. The inaugural meeting of Music Theory Midwest was held on campus in 1990. Instrumentalists flocked to Northwestern for the 1993 International Viola Congress, 1995 International Tuba-Euphonium Conference, 1997 International Double Reed Society Conference, and 1998 North American Saxophone Alliance Conference. In 1999, Richard Ashley hosted the annual conference of the Society for Music Perception and Cognition. Other organizations holding conferences at the school have included the American Liszt Society, the Midwest chapter of the American Musicological Society, and the American Society of University Composers. The National Opera Association called Northwestern's music school its home from 1993 to 1995, with Jeffrey Wright (G83, G91) as its national secretary.

Music Library

Throughout the decade, head music librarian Don Roberts continued to strive to make the Music Library more accessible to the community. Looking to the future, he noted that "the main challenge will be keeping up with the electronic advances made both internationally and nationally to gain better access to special collections. Lack of space will soon become a problem, too."

The Music Library's current holdings of more than 225,000 cataloged volumes include 74,000 scores, 32,000 books, 46,000 recordings, and thousands of manuscripts, microfilms, and periodical volumes. Now internationally renowned for its 20th-century collection, the library houses material from John Cage, the ONCE Group, and other distinguished figures. Roberts, focusing on electronics and computerization as bridges to the future, is determined that the Music Library "always be in tune with what is happening in the current period."

ABOVE

Tubas on parade during the International Tuba-Euphonium Conference in June 1995

BELOW

A soccer game in Deering Meadow, with Deering Library in the background

ennial Celebration

95 the school began celebrating its 100th birthday. The festivities started with
coff by Dean Dobroski at the Homecoming Concert in October 1995. The 15-
h celebration brought in such guests as composers Gunther Schuller, Ned
Rorem, and Pauline Oliveros as well as guitarist Paco de

Lucia, pianist John Browning, the London Brass, Chicago Symphony Orchestra chamber ensembles, and I Musici de Montreal with faculty member Sylvia Wang as piano soloist. On March 1, 1996, Chicago's Orchestra Hall hosted an all-school gala concert that featured faculty mezzo-soprano Mignon Dunn, the Symphony Orchestra under conductor Victor Yampolsky, and a combined chorus led by Robert Harris. That spring, voice pro-

fessors Sunny Joy Langton and Karen Brunssen produced the
ol's "Birthday Bash." The Evelyn Dunbar Memorial Early Music Festival and the
nuing education series Score Order began in 1996 as part of the centennial
ration as well.

Other special events included the release of recordings by the Symphonic
. Ensemble, Marching Band, Symphony Orchestra, Samaris Trio, and Kwak-
g Piano Duo. Faculty composers M. William Karlins, Michael Pisaro, Stephen
ud, Amnon Wolman, and Jay Alan Yim wrote pieces for the school; Karel Husa
lumni Joseph Schwantner, Augusta Read Thomas, and Mark Camphouse also
osed works for the occasion. The festivities included an alumni organ series,
rmances by pop and jazz artists, and a series of lecture-demonstrations by out-
ing alumni, faculty, and special guests. Ursula Oppens helped wrap up the cele-
on with the premiere of Tobias Picker's *Four Etudes for Ursula* — commissioned
ppens and the School of Music in honor of the school's centennial — at her
egie Hall recital on February 4, 1997.

TOP
The centennial Homecoming concert
CENTER AND BOTTOM
CDs and brochure issued in honor of
the School of Music centennial
LEFT
Choristers performing at a centennial
concert

A Vision for the Future

From modest music lessons to a full-fledged music school, Northwestern University's School of Music has grown in stature and size, programs and pupils, and faculty and staff. Like all centenarians, it has witnessed the advent of technological changes, from phonographs to computers. It has survived Prohibition, the sexual revolution, the roaring '20s, the "conservative" '50s, and the "postmodern" '90s. It has seen music in the United States come of age; orchestras and community bands rise and fall; opera and choral traditions flourish; and new musical venues emerge amid the 20th century's ever-changing opportunities.

Yet through it all — the world wars, financial fluctuations, and social change — the school has remained consistently loyal to its founder's vision and drive: to prepare well-rounded musicians for the challenges of daily life amid a culturally rich environment. It has adjusted and added programs to maintain competitiveness within an ever-changing music world. It has continued to reach and educate the broader community.

Now, as the School of Music welcomes a new millennium, it strides ahead with a mission rooted firmly in the past. "Of our legacy's forebears, none was more creative, dynamic, and clear-sighted than Dean Lutkin," wrote Dean Dobroski in the fall 1995 *Fanfare.* "A handwritten essay found among his papers in the library is as appropriate today as it was when set down nearly 100 years ago. We are truly united in purpose and efforts across time and space."

The study of music in connection with a university cannot but exert a broadening and most wholesome influence. The music student is continually reminded that there are other cultural values besides those he has chosen for his life's work, and college discipline and college tradition are constant incentives to close application. Opportunity is afforded for the pursuit of subjects which have a collateral bearing on music study, such as modern languages, physics with its attention to acoustics, and history both general and in its relation to the fine arts. With an exacting course he must necessarily devote his whole time to the work, and such intricate subjects as advanced harmony, counterpoint, and composition will receive that time and attention without which no lasting benefit accrues.

The adoption of the study of music into the college curriculum and the establishment of schools of music under university auspices is a movement of deep import to the future development of music in America. It places the study of the art on a higher intellectual plane, and it will tend to make the musician of the future a man of wider vision and greater culture. It will encourage that thorough and scientific pursuit of the subject that results in composition of the highest order, in criticism that is intelligent and discriminating, in musico-literary work that evinces both technical knowledge and good English, in research work that will trace the cause and effect of indigenous art, in standards of performance which seek to expose the real intent of the composer rather than to exploit the virtuosity or personality of the performer. Through lectures, recitals, concerts, and music festivals the student body as a whole will come in contact with the highest expression of musical art, and that at a period in their lives when their receptive capacity is greatest and their enthusiasm the keenest. These thousands of students will go forth as musical missionaries to their various communities and will serve as a powerful leavening in the lump of popular appreciation of music in our broad land.

— From *Music in Its Relation to the University,*
undated holograph essay by Peter Christian Lutkin, c. 1910

Faculty Hall of Fame

PAUL A. ALIAPOULIOS

Born on December 6, 1935, in Manchester, New Hampshire, Paul Aliapoulios began his musical career as a clarinetist, saxophonist, conductor, and vocalist. He received his bachelor's degree from the University of New Hampshire in 1957. After stints as a public-school music teacher and army officer, he began graduate study at Boston University, where he taught woodwind classes, conducted the Varsity Band, and supervised student teachers. He completed a master of music in 1961 and a doctor of musical arts in 1970.

Aliapoulios was choral director at Weymouth High School from 1962 to 1966. From 1966 to 1972 he served on the faculty at East Carolina University, rising to associate professor and assistant dean in 1970. After chairing the music department at Miami University from 1972 to 1976, he joined the Northwestern conducting and music education faculty in 1976. At the School of Music he held a variety of administrative positions: associate dean of undergraduate studies (1976–84), associate dean of academic affairs (1984–94), acting dean (1989–90), acting chair of voice and opera (1991–94), cochair of performance studies (1994–96), and chair of academic studies and composition (1997–2001). For his last seven years on the faculty, Aliapoulios carried a full teaching load as professor of music education. In 2000 the Northwestern Alumni Association honored him with its Excellence in Teaching Award.

Conductor of nearly 20 choral groups across the United States, Aliapoulios founded and led the Weymouth Civic Chorus and the Greenville (North Carolina) Community Chorus. He also conducted the Braintree (Massachusetts) Choral Society, the Frederick Smyth Chorale, and the Music Center of the North Shore Summer Chorale as well as the East Carolina Chamber Singers and the A Cappella Singers of Miami University. At Northwestern he served at various times as conductor of the University Chorus, University Singers, Women's Chorus, and Chorale. From 1984 to 2001 he was also music director of Kenilworth Union Church.

While on the faculty, Aliapoulios performed often as a baritone soloist and played saxophone in the Old Man's Jazz Band. He also served as an adjudicator and clinician for choral and instrumental ensembles throughout the United States. His wife, Janet, taught in the Winnetka Public Schools; they have three sons (all of whom earned degrees from Northwestern) and six grandchildren. Aliapoulios retired in 2001 after 25 years on the Northwestern faculty.

HERMANUS BAER

Born November 9, 1902, in Beaver City, Nebraska, Hermanus Baer received his bachelor's degree from the University of Nebraska — where he also met his future wife, Rachel Clem. A year after graduation, the 23-year-old Baer started his teaching career as a voice professor at North Central College in Naperville, Illinois. He remained there for 16 years, meanwhile earning his master's degree from the American Conservatory of Music in 1936. In 1941 he accepted an offer to teach at Northwestern, and five years later he became chair of the voice department. A member of the Chicago Singing Teachers Guild, National Association of Teachers of Singing, and Society of American Musicians, Baer sang on radio and was active as a recital, concert, and oratorio soloist. After retiring in 1973, he settled in Bradenton, Florida.

Baer is best remembered for his special technique of "drinking in the breath," which he developed in 1960 after extensive research into new teaching methods. He adapted ideas from

German instructors to create a more natural balance between the muscles of inhalation and exhalation. Accompanied by Baer's supportive teaching approach, this technique helped his students achieve widespread success as performers — at the Metropolitan Opera, Lyric Opera of Chicago, San Francisco Opera, Seattle Opera, Houston Opera, Covent Garden, and opera houses in Cincinnati, London, Hamburg, Munich, Vienna, Lisbon, Barcelona, and Stockholm.

Baer died in Bradenton, Florida, on September 10, 1996.

JILL BAILIFF

Jill Bailiff came to Northwestern in 1957 to join the faculty as a teaching associate in harp. Previously she taught at the University of Texas at Austin and played with the Austin Symphony from 1952 to 1955. Before her stint in the Lone Star State, Bailiff played with the La Scala Opera Company from 1947 to 1952. She also played for five years with the Philadelphia Orchestra and for seven seasons with the Salzedo Summer Harp Colony in Camden, Maine.

Born on May 20, 1925, in Mullens, West Virginia, Bailiff earned her bachelor's degree and certificate in music in 1949 from Philadelphia's Curtis Institute of Music, where she belonged to Mu Phi Epsilon. Before arriving at Northwestern, she spent a year in Paris on a Fulbright scholarship, studying chamber music with Lily Laskine and Micheline Kahn.

Bailiff taught at Northwestern until 1966. Her late husband, Angel Reyes, taught at the University from 1955 to 1965, serving as chair of the string department and professor of violin. He left Northwestern to chair the violin department at the University of Michigan.

GLENN CLIFFE BAINUM

Born January 6, 1888, in Olney, Illinois, Glenn Cliffe "Rusty" Bainum began his lifelong love affair with bands as a child. As a 10-year-old in Paxton, Illinois, Bainum played both trombone and upright alto horn in the Paxton Silver Cornet Band. He continued to participate in band as a student at the University of Illinois, though he took time off before graduation to teach English and engineering science in Piper City, Momence, and Melvin, Illinois.

At the University of Illinois, band leader A. A. Harding took Bainum under his wing, appointing him first percussionist and bass drummer in the band and later making him the first assistant conductor of Illinois bands. After graduating in 1913, Bainum spent a year teaching at West Aurora High School before moving to Southern Illinois Normal University (now Southern Illinois University), where he served as director of music from 1914 to 1922 except for two years as an officer in the U.S. Army infantry.

Returning to the University of Illinois, Bainum worked on a BA in music from 1922 to 1924. He then moved to Grand Rapids, Michigan, to direct music programs in the city's public schools and junior colleges. It was in Grand Rapids that Bainum first worked under future School of Music dean John Beattie.

Bainum followed Beattie to Evanston in 1926 at the urging of Dean Peter Christian Lutkin, who appointed Bainum professor of music, director of bands, and director of the men's and women's glee clubs. He taught classes in conducting, band arranging, instrumentation, and band techniques. In his first two years, Bainum expanded the band from 17 to more than 100 members.

Among Bainum's most noteworthy achievements were his innovations on the marching field. He was the first to use charts to teach band members marching maneuvers, and he originated electrically illuminated marching pageantry for night formations at the all-star football games at Soldier Field. Bainum also created the 200-piece College All-Star Marching Band and encouraged students' compositional efforts by performing their music during football games.

His activities were not limited to the School of Music. Bainum conducted the Waa-Mu Show orchestra. He was Frederick Stock's associate conductor in the North Shore Music Festival and also conducted the Grant Park Symphonic Band and weekly programs on Chicago radio station WMAQ. As chief of the Overseas Music Branch of Special Services for the U.S. Army from 1942 to 1945, he was responsible for music in the European theater of operations.

Students from the era have fond memories of Bainum's humorous teaching phrases and methods. Loren McDonald (G42) recalls his descriptions of an alto horn as a "flat wheel on the streetcar" and an oboe as "the ill wind that nobody blows good."

Bainum retired in the spring of 1953 but went on to teach and conduct in all 50 states. His new charges ranged from elementary school children to music professionals. When he died in 1974 at age 86, he was the honorary life president of the American Bandmasters Association, of which he had served as president, secretary, and treasurer.

After Bainum's death his successor, John Paynter, recalled their initial encounter. "It was a matter of only a few minutes after my first meeting with Glenn Cliffe Bainum that I was employed by the Northwestern University Band as a member of the student staff," Paynter said in a memorial tribute. "My clarinet audition on that fall day of 1946 surely could not have impressed this small, thinly built, white-haired man who glowingly convinced me otherwise as he sped me into his office, hurried me through the playing, and hustled me out again in less than four minutes. Before I could put my clarinet in the case, his door swung open. 'You look like a bright guy with a lot of energy. Do you know how to run a mimeograph machine?' Of course I didn't, and of course I never told him so. If he found out, Mr. Bainum never let on. He was content to build the ego and bolster the sense of belonging for a bumbling kid from a small town who was trying to adjust to the life of a large urban university."

Paynter observed that Bainum was as fondly remembered for his concern for others as for his musical talents. "The secret was his uncanny capacity for saying just the right thing in such a uniquely original way that, punctuated with the warm intensity of his sparkling eyes and possessing smile, you just knew he meant every word of it. . . . He had the capacity for making everyone he met feel a little bigger, to know a little more happiness, to love with more fullness. Glenn Cliffe Bainum truly fulfilled his purpose on this earth."

HANS BALATKA

Conductor of the Philharmonic Society — precursor to the Theodore Thomas Orchestra, which in turn became the Chicago Symphony Orchestra — Hans Balatka served on the Conservatory of Music faculty in the 1870s. According to the 1875 University catalog, he taught "quartette singing," "drilled" choirs, and served as conductor of choral and "concerted" music. Balatka was born on February 26, 1825, in Moravia and studied and conducted in Vienna before coming to the United States in 1849. After founding the German Musik-verein in Milwaukee and conducting it from 1851 to 1860, he moved to Chicago to lead the Philharmonic Society and the Musical Union. Active as a composer and as director of other Milwaukee and Chicago musical organizations, he died in Chicago on April 17, 1899.

Dean JOHN WALTER BEATTIE

When Dean John Walter Beattie retired from Northwestern, the heartfelt messages of gratitude and good wishes that poured in from fellow faculty members, friends, and alumni all over the country

filled a bound scrapbook five inches thick. They spoke of the educator's intelligence, integrity, and dedication.

Sadie Rafferty, then director of music at Evanston Township High School and a School of Music faculty member, wrote new words to Gilbert and Sullivan's "Modern Major General" that summed up the sentiments of many:

> You are the very model of a modern School of
> Music dean,
> You're filled with ideas, projects, plans, and all
> of them are very keen,
> You write a book, you teach a class, you play a
> bit of golf, I ween,
> And through it all, I do declare, you never lose
> your deanly mien.

Born November 26, 1885, in Norwalk, Ohio, Beattie received a bachelor's degree in classical languages from Denison University in 1907 and a master's in education from Columbia University in 1923. As a student he participated in a variety of activities, from glee clubs to managing the football team.

The ardent and involved student went on to become an administrator with the same qualities. He started his career as supervisor of music for the public schools of Xenia, Ohio. In 1912 he moved to the same position in Grand Rapids, Michigan, where he remained for 12 years. Appointed Michigan's state supervisor of music in 1924, he held the position in Lansing just one year before accepting a professorship of public school music at Northwestern in 1925.

After Carl Milton Beecher resigned as dean in 1934, Beattie was named acting dean, then promoted to dean in 1936. In addition to maintaining his teaching duties and serving as supervisor of music education in the Evanston elementary schools, Beattie served as the School of Music's placement director from 1925 to 1950 and director of the summer program from 1926 until his retirement in 1951.

Especially interested in Latin American music, Beattie collected folk songs from the region and incorporated them into his educational publications. In 1941 he was chosen to represent the Pan American Union on a two-month tour of seven South American countries to research music education methods and the possibilities for cooperation between those countries and the United States.

Beattie received numerous awards throughout his career, but the greatest honors came from students and colleagues who remembered his invaluable advice, his steady golf swing, the time he took from his busy schedule to help a student, and his sincere friendship. Those who knew him will never forget his patience, hard work, intelligence, and dedication to his field.

"We all remember you as a real friend, wonderful adviser, and teacher. Maybe you will remember me as the 'gal' who was told, 'Don't bust my car,' when she borrowed your personal automobile for an application trip," joked Genevieve Rystrom More (35).

Esther M. Hoffman recalled a statement he had made to future teachers in her last class with him: "You have been taught many methods of teaching music. Go out and find your own."

Howard Kilbert (41, G46) wrote, "I remember the first meeting of your class in music supervision. You told us to forget about being supervisors — the course would be concerned with more useful material. It was only necessary to have such a course title on a transcript since so many states required it."

"Talking with you in your office or meeting you in the halls of 1822 et al. was always a dramatic experience in sincere cordiality and human interest and understanding," remembered E. Lawrence Barr (31, G40). "You liked us all, knew our strengths and shortcomings, [and] placed us in jobs where we could do our best."

Beattie's first wife, Maude Hayes Thayer, died in 1950; he later married Clara Kanne Blondoit. He died on November 23, 1962, and Clara died two days later.

Dean CARL MILTON BEECHER

School of Music legend has it that the school's second dean disappeared one day, turning up years later in Tahiti married to a woman from the islands. Carl Milton Beecher did not actually "disappear," but the exotic trajectory of his musical career did include a lengthy stay in the South Pacific.

Beecher was born in Lafayette, Illinois, on October 22, 1883, and began his musical training at an early age. At 16 he came to Northwestern and studied in the College of Liberal Arts before devoting himself to music as a piano and composition student of Arne Oldberg.

In 1908 Beecher became the first to earn Northwestern's five-year bachelor of music degree. Following four years of study in Europe with Russian pianist Josef Lhévinne and Russian composer Paul Juon, Beecher returned to his alma mater in 1913 to teach piano and theory. In 1920 he and Mark Wessel received the first two master of music degrees conferred by Northwestern. By 1924 he was named the School of Music's administrative director. During his years at Northwestern, he composed chamber and vocal works and studied Polynesian music.

Lutkin supported Beecher's appointment as dean in 1928. The former dean wrote, "It is only the natural order of things that a talented alumnus, a longtime prominent faculty member, and a highly successful administrative director should make the best possible candidate for the exacting office of dean." Beecher held the position for only six years before his departure for Tahiti. He tendered his resignation in February 1934 to "devote himself to research projects in music and to composing" and asked for a year's leave of absence beginning that May. In March 1936 he requested an indefinite leave without salary.

That Beecher ended up in the Polynesian islands was not a total surprise. He had already taken several trips there to make recordings of the local music, attempting to create — as he told the *Chicago Daily News* in 1936 — a "motion-picture record of the ordinary native life of the Society Islands, trying to escape any falseness or unnaturalness." His research included study of the language and culture as well as the music. Beecher was particularly taken with the culture of islands less influenced by the West; he noted that while a strong economy drove the islands to "the less desirable kind of white culture," recessions produced "a boon for the natives" by forcing them back to a self-supportive agricultural lifestyle.

Some 16 years after Beecher's departure, a 1948 *Daily Northwestern* article chronicled his experiences with Polynesian life and music. "It is a rather ideal spot for older men with mental work to do," observed the *Daily* writer, "for they can work without being bothered by the demands of big-city life. Dr. Beecher mentioned James Norton Hall, noted anthropologist, as one who came to Tahiti for this reason. Other musicians, painters, and writers are in Dr. Beecher's circle of friends."

Beecher's student Emily Boettcher (26, G38) was one of the few to keep up with his post-Northwestern life. He wrote her from Tahiti, "I think of you and a few other choice souls and forget all the rest of those soul-trying years at Northwestern. How dim and far away most of that experience seems to me now."

Beecher directed a plantation that produced vanilla and copra (dried coconut meat yielding coconut oil) and continued performing with other musicians who had settled in the islands. In 1953 Boettcher wrote to a friend of her former professor: "On the island of Moorhea, he built himself a large, airy house, married Ahnura, and begot two children. Toward the end of the war, when living in a French colony became impossible, he went back to the states and settled in his father's house in Portland, Oregon. He has two lovely daughters, Louise and Helen. He says they are his best opus!"

Beecher remained in Oregon, where he taught theory at a local college, until his death in 1968. In a 1953 Christmas letter to Boettcher, he wrote, "Music is the greatest thing invented by man."

FELIX BOROWSKI

Born March 10, 1872, in Kendal, England, Felix Borowski joined the faculty in 1933 as a lecturer on musical form and history and became a professor of musicology in 1937. As professor emeritus after his official retirement in 1941, Borowski served as a lecturer from 1942 to 1947. He died on September 6, 1956.

Educated in London and Cologne, Borowski began his career in Aberdeen, Scotland. He came to the United States in 1897 to teach violin, composition, and history at Chicago Musical College, where he served as president from 1916 to 1925. Active as a composer and critic, he also served for several years as a program annotator for the Chicago Symphony Orchestra. Borowski succeeded George P. Upton at the *Chicago Tribune* as the city's leading music critic and expanded two Upton works as the books *The Standard Operas* and *The Standard Concert Guide,* republished together in 1936. He was also responsible for building the music collection of the Newberry Library, beginning soon after his arrival in Chicago and continuing as a part-time staff member from 1920 to 1956.

Lillian Sellars (38), a former student, wrote that Borowski was one of her favorite teachers at Northwestern: "Felix Borowski told one anecdote after another about composers, conductors, musicians, and the history of music, which I remember to this day and never pass along to my piano students without thinking of him. There seemed to be an endless bounty of stories and tales which came alive as he sat on a high stool and lectured with his skilled, faultless diction and wit. He made music history fascinating."

CLIFTON BURMEISTER

Born in 1913 in Mason City, Iowa, Clifton Burmeister received a BA from Carleton College in 1933, a master's from Northwestern in 1941, and a PhD from the University of Kansas in 1953. Before joining the Northwestern faculty in 1952, he served as an officer in the U.S. Air Force Convalescent Training Program during World War II and taught in Iowa, Ohio, and Missouri.

At Northwestern, Burmeister chaired the music education department, directed the School of Music placement office, and served on the committee planning the University's lakefill fine arts facilities. Director of music for Evanston's School District 65 from 1952 to 1960, he also played trombone in the Evanston Symphony Orchestra and in concert and dance bands, sang tenor in a church quartet, and conducted church choirs.

Burmeister's publications included *Music Research Handbook* with Hazel B. Morgan (1962) and a chapter in *Basic Concepts of Music Education* (1958). He served as a consultant for the Birchard Music Series in 1962 and as a member of the state committee preparing a curriculum guide for secondary school music in the 1960s.

Guest conductor, clinician, speaker, and adjudicator for various musical and educational events, Burmeister served on the editorial board of the *Music Educators Journal* and as an adviser to the National Education Association's Educational Policies Commission. He was a member of the Music Educators National Conference, serving as North Central Division president and first vice president. He was also MENC's national counselor of student chapters and national chair of the commission on music in higher education.

In 1963 Burmeister became the first professor to hold the John W. Beattie Chair of Music. In 1969 Steinway & Sons presented the Steinway Award to Burmeister for his outstanding contributions to music education, and in 1996 Northwestern's School of Music presented him its Legends in Teaching Award. He died in Ames, Iowa, on November 8, 2001, at age 88.

WALTER CARRINGER

Born in 1924, Walter Carringer began his formal music studies with piano lessons in high school. Though he had been singing since childhood, it wasn't until after entering the army in 1943 that he thought of becoming a professional. Performances in USO shows and chapel services while he was stationed in Florida convinced him to major in music on the GI bill after his enlisted duty ended. He enrolled at Wesley-Carolina College but was encouraged by a librarian there to transfer to Columbia University, where he continued to major in music but was obliged to study voice on his own because the performance department was so small. As a senior, Carringer began singing with the Robert Shaw Chorale, and soon afterwards he was signed by a New York manager. Within a few years he was in worldwide demand as an oratorio soloist and had launched a successful recital career. On the operatic stage he appeared in the American premiere of Rossini's *Semiramide* with Joan Sutherland and Marilyn Horne.

Carringer continued to perform after joining the Northwestern voice faculty in 1964, giving yearly campus recitals that were accompanied and coproduced by piano professor Laurence Davis. Fond of singing new music, he premiered works by Lukas Foss and sang pieces by fellow faculty members Anthony Donato and Alan Stout. Carringer also encouraged students to be more adventurous in their choice of repertoire. His book *The Singer's Primer* was issued by Hinshaw Music in 1979.

Since retiring from Northwestern in 1987, Carringer has made his home in Flat Rock, North Carolina.

VINCENT CICHOWICZ

Born on August 27, 1927, in Chicago, Vincent Cichowicz began his musical career at age 17 in the Houston Symphony Orchestra. He began studies in Chicago with Renold Schilke at Roosevelt University and with Adolph Herseth on a Civic Orchestra of Chicago scholarship while playing first trumpet in the Grant Park Symphony Orchestra one summer. After a brief military service in the United States Fifth Army Band, he resumed his musical career in the Chicago area while attending Roosevelt University. In 1952 he became a member of the Chicago Symphony Orchestra, where he remained for 23 years. During that time he was a member of the Chicago Symphony Brass Quintet and a participant in the Grammy Award–winning Columbia recording of Giovanni Gabrieli's *Antiphonal Brass Music*. He joined the Northwestern faculty in 1959 and retired in 1997. A member of the Chicago School of Music faculty from 1946 to 1961, he has also taught for the National Youth Orchestra of Canada since 1980 and the Brass Seminar program at Le Domaine Forget in Quebec since 1986.

Cichowicz has written articles for the *Instrumentalist* magazine, arrangements for Crown Press, and a pamphlet, published by Selmer, on the piccolo trumpet. A member of the steering committee responsible for founding the International Trumpet Guild, he also served on the advisory board of the *Instrumentalist*. In 1995 he was appointed music director of the Millar Brass Ensemble. Regarded as one of North America's foremost experts in brass pedagogy, he has conducted numerous workshops and clinics throughout the United States, Canada, Europe, and Japan.

SADIE KNOWLAND COE

Born October 9, 1864, in San Francisco, Sadie Knowland began piano lessons at age nine. According to her husband, the lessons were started "as they do with most girls whose mothers value music as an accomplishment." But once she began studying with Ernst Hartmann of San Francisco, she became passionate about music. In 1885 she set off for Boston to study piano with Carl Baerman and composition with John W. Tufts. During her two-year stay there, she met her future husband, George Coe, later a professor at Northwestern. They were married on September 3, 1888, and both first taught in Los Angeles at the University of Southern California. Overseeing the musical and business aspects of the music department, she won the respect of her colleagues by turning the financial tide and ended up with a salary almost equal to her husband's. In the musical realm, she founded a music library and stressed theory and history, both of which she taught in connection with piano.

In 1890 the Coes went to Germany. While there Mrs. Coe attended the Royal College of Music and studied with Heinrich Barth, Woldemar Bargiel, and Moritz Moszkowski. She also developed a lifelong love for the music of Wagner. Though in 1891 her husband received a call to teach at Northwestern, she remained in Germany to finish her studies.

Sadie Coe came to Northwestern in 1893 and stayed until her death in 1905. Initially a piano instructor, she also helped make music history an integral part of the curriculum. Her husband wrote that "at first, she taught the subject for the love of it." In addition to reading widely in music history, biography, and criticism, she began procuring books for a music library. Coe gave lectures and lecture-recitals, wrote for the press, and composed. Most of all, she loved to teach. She constantly sought new material and went out of her way to help students, whether academically or financially. In 1901 she was promoted from instructor to professor, and she later received a lectureship in the College of Liberal Arts.

Coe also chaired the music department of the Illinois Federation of Women's Clubs for two years and led the musical work of the Evanston Women's Club for four seasons. Just before her death on August 24, 1905, she published "The Melodrama of Hiawatha" for speaking voice and piano. Her works and mission live on in the Sadie Knowland Coe Music Collection at the Evanston Public Library. The purpose of the collection is "to perpetuate the work of popular music culture carried on in Evanston by Mrs. Coe for 12 years."

FRANK BARTON COOKSON

Born in Wigan, England, on September 27, 1912, Frank Cookson moved to Detroit with his parents when he was a year old. He began studying music on a scholarship at Oberlin College but dropped out when his mother died in a car accident. He remained with his father until eventually attending Northwestern's School of Music, where he earned his bachelor's and master's degrees. In 1947 he received a PhD from the Eastman School of Music.

Cookson joined the Northwestern faculty at age 27 and taught theory and composition for 23 years, chairing the department for a decade. He edited and (with Arrand Parsons) co-authored the two-volume textbook *Creative-Analytical Theory of Music*. He also served as managing editor of the School of Music's *Educational Music Magazine*. Choirmaster, organist, composer, author, and nationally recognized educator, he was listed in *Who's Who in America*, *Who's Who in Music*, and *Contemporary Authors*. In 1961 he became the first dean of fine arts at the University of Connecticut at Storrs. After his death in 1977, that school's music library was renamed the Frank B. Cookson Music Library.

FRANK CRISAFULLI

Born on January 15, 1916, in Chicago, Frank Crisafulli began studying trombone in high school with his father, a trombonist for the Chicago Opera Company and the WGN radio orchestra. While a student in the College of Liberal Arts at Northwestern, he played with the Civic Orchestra of Chicago. He joined the Chicago Symphony Orchestra in 1938 and within a year was named principal trombone — a position he retained, with a break for military service (1945–46), until 1955. Crisafulli remained a member of the CSO until his retirement in 1989 and was a member of the Chicago Symphony Brass Ensemble from its inception.

After teaching at Chicago State College, Crisafulli joined the Northwestern faculty as professor of trombone in 1953 and taught until retiring in 1998. His standard advice to students was to pursue double majors, become teachers, and, above all, keep practicing.

Crisafulli's students, many of whom now hold positions in some of the world's top-ranked orchestras, affectionately called him "Mr. C" (earlier students called him "Cris"). He treated every pupil like part of his family and was famous for inviting students to his house for Thanksgiving dinner if they were stranded on campus.

Lessons lasted as long as needed, and he sneaked his students into CSO concerts so many times that orchestra officials began to think they worked there.

After his death in Evanston on November 5, 1998, tributes were plentiful. Hank Keating (c4, G55) said, "While lots of people remember him as a musician, to me he was the best example I have ever known of what a fine, first-class human being should be." Associate professor of tuba Rex Martin commented, "Frank was a tremendous man, and he had a great influence on my playing, my teaching, and even my driving. He was as honest and upfront as any man, and he was more encouraging to his students than anyone I've known."

LOUIS CROWDER

Born July 5, 1907, in Springfield, Illinois, Louis Crowder received his bachelor's degree from Pittsburgh's Carnegie Institute of Technology in 1930. He then studied piano in Europe for four years — with Eugen d'Albert and Egon Petri in Berlin and Robert Casadesus in Paris.

His career soon took off, with concert tours to major cities in the United States as well as to London, Vienna, Berlin, Budapest, and Leipzig. He performed as a soloist with the Chicago Symphony, Pittsburgh Symphony, and Leipzig Philharmonic Orchestras and at universities across the country. Crowder was also a visiting artist with the arts program of the Association of American Colleges for 12 years. In 1959 he was elected president of the Society of American Musicians — at the time, a 250-member group of teachers and performers.

Crowder taught at Mount Union College in Alliance, Ohio, from 1935 to 1937 and at Iowa State Teachers College in Cedar Falls before coming to Northwestern in 1941. He remained on the faculty for 24 years, including nine years as chair of the piano department. His wife, Lucille, also taught piano at Northwestern.

GEORGE DASCH

Cincinnati native George Dasch was born on May 14, 1877, and attended the University of Cincinnati College-Conservatory of Music as a violin major in 1894–95, earning a diploma, a teacher's certificate, and the Springer Medal. He served on the faculty there and played in the Cincinnati Symphony Orchestra for three years.

In 1898 he joined the Chicago Symphony Orchestra, playing under conductors Theodore Thomas and Frederick Stock and such guest conductors as Richard Strauss, Edward Elgar, Camille Saint-Saëns, Vincent D'Indy, Victor Herbert, Pietro Mascagni, and Sergei Rachmaninoff. For three years he also served as assistant conductor of the Chicago Civic Orchestra under Stock.

In 1921 he cofounded the Little Symphony Orchestra of Chicago, which so flourished that after two years he resigned from the CSO. For 15 years the Little Symphony gave concerts and radio performances in the Chicago area and throughout the country.

In 1928 Dasch was appointed conductor of the Northwestern University Symphony Orchestra — the group's first truly professional leader. He also conducted the Chicago Business Men's Orchestra, Iowa's Waterloo Symphony Orchestra, and a symphony orchestra in Joliet, Illinois. In 1943 he was named director of the Evansville Philharmonic Orchestra in Evansville, Indiana, where he also taught violin at Evansville College.

Dasch retired from Northwestern University in 1945 after directing NUSO for 17 years. He died in in his home in Glenview in April 1955, just a month before he would have turned 78.

LYNDEN DeYOUNG

Born on March 6, 1923, in Chicago, Lynden DeYoung began his career as a jazz trombonist and arranger in the Chicago area and continued to play professionally while at Northwestern. A special

services trombonist-arranger in the U.S. Army from 1943 to 1946, he received a bachelor's degree in composition in 1949 and a master's in the same field in 1950 from Roosevelt University, where he then taught. After teaching fifth through eighth grades (including classes in language arts and science) in Illinois public schools, DeYoung came to Northwestern, where he served as a teaching assistant while pursuing a doctorate in composition. He received the degree in 1966 and was named to the composition faculty that same year.

DeYoung's students recall his encouraging and uplifting teaching style, gentlemanly ways, and kind nature. Chair of the theory and composition department from 1967 to 1975, he taught numerous courses, including aural skills, orchestration, musicianship, baroque counterpoint, Jazz and the Swing Era, Materials of Modern Music, and private composition lessons. His compositions included a brass quintet commissioned for the Chicago Symphony Brass Quintet. He also wrote magazine articles; his research interests included baroque counterpoint and 20th-century music. DeYoung's nonprofessional pursuits ranged from photography to fishing.

In 1988 he retired after 22 years at Northwestern.

LUTHER DIDRICKSON

Born on July 19, 1938, in Chicago, Luther Didrickson received a bachelor's in music education in 1960 and a master's in music in 1961 from Northwestern. In 1964 he was invited to join the faculty as a trumpet instructor. In addition to studio lessons, Didrickson has given many in-house trumpet master classes as well as courses on brass repertoire, brass history, and related topics. He also organized the trumpet solo class, which allowed trumpeters to perform for their peers and hear new repertoire.

As a performer Didrickson has appeared with Chicago's major performing ensembles, including the Chicago Symphony Orchestra, Grant Park Symphony Orchestra, Lyric Opera of Chicago, Chicago Little Symphony, and Contemporary Chamber Players of the University of Chicago. With the CSO he was chosen to record the off-stage solos in Mahler's Symphony no. 2 on recordings conducted by both Sir Georg Solti and Claudio Abbado. He has toured with the orchestra to places ranging from Carnegie Hall and Lincoln Center to Tokyo, Hong Kong, Moscow, and Vienna.

In 1960 Didrickson was invited to join the Peninsula Festival Orchestra in Door County, Wisconsin, by its founder, Thor Johnson. He became a regular member in 1968 and was named solo trumpet in 1972. In the late 1960s he formed the brass ensemble Brassworks Chicago, which he directed through the early '80s. The group varied in size from a sextet to a nonet plus organ and performed concerts and recitals all over the Midwest. Many arrangements and transcriptions that Didrickson made for the group were published by Crown Press.

Didrickson died on August 1, 2001, at age 63.

Dean BERNARD J. DOBROSKI

He's a Wildcat through and through. Bernard J. Dobroski loves Northwestern and exudes pride every time he talks about the school.

Born on September 29, 1946, Dobroski received a bachelor of fine arts degree in music performance from Carnegie Mellon University in 1968 and a master's in music performance and music history from Catholic University of America in 1972. From 1968 to 1972 he performed as a tubist and keyboardist with the U.S. Navy Band in Washington, D.C., as a soloist with the U.S. Navy Concert Band, as a conductor and performer with the U.S. Navy Ceremonial Band, and as a leader of the U.S. Navy Brass Quintet. He was an instructor and director of the Preparatory Wind Ensemble of the Washington Youth Orchestra from 1969 to 1972.

As a Danforth fellow, Dobroski could attend virtually any school for his doctoral studies. He chose Northwestern after Jack Pernecky, then associate dean of graduate studies, assured him he could follow the program he wanted and study tuba with Arnold Jacobs. He earned an interdisciplinary PhD in 1984.

Almost immediately upon arriving at Northwestern, Dobroski began working as an assistant to Dean Thomas Miller. He was named assistant dean and director of undergraduate studies in 1975 and promoted to associate dean for administration in 1981. In 1986 he became dean of the School of Music at the University of Oregon. During his four years there he was also the administrator for the Oregon Bach Festival, charter president of the Pacific Northwest Chapter of the College Music Society (1987–89), and president of the Oregon Music Administrators Association (1988–90). In 1990 he returned to Northwestern as dean of the School of Music, where he will serve as John Evans Professor of Music after passing the deanship to his successor in 2003.

Dobroski was the founding editor of *Accent*, a national music education publication that he edited from 1975 to 1982. Author of numerous articles in research journals and other music publications, he edited the *College Music Society National Newsletter* from 1972 to 1980 and has contributed to the *Instrumentalist* magazine since 1985. He appears frequently as a lecturer, conductor, adjudicator, and clinician and has given professional performances as a tubist, conductor, and keyboardist throughout the United States. Dobroski has given lectures for the Chicago Symphony Orchestra, the Ravinia Festival Orchestra, the San Francisco Symphony, and the Distinguished Pianist Symphony Series at Carnegie Hall. He frequently presents musicales and continuing education classes for adults and senior citizens in the Northwestern and North Shore communities.

Dobroski is active in numerous academic organizations, including the National Association of Schools of Music, Society for Values in Higher Education, and Music Educators National Conference. Secretary of the Lyric Opera Center for American Artists board, he serves on the board or on visiting committees for the Chicago Symphony Orchestra, Ravinia Festival, Illinois Arts Council, Chicago Center for Arts Policy, Center for Black Music Research, University of Chicago, Carnegie Mellon University, Lira Singers, and Rembrandt Players. He is also the coordinator of the Seven Springs Group, a consortium of 11 major music schools.

In 1992 the Evanston Arts Council presented Dobroski its Arts and Youth Award for the School of Music's popular Kids Fare series. In 1999 he received the Excellence in Opera Award for distinction in the pursuit of operatic education and opera production from the National Opera Association as well as the Alumni Service Award from his alma mater, Carnegie Mellon University.

Louis Norton Dodge

Born in Lone Rock, Wisconsin, in 1873, Louis Norton Dodge bounced between Tacoma, Washington, and Evanston, Illinois, throughout his student years. After beginning his schooling at the Tacoma Academy, he graduated from Northwestern Academy in 1892 and the following year entered Northwestern's College of Liberal Arts, where he gained band and orchestra experience. Dodge then studied piano with Robert Weisbach in Tacoma from 1896 to 1897 before reentering Northwestern to study piano, organ, and theory with Dean Peter Christian Lutkin and organ with Clarence Dickinson in the School of Music.

Even before graduation, Dodge taught piano and harmony at Northwestern during a break in his studies. Upon earning a graduate in music degree in 1903, he was appointed head of the school's preparatory department, where he taught piano and theory until 1917 and ensemble playing from 1915 to 1917. Dodge went on to serve as assistant professor of theory and instructor in piano from 1917 to 1920, associate professor of theory from 1920 to 1924, and professor of theory (also teaching piano and ensemble playing) from 1924 to 1938, when he retired and was named professor emeritus of theory. Two banquets celebrated his Northwestern career, one given by the faculty and the other by his former students.

Dodge's work extended beyond the classroom; he coached piano ensemble and served as an accompanist in addition to writing a keyboard harmony text and composing piano pieces and songs. He was also organist at the Church of the Messiah in Chicago and St. Mark's Episcopal Church in Evanston. Dodge died at age 78 on May 14, 1951.

Anthony Donato

Born March 8, 1909, in Prague, Nebraska, composer and violinist Anthony Donato earned all his degrees at the Eastman School of Music: a bachelor's in 1931, a master's in 1937, and a doctorate in 1947. In addition to pursuing violin studies, he studied composition with Bernard Rogers and Howard Hanson and conducting with Eugene Goossens.

Prior to joining the Northwestern faculty in 1947, Donato headed violin departments at Drake University in Des Moines (1931–37), where he also conducted the orchestra; at Iowa State Teachers College, now Northern Iowa University (1937–39); and at the University of Texas (1939–46), where he also taught composition. He remained at Northwestern until 1976, when he became an emeritus professor. From 1947 to 1958 and in 1961, he directed the University Chamber Orchestra.

As a Fulbright fellow, Donato lectured on contemporary American musical composition at Birmingham University in England during the 1951–52 school year. He was a Huntington Hartford Foundation Fellow during the summer of 1961, furthering his research in musical composition. Donato also received numerous commissions, including those for *Solitude in the City* (1954) from the Cincinnati Symphony Orchestra and *Serenade* (1962) from the Chicago Little Symphony Orchestra.

As a violinist, Donato performed as a member of the Rochester Philharmonic Orchestra from 1927 to 1931 and the Hochstein Quartet from 1929 to 1931, in addition to founding his own quartet. He made many appearances as soloist and chamber player throughout the United States, frequently accompanied by his wife, pianist Carolyn Scott Donato. A prolific composer, he wrote works for orchestra, band, chorus, opera, various chamber ensembles, piano, organ, solo voice, and various instruments with piano. Donato died in Bradenton, Florida, on October 29, 1990.

Emil Eck

Born March 14, 1899, in Elberdeld, Germany, Emil Eck received a bachelor of music degree in 1921 from the Cologne Conservatory, where he studied flute and piano. He performed with the Cologne Symphony Orchestra before coming to the United States, where he was a member of the Chicago Symphony Orchestra flute section from 1923 to 1952. He taught flute at Northwestern's School of Music from 1931 until 1965.

Eck's research interests included flute and other woodwind literature and the history and development of the flute. Belwin Mills published his *Practical Studies, Quartett Album, Arrangements of Flute Soli,* and two-volume *Flute Method*. He was a member of the International Society of Contemporary Music. Eck died on April 4, 1977, in St. Petersburg, Florida.

Richard Enright

Greatly admired by students, Richard Enright not only challenged them professionally but also went to great lengths to help them personally. He was a teacher who cared about the entire person, taking time to inquire about all facets of students' lives and genuinely listening to all they said.

Born on November 29, 1923, in Freeport, Illinois, Enright studied organ at Iowa's University of Dubuque from 1941 until the war intervened in 1943. After serving three years in the U.S. Army, he enrolled at Northwestern, where he received a bachelor's in organ in 1948, a master's in organ in 1949, and a doctorate in church music in 1961. He also studied at the Royal School of Church Music in England in 1954 and the Staatliche Hochshule in Frankfurt, Germany, in 1963.

In 1949 Enright began teaching organ part-time at Northwestern and became associate organist and choirmaster at the Fourth Presbyterian Church in Chicago. Also an instructor at the University of Wisconsin–Madison from 1960 to 1961, he was named chair of Northwestern's department of church music and organ in 1962. As organist for 22 years (and choirmaster for 17 years) at the First Presbyterian Church in Evanston and organist at the First Presbyterian Church in Lake Forest from 1970 to 1993, he provided his students with many opportunities to play during services.

A member of Pi Kappa Lambda, Enright was dean of the North Shore Chapter of the American Guild of Organists from 1964 to 1965. He gave organ recitals in Chicago and across the country, performing at New York's Riverside Church, Washington's National Cathedral, the Cleveland Museum of Art, and numerous colleges and universities. His widely used instruction book *Fundamentals of Organ Playing: Two Practices* was issued by Concordia Press in 1988.

Enright retired as professor of music in 1989.

LOUIS FALK

A noted church and concert organist, Louis Falk taught at the Conservatory of Music during the 1870s. Born in 1848 in Germany, Falk was raised in Pittsburgh and Rochester, where he established himself as an organist. In 1861 he moved to Chicago. After studying in Hamburg and Leipzig from 1865 to 1869, he returned to Chicago, where he also served as head organ teacher at Chicago Musical College. Falk died in 1925.

GRIGG FOUNTAIN

Born on October 25, 1918, in South Carolina and raised in North Carolina, Grigg Fountain began his musical career mimicking his older sister's piano playing. In those Depression years the family could only afford to pay for one child's lessons, so young Grigg was left to his own devices until he was in junior high, when a church organist offered him free lessons.

Fountain received his AB from Furman University in 1939. He went on to study organ, theory, and history with Luther Noss at Yale, where he earned his bachelor of music in 1942 and master's degree in 1943, followed by a stint as a Fulbright scholar.

After a brief tenure as organist at the W. M. Bobo Funeral Home in Spartanburg, South Carolina, and an unsuccessful attempt to join the U.S. Army (he failed the entrance exam because of poor vision), Fountain became a teacher and organist at Oberlin College, remaining there from 1946 to 1961. While at Oberlin he met and worked with Robert Shaw.

Fountain came to Northwestern in 1961, first serving as organist for Lutkin Hall chapel services and then helping build a flourishing program as musical director of Alice Millar Chapel after it opened in 1963. Frequently taking on major projects, he set a high standard in diverse repertoire that included works by Bach, Beethoven, Strauss, Schoenberg, and composition professor Alan Stout. In 1967 he prepared the Chapel Choir for a performance of Bach's Mass in B Minor conducted by Robert Shaw. In developing the Millar choral program, Fountain made it a point to involve non-majors and instrumental majors. He also created small ensembles and appointed student conductors to lead them.

After his retirement in 1985, Fountain served for a year as visiting professor and choir director at Duke University.

ROBERT GAY

Born November 5, 1913, Robert Gay began his opera career as a singer and by age 25 was performing with the Philadelphia Opera Company. After four years in the infantry during World War II, he went to Tanglewood in the summer of 1946 to work with his friend and mentor Boris Goldovsky; while there he met his future wife, Nancy Trickey. Gay earned his bachelor's and master's degrees from Boston University and sang lead baritone roles in the New England Opera Theater under Goldovsky's direction. In 1958 he accepted a joint appointment on the Northwestern music and theater faculties as director of the Opera Workshop.

At Northwestern, Gay was responsible for the School of Music's opera programs for 25 years. Increasingly in demand as a judge and consultant, he became a major force in the growth of college opera programs throughout the Midwest. His 1974 staging of the American premiere of Sir Michael Tippett's *The Knot Garden* brought an international audience to the school, and he brought further exposure to the program by arranging for his students to perform with orchestras and on radio and television. On January 17, 1998, the National Opera Association honored Gay for his life's work in opera. He died June 9, 1998.

NORMAN GULBRANDSEN

Born on October 3, 1918, Norman Gulbrandsen grew up in Salt Lake City. At age 16 he walked to the University of Utah campus to hear a concert by Metropolitan Opera bass Ezio Pinza, later to star in *South Pacific* on Broadway. Gulbrandsen was so mesmerized that afterward he prayed to be able to teach someone to sing as beautifully as Pinza. As a University of Utah student he studied music education, conducting, and choral music and became the youngest member of the Mormon Tabernacle Choir. He graduated in 1943 and two years later received his master's in music education from Northwestern. Gulbrandsen later studied musicology on a fellowship at the University of Southern California and voice with Hermanus Baer at Northwestern.

Particularly interested in choral conducting, Gulbrandsen directed glee clubs while at USC and from 1945 to 1951 served as the first director of choral activities at Montana State University, where 10 percent of the 3,000-member student body sang in his choral ensembles. From 1951 to 1960 he directed choruses at Brigham Young University in Utah.

Gulbrandsen returned to Northwestern as a faculty member in 1963. While at the University he also directed the music program at Glenview Community Church, participated in the Chicago Singing Teachers Guild, and conducted master classes throughout the country. A resident of Lake Forest, Gulbrandsen joined the ranks of Northwestern's emeritus professors with his "retirement" in August 1989. But that September Frederick Miller, then dean of the DePaul University School of Music, invited Gulbrandsen to join the DePaul faculty part-time "for as long as you want to teach." He now teaches there full-time in addition to teaching privately.

FREDERICK L. HEMKE

Frederick L. Hemke was born in Milwaukee, Wisconsin, on July 11, 1935. In 1956 he became the first American to receive the Premier Prix du Saxophone from the Conservatoire National de Musique in Paris. Hemke earned a bachelor's degree from the University of Wisconsin–Milwaukee in 1958 and a master's in music education from the Eastman School of Music in 1962. He joined the Northwestern faculty in 1963 and went on to receive a doctor of music degree from the University of Wisconsin–Madison in 1975. At Northwestern he chaired the Department of Music Performance Studies until 1994 and is currently senior associate dean for administration.

An internationally recognized saxophonist, Hemke has performed and presented master classes and lectures throughout North America, Europe, and the Far East. He has appeared as a soloist with the Chicago Symphony Orchestra, Saint Louis Symphony Orchestra, Minnesota Orchestra, Stockholm Philharmonic Orchestra, Tokyo Metropolitan Symphony Orchestra, New Zealand Philharmonic Orchestra, and Korea Philharmonic Orchestra. An invited soloist at every World Saxophone Congress since the event's inception, he has served as an adjudicator for numerous national and international competitions and as a visiting professor at the Conservatoire National de Musique in Paris, the Sweelinck Conservatory of Music in Amsterdam, the Basel Conservatory of Music in Switzerland, and numerous U.S. universities.

Hemke's recordings include solo albums, chamber music, and six recordings with the Chicago Symphony Orchestra, including Mussorgsky's *Pictures at an Exhibition*. An editor for the Southern Music Company, he serves as a consultant for the Selmer Company and the La Voz Corporation, which manufactures the Frederick Hemke Premium Reed.

Dean GEORGE HOWERTON

George Howerton was born on October 28, 1905, in Milton, Kentucky. His life in music began at age five, when his parents saw him "playing" the windowsill like a piano and decided to give him lessons. Growing up in Springfield, Missouri, Howerton taught piano and started organ lessons as a high school freshman.

Because his father considered music a "fancy" vocation, Howerton attended William Jewell College in Liberty, Missouri, as an English literature major and French minor while studying music on the side. Graduating in 1926, he then earned an MA in music education at Columbia University Teachers College. He also studied at the University of Southern California, New York University, and Harvard University as well as with Marcel Dupré in Paris.

Howerton joined the School of Music faculty in 1939 and served as director of choral activities, conducting the A Cappella Choir in many national broadcasts on Chicago radio station WGN and the ABC, NBC, and Mutual radio and television networks. He prepared choruses for performances with the University Symphony, Chicago Symphony Orchestra, and Ravinia Festival, and his choruses sang under such conductors as Bruno Walter, Pierre Monteux, William Steinberg, and Sir Georg Solti. A guest conductor, clinician, and adjudicator for various events, he wrote textbooks and arranged compositions for choral groups. He was also organist and director of music for Northwestern's chapel services.

In 1951, a year after completing his PhD at Northwestern, Howerton became the School of Music's fourth dean. One of his most significant contributions was a program that brought prominent musicians to the University for performances and master classes. Among them were Dupré, duo-pianists Vitya Vronsky and Victor Babin, soprano Lotte Lehmann, and composer Aaron Copland. He also strengthened the school's Opera Workshop and built up the music library's holdings of books and manuscripts.

During his academic career, Howerton was vice chair of the Ravinia Festival Association, a governing member of the Chicago Symphony Orchestral Association, a member of the educational committee of Lyric Opera of Chicago, national president and a member of the board of regents of Pi Kappa Lambda, and national vice chair and a member of the board of directors of the Met's Central Opera Service. In 1967 he received a Steinway Award for his contributions to the field of music education.

After his retirement in 1971 he and his wife, A'Louise, moved to Salida, Colorado. Howerton remained involved in music, helping establish the Salida-Aspen Concert Series, which each summer brings Aspen concert artists to perform in the community. He died in Salida on April 8, 1999.

DONALD ISAAK

Born on October 23, 1927, in Elk Point, South Dakota, Donald Isaak graduated from the University of South Dakota in 1949 and served in the U.S. Navy from 1950 to 1954. He also studied at the Juilliard School with Carl Friedberg, taking academic courses at Columbia University. Isaak then studied for a year at the Musik Akademie in Vienna before beginning graduate work at Northwestern, where his teachers were Harold van Horne, Dorothy Lane, and Gui Mombaerts. He received his doctor of music degree from Northwestern in 1963, a year after he began teaching at Arizona State University. Isaak returned to Northwestern in 1971 and taught until his retirement in 1996; many summers he also taught at the Adamant School of Music in Vermont. He died at age 68 on July 25, 1996.

While at Northwestern, Isaak performed widely, received the School of Music's first Exemplar in Teaching Award, and served for 25 years on the executive board of directors of the Illinois State Music Teachers Association. Active as a solo recitalist, chamber player, and vocal accompanist throughout the United States and in Vienna and Edinburgh, he appeared as soloist with the New York Philharmonic and other orchestras. He was featured as an accompanist on 12 recordings issued on the EbSko label. Beyond performing, Isaak reached people around the nation with his love for music. He gave master classes and workshops, presented continuing education programs and programs for retirement and nursing homes, and adjudicated state, national, and international piano competitions.

ARNOLD JACOBS

Before Arnold Jacobs even thought about the tuba, he considered becoming a singer. But fortunately for the world of brass instruments, he decided against it. Born on June 11, 1915, in Philadelphia and raised in California, he progressed from bugle to trumpet to trombone and finally to tuba before entering his native city's Curtis Institute of Music as a 15-year-old scholarship student.

After graduating from Curtis in 1936, Jacobs was engaged as the Indianapolis Symphony's tuba player under Fabien Sevitzky for two seasons and then took the same post with the Pittsburgh Symphony under Fritz Reiner from 1939 to 1944. He joined the Chicago Symphony Orchestra in 1941 and three years later became principal tuba, a position he held until 1988. Jacobs toured the country in 1941 with Leopold Stokowski and the All-American Youth Orchestra and toured England and Scotland with the Philadelphia Orchestra in the spring of 1949. In 1962 he was the first tuba player invited to play at the Festival Casals under Pablo Casals in San Juan, Puerto Rico.

Jacobs joined the Northwestern music faculty in 1956 and continued to give workshops at the school until his death. A founding member of the Chicago Symphony Brass Quintet, he presented lectures and clinics throughout the world, including clinics in Tokyo during the CSO's 1977 and 1986 Japanese tours. In 1984 the Second International Brass Congress presented him its highest award, and in 1986 he was awarded an honorary doctor of music degree from Vandercook College. In 1995 Northwestern honored him with its first Legends in Teaching Award. He died October 6, 1998.

THEODORE KARP

Born in New York City in 1926, Theodore Karp earned a diploma in piano from the Juilliard School in 1946 and a bachelor's degree from Queens College in 1947. In addition to graduate work at Juilliard, he pursued further studies at the Université catholique de Louvain, the Université libre de Bruxelles, and New York University, where he earned a PhD in 1963. His academic honors include election to Phi Beta Kappa, a Fulbright grant, a Queens College Scholarship, an Ogden Butler Fellowship, and senior fellowships from the National Endowment for the Humanities and the Institute for Research in the Humanities at the University of Wisconsin–Madison.

Before coming to Northwestern in 1973 as professor of music history and literature and department chair, Karp served on the faculty at the University of California, Davis, from 1963 to 1973, rising from assistant to full professor and department chair.

Active in professional societies, Karp served on the council of the American Musicological Society in addition to chairing its Northern California and Midwest chapters. He was editor and consultant to the Grolier Society from 1961 to 1970.

Karp has delivered many papers at various universities and for international, national, and regional meetings of scholarly societies. His numerous published works include the books *Dictionary of Music* and *The Polyphony of St. Martial and Santiago de Compostela* as well as articles, reviews, and contributions to *Encyclopedia Americana* and other reference works.

HAROLD E. KNAPP

Harold Knapp began his 36-year tenure on the Northwestern University faculty in 1893, when the music program was not yet a school. Born on August 23, 1867, in Neponsett, Illinois, he graduated from Oberlin College and studied with Hans Sitt at the Leipzig Conservatory in Germany.

Shortly after arriving at Northwestern, Knapp organized a string quartet consisting of himself as first violinist, his brother William H. Knapp as cellist, Joseph Biehl as second violinist, and Carpan Gribbenger as violist. The University String Quartet, also known as the Knapp String Quartet, performed widely and was featured in the dedicatory concert of the Music Hall in 1897.

Chair of the violin and ensemble departments, Knapp also directed and assisted in developing the Northwestern University Symphony Orchestra. Its varied repertoire included works by Beethoven, Brahms, Dvořák, Haydn, Mendelssohn, and Wagner. Under his leadership the orchestra — made up of students, players from the North Shore, and eventually some Chicago Symphony Orchestra members — attracted much attention and performed in the North Shore Music Festivals. Local newspapers followed his musical activities with admiration.

Well-known and liked in Evanston, Knapp was a member of the city's University Club. His wife, Hila Verbeck Knapp, received a graduate in music degree in 1904; she also served as an assistant piano instructor in Northwestern's preparatory department. Knapp died on February 10, 1950, in Orlando, Florida.

WALFRID KUJALA

Born on February 19, 1925, in Warren, Ohio, Walfrid Kujala started flute lessons at the age of 13 when his bassoonist father steered him away from the bassoon to spare him the headaches of making reeds. Raised in Ohio, he began his performing career in high school, playing second flute in the Huntington Symphony while studying with its principal flutist, Parker Taylor. He attended the Eastman School of Music as a student of Joseph Mariano, receiving his bachelor's in flute performance in 1948 and his master's in 1950. Kujala joined the Rochester Philharmonic under Erich Leinsdorf and taught at Eastman until accepting the assistant principal flute position in the Chicago Symphony Orchestra under Fritz Reiner in 1954. In 1957 he switched to piccolo. From 1955 to 1960 he also served as principal flute of the Grant Park Symphony Orchestra.

Kujala has appeared as soloist with the CSO under Reiner, Sir Georg Solti, Antonio Janigro, and Seiji Ozawa as well as at the Stratford and Victoria Festivals in Canada. He is active as a chamber musician and gives recitals and master classes throughout the country.

Since 1962, Kujala has been professor of flute at Northwestern. In honor of his 60th birthday, his students and colleagues commissioned a flute concerto from Gunther Schuller. Kujala and the Chicago Symphony premiered the work in 1988 under Solti; he also performed it at Northwestern in 1995 in honor of Schuller's birthday. In 1990 he gave the premiere of a flute concerto by Finnish composer Einojuhani Rautavaara at the National Flute Association convention.

FRANCES LARIMER

Born on May 13, 1929, in Tavares, Florida, Frances Larimer received her bachelor's degree in 1952 and her master's in 1954, both in piano performance from Northwestern. She then taught part-time in the school's piano and preparatory piano departments except for a year (1963–64) as visiting professor at Louisiana State University. In 1967 she was promoted to full-time assistant professor at Northwestern and in 1973 was named associate professor of piano and director of piano pedagogy. She retired in 1998.

At Northwestern, Larimer developed a master's program in piano performance and pedagogy in 1972 and a doctoral program in 1977, serving as director of these programs for more than two decades. She also initiated a master's program in music education and piano pedagogy in 1989. Larimer has received research grants to develop instructional techniques in piano pedagogy and college-level group piano. In 1985 she reorganized the preparatory department; it went on to achieve national and international recognition, expanding its offerings to include preschool classes, evening adult piano classes, and piano classes for nonmusic majors. Larimer was also instrumental in acquiring the school's first piano laboratory in 1970 and keeping it up to date. Her pedagogy students have won national competitions for young teachers, and graduates from her programs hold teaching positions in colleges, universities, and community schools throughout the United States and abroad.

Larimer has served a four-year term as national group piano chair for the Music Teachers National Association and has written numerous articles for music periodicals and professional journals. She is coauthor of *The Piano Pedagogy Major in the College Curriculum* (National Conference on Piano Pedagogy, 1984 and 1986).

Since 1993 Larimer has organized annual summer piano institutes for American students and teachers in St. Petersburg, Russia, and in 1994 she was named a member of the St. Petersburg International Center of Russian Musical Culture and the organization's U.S. representative. She was also guest professor for three summers at the Rubin Academy of Music in Jerusalem.

PAULINE LINDSEY

Born Pauline Manchester to American parents in Cuba on October 22, 1906, she attended Northwestern as an undergraduate, receiving her bachelor's in French in 1927. She studied piano with Howard Wells in Chicago from 1921 to 1931 and with Artur Schnabel in Berlin from 1931 to 1932, later continuing her studies with Robert Casadesus. Early in her career Lindsey won the 1928 and 1929 Society of American Musicians contests and the 1928 and 1932 Musical Guild Awards. Her performance schedule included concerts throughout the Midwest and Germany as well as appearances with the Chicago Symphony Orchestra under Frederick Stock, the Cedar Rapids Symphony, the Chicago Little Symphony, and the Evanston Symphony Orchestra.

In need of a job when she returned from Europe during the Depression, Lindsey began her teaching career at the Lake Forest Day School, where she went on to serve as director of music before assuming the same position at Ferry Hall Academy and Junior College in Lake Forest. She was also in charge of rhythm and music at the Montessori School in Winnetka. Lindsey came to Northwestern as a substitute piano instructor in 1937 and worked her way up to professor and chair of the department by the time she retired in 1975.

In 1945, shortly after her promotion to assistant professor, Lindsey took a leave of absence to make a seven-month USO concert tour of Europe. The *Chicago Tribune*, describing tour conditions, noted that her concerts "often were presented from a special army truck or in some roofless, bombed-out concert hall, so cold that she wore heavy army slacks under her evening gown. She often sat on a chemical heating pad as she played." In recognition of her wartime efforts, Lindsey received the Civilian Service Medal and the Northwestern Alumni Service Award.

Lindsey died on October 3, 1997. At her request, her ashes were buried in a secluded spot between the Music Administration Building and Lutkin Hall.

OREN E. LOCKE

Born on January 22, 1837, in Chester, Vermont, Oren E. Locke studied music in Leipzig and Weimar, Germany. He began his musical career in his native state, assuming a teaching position in 1860 in Springfield, Vermont. After directing the department of music at New York's Genessee College in 1867, he became director of the Boston Conservatory of Music, serving from 1868 to 1877. That year he was named director of Northwestern's Conservatory of Music. It was during Locke's directorship that his successor, Peter Christian Lutkin, first taught at the conservatory. Locke left Northwestern in 1891 and died in California on December 17, 1926.

Dean PETER CHRISTIAN LUTKIN

Peter Christian Lutkin discovered music at an early age. Recalling the moment when he stumbled into a cathedral choir during his childhood, Lutkin said that "music stirred his youthful soul" and "determined his life's profession."

Born March 27, 1858, in Thompsonville, Wisconsin, Lutkin was the youngest of six children. In 1863 the family moved to Chicago, where he spent most of his life. At age nine Lutkin joined the boys' choir at the Episcopal Cathedral of Saints Peter and Paul in Chicago. Performing as an alto soloist in oratorios, he grew to love singing.

Lutkin began his Northwestern career in the fall of 1879 as a piano instructor in the Conservatory of Music. After two years, however, he left to study in Europe. When he returned to Chicago, he became organist and choirmaster at St. Clement's Episcopal Church; he later served in the same capacity at St. James Episcopal Church. Lutkin also served for four years as director of the theory department at Chicago's American Conservatory of Music and started his own music school in his home.

Formulating a philosophy of music education ranked high among the many concerns Lutkin addressed when accepting the directorship of Northwestern's Conservatory of Music in 1891. Basing his ideas on the European tradition, he developed a curriculum that provided a strong background in music theory, with individualized instruction adapted to each pupil's specific needs. To implement this program, he set out to hire a faculty with outstanding training. Lutkin himself taught classes in harmony, counterpoint, fugue, musical form, and composition according to a systematic and practical method. At one point he taught all the conservatory's music theory classes, including instrumentation, acoustics, and analysis. He also advocated restructuring the academic requirements for music students seeking a degree, proposing proficiency requirements in English literature, mathematics, and a foreign language of choice.

Lutkin developed many campus musical ensembles, including the Men's Glee Club, Cecilian Choir for Ladies, A Cappella Choir, and Northwestern University Choral Association, superseded in 1894 by the Evanston Musical Club. He served as its only conductor until 1922.

Church and choral music was Lutkin's most ardent passion, and his efforts led to the establishment of a church music department at Northwestern in 1926. Best known as composer of the choral benediction "The Lord Bless You and Keep You," Lutkin also composed church, organ, piano, and vocal music and served as coeditor of the official Methodist hymnal. He lectured nationwide, and his lectures were later published in *Music in the Church.* He also assisted in the compilation of other hymnals and held countless hymn festivals throughout the country.

Lutkin created the annual Chicago North Shore Music Festival in 1908 and served as its director until 1930. He was a founder of the American Guild of Organists and was twice president of the Music Teachers National Association.

Upon his retirement as dean of the School of Music in 1928, Lutkin was named dean emeritus. Northwestern president Walter Dill Scott said, "It is a significant fact that Dean Lutkin has been an active member of our faculty for more than 40 years. But the real significance of this does not lie in the length of service, but the results attained. Within this relatively short period of 40 years, he has created an institution of national and international repute. Frequently a single individual is credited with the honor of the founding and the development of a school in the University but such an expression is merely a gesture and a compliment. In the case of Dean Lutkin, however, such a statement is justified by the facts. He created the School of Music and for 40 years has been the outstanding personality in its development. His going is an irreparable loss to the University and to the whole musical world."

Lutkin died at his son's home in Evanston on December 27, 1931. He was survived by his wife of 46 years, Lelah Nancy Carmen Lutkin; and his son Harris Carmen Lutkin, born in 1886. A younger son, Caryl Cecil Lutkin, was born in 1888 and died at age four.

After Lutkin's death, Bishop George Craig Stewart described him as a humble man "who walked with childlike faith in God." Carl Beecher, Lutkin's successor as dean, wrote that "two marked characteristics of this man will be remembered by all who have known him. . . . One of these was his delightful sense of humor. The other . . . was his intense devotion to and belief in the profession of teaching. To him teaching was a sacred and noble calling, and this belief tinged all of his work in the school which he founded."

Peter Christian Lutkin's legacy extends not only to Northwestern University and Evanston but to musical education in America. As Howard Hanson wrote, Lutkin's "significance in American music stands out like a mountain towering above the plain."

ROBERT MARCELLUS

As a teacher, Robert Marcellus shaped the playing of countless clarinetists at Northwestern, the Cleveland Institute of Music, and beyond. As a symphonic player with the Cleveland Orchestra, he brought clarinet playing to new levels. As a conductor, he gained even more respect and a new following.

Born on June 1, 1928, in Omaha, Marcellus landed his first performing job at age 17 as a member of the National Symphony Orchestra in Washington. The youngest clarinetist ever hired by a major U.S. orchestra, he was named principal clarinetist at 22. In 1953 he joined the Cleveland Orchestra at the request of conductor George Szell, remaining its principal clarinetist for 20 years. During that time he taught, made recordings, and performed under conductors Pierre Boulez, Istvan Kertesz, Louis Lane, Erich Leinsdorf, Lorin Maazel, and Robert Shaw. He also conducted the Cleveland Civic Orchestra, the Interlochen Arts Academy Orchestra, the Peninsula Music Festival in Door County, Wisconsin, and the Scotia Chamber Players in Halifax, Nova Scotia.

Marcellus resigned from the Cleveland Orchestra in 1973 but continued to teach and conduct, even after the onset of blindness in 1984. He was professor of clarinet at Northwestern from 1974 to 1990. In retirement as professor emeritus he lived in Sister Bay, Wisconsin. He died there at the age of 67 on March 31, 1996.

ROBERT MAYER

Born on August 26, 1910, in Grand Forks, North Carolina, Chicago Symphony Orchestra oboist Robert Mayer taught at Northwestern for 15 years, beginning in 1948. At age 19 he became a member of the John Philip Sousa Band, playing second oboe on the band's last tour. His daughter later said that his joining the Sousa Band was "equivalent to running away to join the circus."

Mayer played with a radio station orchestra, a movie palace orchestra, and the Duluth Symphony Orchestra before conductor Frederick Stock hired him for the CSO in 1931. He remained with the organization until 1956. During his tenure at Northwestern, Mayer served as chair of the woodwind, brass, and percussion department and taught oboe and English horn. He was an original member of the Chicago Symphony Woodwind Quintet and an honorary member of the International Double Reed Society.

A resident of St. Petersburg, Florida, after his retirement in 1976, Mayer died on March 9, 1994, at the age of 83.

GEORGE McCLAY

Born on September 28, 1903, in Montana, George McClay received a bachelor of music degree at Northwestern in 1928 and was promptly appointed to the theory faculty. In 1934 he was given the additional job of School of Music registrar, a position he held for 20 years. After earning his master's in church music from the school in 1939, McClay was promoted to assistant professor of theory; he was named associate professor of theory in 1946, associate professor of church music in 1953, assistant dean in 1954, and associate dean in 1964. Among his special interests was the field of organ history and design.

As registrar, McClay was career counselor and adviser to nearly every student in the School of Music, demonstrating an uncanny memory for students' names and studies. Wilbur Simpson (40, G46) recalled meeting McClay on campus and asking for advice about what classes to take the next quarter. Without hesitation McClay proceeded to recite Simpson's course history and remaining requirements for graduation.

McClay served as organist at Chicago's Grace Episcopal Church from 1927 to 1945 and later at Trinity Episcopal Church in Highland Park. He was vice president of the National Association of Schools of Music, also serving on its church music committee, and a member of Alpha Delta Phi, Pi Kappa Lambda, and Phi Mu Alpha Sinfonia.

Shortly after his 1968 retirement, students and faculty showed their appreciation by commissioning a portrait of McClay. Presented to him in 1969, it now hangs in room 101 of the Music Administration Building.

McClay's first wife, Evelyn Van Vactor (Liberal Arts 25), died in 1955. He later married Winifred L. Bell, and they traveled extensively, visiting nearly every continent. After her death in 1985, he moved to Florida to live near his daughter. McClay died on December 25, 1995, in his home in Cocoa Beach, Florida, at age 92.

Dean THOMAS W. MILLER

Born in Pottstown, Pennsylvania, on July 2, 1930, Thomas Miller received his bachelor's in music education from his home state's West Chester University in 1952. After serving in the U.S. Second Army Band from 1952 to 1955 and as director of instrumental music at Susquenita High School in Pennsylvania from 1955 to 1956, he earned his master's in music at East Carolina University in Greenville, North Carolina, in 1957. In 1964 Miller earned his doctor of musical arts degree from Boston University, where he served as assistant conductor of university bands from 1961 to 1962. He then returned to the School of Music at East Carolina University, where he rose from trumpet instructor to dean.

Within a year of his arrival at Northwestern as dean in 1971, Miller led the most sweeping curricular revision in the School of Music's history. By bringing increasing numbers of guest artists and professional conventions to campus, overseeing the construction of two new buildings, promoting Chicago Symphony Orchestra musicians to faculty status, and helping inaugurate new degree programs, he sought to make the school preeminent in its field. After stepping down as dean in 1989, Miller took a year's leave of absence and then continued to serve as professor of music education until his retirement in 1995.

Miller was president and vice president of Pi Kappa Lambda and the National Association of Schools of Music, a member of the NASM executive committee, and chair of the NASM graduate commission. A member of the PKL board of regents since 1979, he was elected an honorary life regent in 1995. He is a member of the College Music Society, life member of Music Educators National Conference, honorary member of Phi Mu Alpha Sinfonia, and honorary life member of NASM. Named a distinguished alumnus of West Chester University in 1975 and a national arts associate by Sigma Alpha Iota in 1988, he is listed in *Leaders of Education and Outstanding Educators of America*, *Who's Who in America*, *Who's Who in American Music*, and *The International Who's Who in Music*. In 1989 he received the Orpheus Award from Phi Mu Alpha.

Miller has served as a consultant to numerous universities and as a member of the accreditation teams for NASM and the Southern Association. He has delivered speeches and presented papers at many professional meetings in addition to serving as guest conductor and adjudicator in several states. A resident of Wilmette, Illinois, he continues to serve as a member of the dean's advisory committee of the University of North Carolina at Greensboro.

GUI MOMBAERTS

Gui (Guillaume) Mombaerts started out playing jazz in Paris and ended up teaching classical piano at Northwestern's School of Music. Born October 6, 1902, in Belgium, he began piano lessons at age eight. Two years later he enrolled in a solfège class at the School of Music–Schaerbeek, after which he studied piano with Arthur de Greef, a pupil of Franz Liszt, at the Royal Conservatory in Brussels. He captured the school's first prizes in solfège in 1916 and harmony in 1918 and went on to receive highest distinctions in piano, chamber music, and keyboard harmony before graduating in 1925.

His penchant for winning prizes did not end with graduation. In 1926 he won the Prix Gunther, a competition for Belgium's top pianists, and in 1927 he was a finalist in the first International Chopin Piano Competition in Warsaw. Subsequently he toured Europe as a soloist and member of the Belgian Piano-String Quartet.

Mombaerts began teaching while still a student. He served on the faculties of Watermael-Boitsfort School of Music (1923–27), the École Normale de Musique in Brussels (1925–27), the Conservatory of Music, La Louvière (1925–40), the School of Music in Molenbeek (1934–40), and the Chapelle de la Reine Elisabeth de Belgique (1938–40).

After the German occupation of Belgium, Mombaerts and the other members of the Belgium Piano-String Quartet escaped to the United States while on a 1940 tour of Portugal. Mombaerts served with the Free Belgium armed forces from 1943 to 1945. After the war he toured the United States and Canada with violist William Primrose and appeared as a soloist with several orchestras.

Mombaerts began his American teaching career as a visiting professor of music at Colorado College from 1941 to 1943. He then taught at Kansas State Teachers College in Pittsburgh, Kansas, from 1945 to 1946 and at the University of Kansas in Kansas City from 1946 to 1948. He joined the Northwestern faculty in 1948, chairing the piano department from 1957 until his retirement in 1971. In 1967 he received a Steinway Award. Mombaerts died in Evanston on June 6, 1993, at age 91.

JAMES MOORE

Jim Moore's door was always open. Whether you were a student in trouble, an alumnus returning for a visit, or a nervous prospective student awaiting an audition, he was quick to make you feel at home.

Born on November 29, 1929, in Detroit, Moore pursued his education in his home state, receiving his bachelor's in music education in 1950 from Wayne State University and his master's and doctoral degrees from the University of Michigan. Before coming to Northwestern, he was a teaching associate at the University of Michigan, assistant professor at Idaho State University, and professor at Cochise College in Arizona. He also directed bands and taught music classes in Michigan high schools for 12 years, led three Michigan church choirs, and directed the Band Training Unit while serving in the 10th Infantry Division Band at Fort Riley, Kansas.

Although he came to Northwestern in 1968 as an associate professor of music education, Moore went on to serve in a variety of areas. As director of field services he administered admissions, managed the placement office, organized the national admissions auditions, wrote the computer program that sends job notices to students, steered the school's national advertising campaign, and edited the school's alumni magazine, *Fanfare*. As director of the summer session he guided the school through a period of extensive change in University program policies. During most summer terms he also served as director of the National High School Institute.

Active in the community, he participated in the Lake Forest Symphony Orchestra and the Northshore Concert Band. He also directed church choirs in Northbrook.

After his retirement from Northwestern in 1994, Moore became a consultant for the National Association for College Admission Counseling. He advises the association on college fairs and often attends them, enjoying the opportunity to see former admissions colleagues and Northwestern alumni.

ALBERT NOELTE

As a child, Albert Noelte was determined to become a musician, despite his parents' wishes. Even though his grandfather was a musician, they allowed him no musical training beyond minimal violin study.

Born March 10, 1885, in Germany, the future composer and Northwestern theory professor ran away to the United States at age 15 with only his violin. A relative in New York City sent him to Troy, New York, to complete his general education, and a church organist there gave him his first real musical training.

At 18 Noelte entered the New England Conservatory of Music, where he studied composition and theory with composers Frederick Converse and George Chadwick while studying English literature at Boston University. After four years Chadwick advised Noelte to return to Munich, where he studied with Felix Mottl and Richard Strauss.

In the 1920s Noelte composed, studied, and taught privately in Germany. He also worked as a music critic for the *München-Augsberger, Abend Zeitung,* and *Boston Advertiser.*

Before his appointment at Northwestern in 1934, Noelte served as dean of Chicago's Institute of Music and Allied Arts from 1929 to 1932. Many of Noelte's compositions — which include symphonic and choral works, songs, and two operas — were performed at Orchestra Hall and elsewhere throughout Chicago. He died on March 3, 1946.

JOHN OHL

Born June 14, 1908, in Chicago, John Ohl spent much of his life at Northwestern. He attended the University as an undergraduate, receiving his bachelor's degree from the School of Speech in 1931. Ohl then attended graduate school at Harvard, earning a master's in 1939 and a PhD in 1944. From 1944 to 1951 he taught at Nashville's Fisk University, where he directed the choir and chaired the music department. Ohl returned to Northwestern to join the School of Music faculty in 1951.

At the school he chaired the history and literature department and taught such courses as Music of the Middle Ages and Renaissance, Music of the Baroque Period, History of Opera, History of Notation, Music of Bach and Handel, Music of the Classical Period, and The Trio Sonata and Concerto Grosso. He also directed the Collegium Musicum and founded the Musicology Club.

Ohl's professional affiliations included the American Musicological Society, Music Library Association, College Music Society, and Society for Music in the Liberal Arts College. His research focused on music of the baroque period and stylistic analyses of Western European music.

Active in the community, Ohl was choirmaster of the Church of the Holy Comforter in Kenilworth and served on the board of the Canterbury House and on the vestry council of St. Augustine's Church in Wilmette. He also participated in the Diocesan Music Commission of the Episcopal Church's Chicago Diocese.

Ohl coedited (with Carl Parrish) the widely used anthology *Masterpieces of Music Before 1750* and edited Norton's *Brahms Chorus*

Book. His other published works included compositions for chorus and piano, program notes, and various articles. Ohl retired in 1973 and died on August 9, 1993, at his home in Winchester, Virginia.

ARNE OLDBERG

Born on July 12, 1874, in Youngstown, Ohio, Arne Oldberg started piano lessons as soon as he could reach the keyboard. His first teacher was his father, an accomplished church organist and noted pharmaceutical authority. By the time the boy was six, he and his father were playing simple four-hand pieces. In 1886 the family moved to Chicago, where the elder Oldberg founded and became dean of Northwestern's School of Pharmacy.

Arne Oldberg continued his piano studies at Chicago's Gottschalk Lyric School. In 1890, at age 16, he won the George M. Pullman Diamond Medal for the best piano playing by a student outside Chicago Musical College, and the next year he received the Ziegfeld Diamond Medal as best pianist in the teachers' certificate class. Upon graduating from the Lyric School with honors in 1892, Oldberg studied in Vienna for two years with Theodor Leschetizky.

At 23 Oldberg joined the Northwestern faculty. One year later he left to study composition with Joseph Rheinberger at Munich's Royal Academy of Art, where he completed the three-year course in one year. He promptly returned to Northwestern in 1899 and remained at the School of Music for the duration of his career. Initially appointed an instructor, he went on to serve as professor of piano and composition (1901–41), director of the piano department (1919–41), director of the graduate music department (1924–41), and emeritus professor (1941–62).

In addition to teaching, Oldberg was active as a concert pianist and award-winning composer. He wrote chamber music, sonatas, piano pieces, and some 25 orchestral works, including six symphonies and concertos for piano, violin, and horn. The Chicago Symphony Orchestra gave its first performance of one of his compositions in 1908; other works were heard at the North Shore Music Festival and in concerts by other major orchestras, often with Oldberg as piano soloist. In 1911 and 1915 he won prizes in the National Federation of Music Clubs' Biennial Prize Competition for American Composers, and in 1915 he was elected to the National Institute of Arts and Letters.

Oldberg's Northwestern honors included an honorary master of arts degree in 1916, an honorary membership in the Iota chapter of Phi Mu Alpha Sinfonia music fraternity in 1939, an honorary life membership in Northwestern's Alumni Association in 1940, and a Northwestern University Alumni Merit Award in 1945. The city of Evanston expressed appreciation to its hometown composer by naming a park in his honor in 1941.

For several summers starting in 1930, Oldberg held the Alchin Chair of Music in the College of Music at the University of California, Los Angeles. It was during that time that he won first prize in the Hollywood Bowl Contest for his Piano Concerto no. 2 in A Major, op. 43.

Oldberg was a charter member of the Chicago Manuscript Society, organized in 1896, and served as president from 1901 to 1903. He was also a charter member of the Cliff Dwellers (then called the "Little Room"), Chicago's club of distinguished writers, artists, and musicians.

Oldberg died on February 17, 1962, at the age of 87. He was survived by his wife, Mary Sloan Oldberg. They had five children: Eric, Karl, Elsa, Richard, and Robert. At his death he was accorded this tribute by Betty and Philip Jacobson: "Arne Oldberg was more than a musician. . . . He was kind. He was considerate. He had great dignity, but the warmth of his humor made him a delightful companion. He was a man of peace."

In 1976 Oldberg was honored posthumously when Mayor Edgar Vanneman and the Evanston City Council designated Friday, December 10, as "Arne and Mary Sloan Oldberg Day," urging all citizens "to give recognition to the many contributions of the

Oldbergs, not only to our community, but also to our civilization." Oldberg's works can be found in the Edwin A. Fleischer Music Collection of the Free Library of Philadelphia, the Los Angeles County Museum, and the Library of Congress as well as the Evanston Public Library.

ARRAND PARSONS

Born July 26, 1918, North Carolina native Arrand Parsons entered the University of North Carolina at age 16. Two years later he transferred to Columbia University's New College. After earning a bachelor's degree there in 1939, Parsons began graduate work at Columbia's Teachers College and then finished his master's in education at the Winnetka Graduate Teachers College.

In 1946 Parsons entered Northwestern to study music composition and was immediately named an instructor. Earning a PhD in music theory in 1953, he chaired the theory and composition department from 1962 to 1966 and served as an assistant dean from 1964 to 1967. On his retirement in 1985, the music library established the Arrand Parsons Collection, consisting of scores from his own library and those donated by friends.

As a faculty member, Parsons focused on the basic instruction of the music major. He was involved in the school's curriculum revision in the 1960s, serving as chair of the curriculum committee and supervising the development of a comprehensive program integrating music history, style, and theory. His interest in curriculum led to his involvement with the Ford Foundation–sponsored Contemporary Music Project, which promoted innovations in music education.

Chicagoans remember Parsons for his role as fifth program annotator for the Chicago Symphony Orchestra. Beginning in 1956, following the death of Felix Borowski, he wrote program notes for Orchestra Hall symphonic and chamber programs for 30 years. He was also program annotator for the Ravinia Festival from 1960 until his retirement in 1992. His other writings included the two-volume *Creative-Analytical Theory of Music*.

From 1966 to 1978 Parsons was heard on radio station WEFM-FM, interviewing nearly 400 conductors, soloists, composers, and other musical celebrities on his weekly program *Chicago Symphony Notebook*. Parsons also hosted a weekly program on WBEZ-FM from 1977 to 1979 and served as a guest interviewer on WFMT-FM.

In 1988 Northwestern honored him with the Alumni Merit Award. He died in Wheaton, Illinois, on June 22, 2001.

WANDA PAUL

Pianist Wanda Paul was born on Independence Day in 1911 in Chicago. After earning her bachelor's in 1930 and master's in 1932 from Chicago Musical College (where she went on to teach from 1940 to 1951), she performed around the country, giving recitals at Town Hall in New York and Jordan Hall in Boston and appearing with the Chicago Symphony Orchestra under Frederick Stock, the Ravinia Festival Orchestra under Artur Rodzinski, the Grant Park Symphony Orchestra under Nicolai Malko, and the Friends of Music Orchestra in Toledo under Hans Lange. She received the Frederick Stock Award, the Society of American Musicians Symphony Award, the Music Arts Piano Award, and the Steinway Piano Award.

Paul joined the Northwestern piano faculty in 1952. Active as a lecturer and adjudicator, she also pursued research in contemporary music. She retired in 1979.

JOHN P. PAYNTER

Named for John Philip Sousa, John P. Paynter was born on May 29, 1928, in Mineral Point, Wisconsin, the son of an amateur bandsman who saw to it that his son received musical training early in life. Paynter earned his bachelor's degree in 1950 and his master's degree in theory and composition in 1951, both from Northwestern; alumni later joked that his blood ran purple. As an undergraduate he was part of the Wildcats' 1949 trip to the Rose Bowl, playing clarinet in the Marching Band and serving as student assistant to director of bands Glenn Cliffe Bainum. In 1951, at age 23, he was appointed to the faculty full-time as director of the Marching Band, assistant director of bands, and instructor of theory. Two years later he succeeded Bainum as the school's second director of bands.

In addition to producing and conducting concerts, Paynter taught classes in band repertoire, conducting, and arranging and served as conductor for the annual Waa-Mu Show and Commencement. Somehow he also found time to compose or arrange more than 400 works.

Through the years Paynter worked to revive the American tradition of community bands — groups comprised of music teachers and trained amateurs. He helped establish the 113-member Northshore Concert Band in 1956 and went on to help organize and inspire hundreds of such bands around the world. Over the course of his career, he logged visits to all 50 states and four continents.

Paynter served as president of the World Association for Symphonic Bands and Ensembles, the Mid-West International Band and Orchestra Clinic (since renamed the Midwest Clinic), the American Bandmasters Association, and the National Band Association, of which he was also cofounder and honorary life president. He was a life member of Music Educators National Conference and Phi Mu Alpha Sinfonia.

His contributions to music were honored with awards from Pi Kappa Lambda, Phi Eta Sigma, Tri-M Modern Music Masters, Phi Beta Mu, Kappa Kappa Psi, Illinois Music Educators, the John Philip Sousa Foundation, the National Band Association, the *School Musician*, the *Instrumentalist*, and the National Association of Music Clubs. In 1987 he was named one of the inaugural recipients of the Northwestern Alumni Association Excellence in Teaching Award, and in 1992 DePaul University granted him an honorary doctorate of humane letters.

Shortly before Paynter's death the Wildcats' 1995 football success brought him back to the Rose Bowl with the Marching Band. Beloved by his family as well as the extended family of his current and former students, he died on February 4, 1996, at age 67, after 45 years of service to the University.

JACK PERNECKY

Born in October 1922 in a Bohemian neighborhood of Chicago, Jack Pernecky started violin lessons at age five with a Bohemian gypsy violinist, learning waltzes, mazurkas, and czardas by rote. In high school he studied violin seriously and played in the all-city orchestra, rehearsing in Orchestra Hall. His teachers eventually included Samuel Arron, Samuel Kruty (former assistant concertmaster of the Vienna Philharmonic and a student of Sevcik), Walter Trampler, and, briefly, Joseph Szigeti.

At Northwestern, Pernecky earned a bachelor's in 1944 and master's in 1945. When a serious skin infection on his chin interfered with his violin playing, he returned to the University to pursue a music education certificate. He then directed high school orchestras and developed string programs in Chicago-area public schools.

In 1956 Pernecky received a PhD in music education from Northwestern. By this time he could again practice violin every day, a development that led to his appointment as assistant professor and head of the string department at Eastern Illinois State College. He also gave recitals and served as concertmaster of the Eastern Orchestra. Concerned that he was risking a return of the infection with this increased performing schedule, Pernecky accepted a position as associate professor of music education at Michigan State University in the late 1950s. There he began to gain administrative experience as director of the Summer High School Youth music program and a member of the committee planning summer session courses and workshops.

Pernecky returned to his alma mater in 1960 as a member of the music education faculty. He soon began to direct the summer high school music program, which at the time had 38 students. Within a few years enrollment grew to 238, with regular faculty members directing ensembles and teaching classes and private lessons. When associate dean George McClay, who directed undergraduate and graduate programs, retired in 1968, Pernecky succeeded him and immediately suggested dividing the position in half. Frederick Miller (later dean of DePaul University's School of Music) oversaw the undergraduate program; Pernecky took over the graduates.

In addition to his administrative duties, Pernecky taught music education methods and string pedagogy (Rolland and Suzuki) courses, string classes, and workshops and classes in college teaching. He held state and national offices in the Music Teachers National Association, American String Teachers Association, Music Educators National Conference, and MENC's National Research Council. His publications include a string method book, a collection of solo string pieces, a collection of pieces for string ensembles and orchestra, and the textbook *Teaching the Fundamentals of Violin Playing*, issued by Warner Publications.

After his official retirement in 1990, Pernecky continued to teach part-time at Northwestern until 1992. He died in Evanston on December 2, 1998.

WILLIAM PORTER

Born on September 8, 1932, in Raleigh, North Carolina, William Porter received a bachelor's degree in music in 1954 from Davidson College, a master's in music history in 1956 from Oberlin College, and a PhD in music history from Yale University in 1962. Elected to Pi Kappa Lambda at Oberlin, he also received fellowships from Yale and a grant for four weeks of study at the Vatican in 1986.

Porter came to Northwestern in 1961 as an instructor of music history and literature. He retired in 1999 as professor, having served as acting chair of music history and literature. He remains active with projects relating to his specialization, late 16th- and 17th-century Italian music.

A member of the American Musicological Society, American Music Library Association, and International Musicological Society, Porter is the author of numerous articles and papers. He is a contributor to the *Encyclopaedia Britannica, New Grove Dictionary of Music and Musicians, Sohlmans Musiklexikon, Studi Musicali, Con che soavità, Essays in Honor of John F. Ohl,* and *Journal of the American Musicological Society,* for which he served on the editorial board.

DUDLEY POWERS

Born on June 25, 1911, in Moorhead, Minnesota, Dudley Powers grew up in a musical family. His father was a voice teacher and head of the music department at Michigan's Central State College, and his mother played piano and organ. As children, he and three siblings formed the Powers String Quartet, which performed throughout the Midwest.

At age 14 Powers finished high school and won a four-year scholarship at the Juilliard Musical Foundation. He came to Chicago in 1930 and joined the Little Symphony of Chicago under George Dasch. In 1933 he joined the Chicago Symphony Orchestra, where he played for 20 years, the last 10 as solo cellist. During that time he performed most of the major cello concertos as soloist with the orchestra. He was also a member of the Mischakoff String Quartet and the Chicago String Quartet.

Powers left the Chicago Symphony Orchestra in 1953 to devote more time to teaching, performing, and conducting. He was appointed conductor of the Chicago Youth Orchestra in 1955 and the Aurora Fox Valley Symphony and Racine Symphony in 1957.

Appointed a part-time faculty member at Northwestern in 1931, when only four cello students were enrolled at the school, Powers was named professor of cello in 1955 and taught a full class of cellists plus chamber music classes. While a member of the Northwestern faculty, Powers played yearly recitals and performed with the Sheridan String Quartet, the Chamber Music Society, and the Eckstein Quartet.

Powers retired in 1979 and lives in Bradenton, Florida.

BENNETT REIMER

Born on June 19, 1932, in New York City, music education specialist Bennett Reimer began his musical career as a clarinetist and oboist. He received his bachelor's degree from the State University of New York College at Fredonia in 1954 and pursued graduate study at the University of Illinois at Urbana-Champaign, where he earned his master's in 1955 and his EdD in 1963 in addition to teaching from 1960 to 1965. From 1965 to 1978 he served on the faculty of Case Western Reserve University, where he held the Kulas Endowed Chair in Music. Reimer joined the Northwestern faculty in 1978, holding the John W. Beattie Endowed Chair in Music and serving as director of the PhD program in music education and the Center for the Study of Education and the Musical Experience, a research group of PhD students and faculty. He retired in 1997.

Reimer's book *A Philosophy of Music Education,* first published in 1970 and issued in a revised edition in 1989 (Prentice Hall), has been translated into French, Japanese, Chinese, Korean, and Greek. Author and editor of a dozen other books, he has written more than 100 articles and book chapters on a variety of topics in music and arts education. His music textbooks for grades one through eight were the most widely used throughout the United States and the world for two decades.

Reimer has served on the editorial boards of all the major music education journals; as national chair of the Music Educators National Conference Committee on Aesthetic Education; as MENC liaison for arts education initiatives; as MENC's representative to the Alliance for Curriculum Reform and to the Aesthetic Education Curriculum Program, sponsored by the U.S. Office of Education; and as a member of the six-person task force that wrote the National Standards for Music Education. Director of a three-year general music curriculum research project sponsored by the U.S. Office of Education, he served for five years on the Rockefeller Brothers Fund Awards Committee for Exemplary School Arts Programs and for six years as codirector and principal consultant for the teacher education project Education for Aesthetic Awareness: The Cleveland Area Project for the Arts in the Schools. In 1986 he spent three months as a research exchange scholar in China studying music education practices from kindergarten through the conservatory level. Reimer presents many keynote addresses and lectures each year throughout the world.

TRAUGOTT ROHNER

Born December 23, 1906, in St. Gallen, Switzerland, Traugott Rohner graduated from Central Wesleyan College as a mathematics major in 1928. After teaching in Minnesota and North Carolina, he earned a master's degree in music education from Northwestern in 1932. The following year he joined the music education faculty, where he taught until 1960.

Rohner also headed the instrumental music department of Evanston public schools, teaching in districts 75, 76, and 202. He made appearances throughout the country as a guest conductor and judged many solo, ensemble, band, and orchestra contests across the Midwest. A member of the Music Educators National Conference, Music Teachers National Association, and American Association of University Professors, he published the *Instrumental Music Primer, Violin Method,* and *Fundamentals of Music Theory* (written with George Howerton) and arranged works for string ensemble. His background in science and mathematics helped him improve and adapt musical instruments to help students learn to play, and his inventions included a mechanical string peg and a five-keyboard piano.

In 1947 Rohner founded and became publisher of the *Instrumentalist,* a national magazine for school band and orchestra directors, and in 1962 he launched *Clavier*, for keyboard teachers and performers. He also produced music education films. Rohner died in Winnetka, Illinois, on September 14, 1991, at age 84.

GERALD SMITH

By the time baritone Gerald Smith came to teach at Northwestern in 1950, he had seen the world while serving in the U.S. Navy and the reserves. Born on March 21, 1921, in Manchester, Iowa, he remained in his home state to earn his bachelor's degree from the University of Dubuque in 1942, then eventually received a master's at the Chicago Conservatory of Music and studied opera and French and German song literature at the University of Colorado. In addition to serving on the Northwestern faculty, he taught at the Chicago Conservatory of Music from 1948 to 1953 and for a year each at Ohio State University and the University of Oregon.

Smith performed as a soloist across the country, including appearances at Town Hall in New York, Town Hall in Detroit, and Orchestra Hall with the Chicago Symphony Orchestra. He also sang in the Grant Park Concert Series, with the St. Louis Municipal Orchestra, and on numerous radio broadcasts, including ABC's *Hymns of All Churches*, NBC's *Dave Garroway Show*, WGN's *Theatre of the Air*, and James Melton's *International Harvester Program*. During the summer of 1973, he presented a series of recitals in Asia through arrangements with the Institute of International Education and the Japanese Consulate in Chicago. He also appeared as an oratorio soloist throughout the country.

Active in area churches, Smith directed the music ministries of Cuyler Avenue Methodist Church in Oak Park, Faith Presbyterian Church in Austin, Highland Park Presbyterian Church, and the First United Methodist Church in Evanston, where over a 21-year period he directed as many as five choirs. He also served as director of the Chicago Wesley Hospital Nurses Chorus, Evanston Hospital Nurses Chorus, Lake County Oratorio Society, and the mass chorus of the Chicagoland Music Festival, sponsored by the *Chicago Tribune*.

Smith also served as president of the Chicago Singing Teachers Guild and as a member of the Chicago Board of Education examining committee for public school music teacher certification as well as the certification committee for ministers of music in the Methodist Church's Northern Illinois Conference. His professional affiliations included the Illinois Music Educators Association, Music Educators National Conference, American Choral Directors Association, National Association of Teachers of Singing, Chicago Singing Teachers Guild, and National Association of Methodist Musicians. Named a national honorary patron of Phi Beta, he served as president of Pi Kappa Lambda and as a consultant for the Methodist Church's National Board of Evangelism. In 1970 he received an honorary doctor of music degree from his alma mater, the University of Dubuque.

Retired from Northwestern since 1991, Smith died in Evanston on July 10, 1999.

RAY STILL

Born on March 12, 1920, in Elwood, Indiana, Ray Still began serious clarinet study at age 14 but switched to the oboe at 16, inspired by Belgian oboist Henri de Busser of the Los Angeles Philharmonic Orchestra. Although he never studied with de Busser, Still was taught by his disciple and longtime assistant, Philip Memoli, also a Los Angeles Philharmonic oboist and a recording musician for MGM studios.

After a year and a half of oboe study, Still began playing in the Works Progress Orchestra, a Depression-era creation of President Franklin D. Roosevelt. At age 19 he was hired for his first professional job, as second oboe in the Kansas City Philharmonic; he held the position from 1939 to 1941.

With the outbreak of World War II, Still studied electrical engineering at Pacific State University from 1941 to 1943 while working at night at the Douglas Aircraft Factory. He served in the U.S. Army from 1943 to 1946. After his discharge he immediately enrolled at the Juilliard School, hoping to study with Robert Bloom. Although Juilliard wasn't a school where the GI Bill would pay Still's tuition, Bloom generously offered to teach him free of charge.

Still stayed at Juilliard for the equivalent of two years. He then held first oboe positions in the Buffalo Philharmonic under William Steinberg (1947–49) and the Baltimore Symphony (1949–1953). While in Baltimore, he taught at the Peabody Institute.

In 1954 Still came to Chicago to play first oboe under Fritz Reiner in the Chicago Symphony Orchestra. He remained with the orchestra for 40 years, making hundreds of recordings and solo appearances. He has performed and coached chamber music extensively at the Aspen and Marlboro Music Festivals, Finland's Festival in Vasa, and other music festivals and continues to conduct master classes and coach wind groups around the world.

Still taught at Roosevelt University in Chicago from 1954 to 1957 and has taught at Northwestern since 1960. He is currently writing a book on playing the oboe.

ALAN STOUT

Born November 26, 1932, in Baltimore, Maryland, Alan Stout is considered one of the most productive composers of his generation. He received his musical training at the Peabody Institute from 1950 to 1954 and completed formal studies in composition and Swedish at the University of Washington in 1959. A year at the University of Copenhagen in 1954 instilled a deep interest in the music and literature of Scandinavia, whose culture has continued to exert a strong influence on his music. His principal teachers were Henry Cowell, Wallingford Riegger, Vagn Holmboe, and John Verrall.

Stout's humanitarian concerns are reflected in his choice of texts and his large body of sacred works. His eclectic musical style displays a personal mixture of experimental and traditional elements. An innovative feature that first appeared in the germinal Second Symphony (1951-66) is the use of large chromatic tone clusters whose constant movement contributes to the overall form. Many of the composer's works since 1960 are written with a continuous rubato, leaving performers free to mold microrhythms within strict meters. His extensive oeuvre includes both instrumental and vocal works.

Stout has written for such publications as *Nordisk Musikkultur*, *Beyond the Square*, and *Music and Musicians*. He has been active on behalf of fellow composers, editing and translating works of Scandinavian composers and promoting performances of neglected 20th-century American masters and young European composers.

The recipient of many major commissions, Stout has served on the Northwestern faculty since 1963 and is active in the Chicago area as a scholar, pianist, and conductor. As a teacher, "Alan Stout has an encyclopedic mind and a certain bent for the silly," related Kurt Hansen (G83). "His courses really brought you to the core of musical structure and all the interesting stories about various works, composers, and performances."

WALTER ALLEN STULTS

Born on November 18, 1884, in Farmer City, Illinois, Walter Allen Stults first studied violin at the Des Moines Conservatory of Music, where he earned a degree in 1899. In 1900 he enrolled at Northwestern, where he focused on vocal studies but also studied piano with Arne Oldberg and theory with Peter Christian Lutkin. He received a graduate in music degree from Northwestern in 1909.

Upon graduation Stults became a member of the faculty as assistant instructor; after successive promotions he was appointed a full professor in 1943. For several years Stults led the musical work at Garrett Biblical Institute and the Swedish Theological Seminary, and he also conducted the Garrett Glee Club and the Northwestern University Glee Club.

In 1916 the Alumni Association of Northwestern's School of Music, as part of a plan to stimulate and reward exceptional musical achievement, appointed a committee to consider establishing a local honor society. Serving on the committee were Stults, Louis Norton Dodge, and Carl Milton Beecher, all of whom in 1918 became founders of Pi Kappa Lambda, soon widely accepted as the national music honor society. Stults served as president of the society from 1918 to 1925, as president of Northwestern's Alpha chapter, and as regent. In the community he was active as musical editor for the *Evanston News-Index* and Chicago correspondent for *Musical America*.

On his retirement in 1948, Stults was named chairman emeritus of the vocal department. He remained active as a singer, teacher, and adjudicator. In 1952 he became president of the National Association of Teachers of Singing, for which he also served as associate editor of the *Bulletin*. Stults went on to teach at North Texas State University (now the University of North Texas) in Denton, serving for three years as visiting professor of voice. After his second retirement he moved to Corpus Christi, Texas, where he opened a private voice studio and in the 1960s taught at the Del Mar College School of Fine Arts. Stults died on April 19, 1976.

SAMUEL THAVIU

Versatility marked the musical career of Samuel Thaviu — violin soloist, concertmaster, chamber musician, conductor, and teacher. Son of a famous Chicago bandmaster, Thaviu was born in Chicago on August 18, 1909, and attended Chicago Musical College, graduating in 1935. By then he had already won the Lyon-Healy Award (the prize was a violin) at 15 and the National Federation of Music Clubs' National Award at 22.

A student of Leon Sametini, Jacques Gordon, and Mischa Mischakoff, Thaviu accumulated quite a resume before returning to the Chicago area in 1966 to accept an appointment as professor of violin and chair of the string department at Northwestern. He spent the early years of his career as a member of the Chicago Symphony Orchestra and the Mischakoff String Quartet. He went on to serve as concertmaster of the Kansas City Philharmonic, the Baltimore Symphony, the Pittsburgh Symphony under Fritz Reiner and William Steinberg, and the Cleveland Orchestra under George Szell. Thaviu was also associate conductor of the Kansas City and Baltimore Symphony Orchestras and a faculty member at the Carnegie Institute of Technology and West Virginia University.

While on the Northwestern faculty, Thaviu performed the cycle of the 10 Beethoven violin and piano sonatas twice on campus and numerous times elsewhere. As professor emeritus after his 1977 retirement, he received two Fulbright grants that took him to Lima, Peru, and Montevideo, Uruguay, to give master classes and perform. Thaviu also continued to teach as a visiting professor and to perform as chamber musician, guest conductor, and guest concertmaster.

Residents of Highland Park, Illinois, Samuel Thaviu and his wife, Elinor, gave Northwestern $100,000 for the Thaviu-Isaak Endowed Scholarship Fund for Piano Performance. He died in Evanston on July 1, 2000, at age 90.

HAROLD VAN HORNE

Born May 30, 1908, in Cañon City, Colorado, Harold Van Horne came to Chicago to attend the American Conservatory of Music, where he received a bachelor's degree in 1932 and a master's in 1936. While still a student he was appointed to the piano faculty there, serving from 1930 to 1941. He came to Northwestern in 1938 and taught on the School of Music faculty until his death in 1957.

Van Horne's performing career corresponded with the rise of radio. Even before he began teaching, Van Horne was heard as a staff pianist on Chicago radio — for WQJ in 1925, WENR in 1926, WMAQ from 1927 to 1932, and the Chicago studio of NBC from 1932 to 1938. A touring soloist and ensemble artist with the Civic Concert Service and National Concert League, he performed as a soloist with the Chicago Symphony Orchestra under Frederick Stock and with the NBC Orchestra. He also accompanied such performers as Jacques Gordon, Mischa Mischakoff, Gladys Swarthout, and Nathan Milstein. Van Horne died in Chicago on August 24, 1957.

KLAUS WACHSMANN

Known as one of the world's most distinguished ethnomusicologists, Klaus Wachsmann was born in Berlin on March 8, 1907, and began his musicological studies in 1930 in Germany under Blume, Schering, Hornbostel, and Sachs. In 1934 he left Germany because of the political situation and continued his work in Switzerland, earning a doctorate in 1935 with a dissertation on pre-Gregorian chant. His work in linguistics began the following year at London's School of Oriental and African Studies, where he specialized in the Bantu languages.

From 1948 to 1957 Wachsmann worked in Uganda, supervising missionary education there until his appointment as curator of the new Uganda Museum in Kampala. From 1958 to 1963 he served as a scientific officer in charge of ethnological collections at the Wellcome Foundation in London. His first American academic appointment took him to the University of California, Los Angeles, where he taught in the department of music and the Institute of Ethnomusicology from 1963 until accepting a dual appointment in the School of Music and College of Arts and Sciences (now Weinberg College of Arts and Sciences) at Northwestern in 1968.

Although he was primarily known as an authority on African music, Wachsmann's interests were exceptionally broad. In later years he was increasingly preoccupied with writing the musical history of nonliterate cultures, and he edited a collection of articles on the subject that was published in 1971 by Northwestern University Press. He also presented seminars with a friend, American musicologist Charles Seeger, to challenge commonly held aesthetic and social conceptions about music and music making.

In 1973 Wachsmann became the first ethnomusicologist to receive the Huxley Medal from the Anthropological Institute of Great Britain and Ireland. During the School of Music's curriculum revision in 1972, he helped plan and implement the World Music course in the Musicianship sequence.

Wachsmann was named a professor emeritus upon his retirement from Northwestern in 1975. He died on July 17, 1984, at his home in Sussex, England.

LEONA WILKINS

Born in Winston-Salem, North Carolina, in February of 1922, Leona B. Wilkins earned a bachelor of arts in 1941 from North Carolina Central University and a master of music in 1944 from the University of Michigan, where she received a PhD in 1971. She also studied at the University of Southern California, Oberlin College, and the Sorbonne in Paris.

Before accepting a position as associate professor of music education at Northwestern in 1972, Wilkins taught for 11 years in North Carolina, St. Louis, and Detroit public schools. She also held college appointments at Hampton Institute in Virginia, Bluefield State College in West Virginia, Tennessee State University, Eastern Michigan University, and Temple University in Philadelphia, where she directed an internship in inner-city schools that was required of all music education majors prior to student teaching.

At Northwestern her main assignment was elementary and junior high school pedagogy. She also taught graduate courses in music pedagogy, individualized instruction, music administration and supervision, and music in urban education as well as the first team-taught interdisciplinary arts course for music and other arts teachers. Wilkins worked closely with the Evanston school system, serving as a consultant for the music department. Throughout her life she has stressed the importance of music and the role it plays in improving the quality of life for children.

Other career activities included directing workshops and clinics and serving as a consultant for Silver Burdett Publishers. She also served on the Role of the Arts Committee Task Force at the U.S. Office of Education, the Bicentennial Commission for Music Education, the National Assessment of Educational Process, and the committee revising the National Teachers Examination in Music Education for the Educational Testing Bureau.

Since her retirement in 1988, Wilkins has continued her involvement with students. With her North Carolina Central alumni chapter, she has presented "career-images workshops" for students enrolled in Chicago GED programs and has organized activities to provide scholarships for inner-city students.

THOMAS WILLIS

One of the Midwest's best-known music critics and educators, Thomas Willis was born on April 24, 1928, and raised in Flat Rock, Illinois. He received his BMus from Northwestern in 1949 and was a Yale scholar in music history from 1949 to 1952. After serving on the music faculty of Sweet Briar College, he returned to Northwestern in 1954 to pursue a PhD. As a graduate student he formed Cameo Opera, a chamber opera ensemble, and produced some 20 works ranging from Monteverdi's *L'Incoronazione di Poppea* to Weisgall's *The Stronger.* He earned his PhD in 1966.

Willis joined the staff of the *Chicago Tribune* in 1957 and was named assistant theater, music, and dance critic in 1960. He became arts editor in 1970, continuing to review music and dance. In 1974 he returned to full-time music criticism.

From 1967 to 1977 Willis held a lectureship at the School of Music. He left the *Tribune* in September 1977 to expand his activity at Northwestern, becoming concert manager and associate professor of music history and literature. Also that year he became the Ravinia Festival's coordinator of educational programming, a post he held until 1981. In addition, Willis served for a year as classical music editor and columnist for *Chicago* magazine.

In 1981 Willis took a leave of absence from Northwestern to become general manager of the Chicago International Festival, arranging some 40 international presentations for a projected 1982 performance. After the project was abruptly aborted by Chicago's Mayor Jane Byrne, he continued as a consultant for the Mayor's Office of Special Events until fall 1982, when he returned to the School of Music as special assistant to the dean and associate professor of music history and literature. He also taught a course in arts management for the Kellogg Graduate School of Management.

In addition to his academic duties, Willis continued to write on music and the arts. Since 1985 he has served as book editor and Chicago correspondent for *Musical America.* Author of the 1974 book *The Chicago Symphony Orchestra,* he appeared regularly as a commentator for Chicago radio station WEFM and television station WTTW as well as on a 1980 series for the Bravo cable network.

In recent years Willis has been in demand as an arts management consultant, with clients including the Cheswick Foundation in Boston, the Peninsula Music Festival in Wisconsin, and the Art Institute of Chicago. Since his retirement in fall 1999 he has remained active as a speaker, guest critic, and adjudicator.

RUTH FOX WYATT

Soon after 18-year-old Ruth Fox's 1927 marriage to lawyer Harry Wyatt, she finished a bachelor's degree in English and Spanish at the University of Chicago. She was also taking voice lessons at a studio in the Loop, but when the Wyatts moved to Evanston, Harry suggested she spare herself the trip downtown by registering at Northwestern. Thus began her long affiliation with the School of Music.

Born August 25, 1906, in Chicago, Ruth Fox Wyatt blazed an unusual trail at Northwestern. While pursuing a bachelor of music education degree, she was asked to help prepare exams, and on receiving the degree in 1931 she was named the school's director of tests and measurements. Her work in the field led to courses in the psychology of measurement and then to two more degrees — a master's (1935) and PhD (1941) in psychology from Northwestern. She went on to serve as professor of psychology and physics of music until 1960, in addition to teaching psychology in the College of Liberal Arts from 1941 to 1945. Her contributions to the field can still be found in textbooks.

Wyatt died on January 18, 1989, but continues to help students through the Harry N. and Ruth F. Wyatt Student Composers Fund, which awards grants to composition students.

ELIZABETH WYSOR

Born in Easton, Pennsylvania, on May 14, 1912, contralto Elizabeth Wysor grew up loving to sculpt, paint, and write. Although singing was the last talent to present itself, she said that "music drew me more than anything else." As she followed her dreams to the Juilliard School and the Akademie der Tonkunst in Munich, Wysor discovered the love of Europe and the passion for opera that would take her across the Atlantic 13 times during her career.

After her Town Hall debut in 1938, Wysor went on to give five concerts there as well as six at Carnegie Hall with the New York Philharmonic and the Boston Symphony Orchestra. She achieved prominence throughout North America and Europe, appearing with most of the important festivals, orchestras, and opera companies on both continents. Wysor's forte was Wagner, particularly Venus in *Tannhaüser,* Ortrud in *Lohengrin,* Brangäne in *Tristan und Isolde,* Erda in *Das Rheingold,* and Fricka and Grimgerde in *Die Walküre.* Yet she was also successful in such lighter roles as Cherubino in Mozart's *Marriage of Figaro* and Bertha in Rossini's *Barber of Seville.*

Wysor taught at Mary Washington College of the University of Virginia in the late 1940s before joining the Northwestern faculty in 1953. Her international singing career equipped her well for offering English, Italian, German, and French diction classes in addition to private voice lessons.

After retiring to Cape Cod in 1973, Wysor continued to teach and sing on a reduced scale. She also lectured, traveled, enjoyed art, and wrote poetry (her book *Moments of Radiance* was first published in 1976 and reprinted in 1984). Later she moved to Bethlehem, Pennsylvania, where she died on October 6, 2000.

Donor Hall of Fame

As donations to the School of Music increased during the latter half of the 20th century, the school was able to launch new initiatives, expand the faculty, and erect new facilities. The following donors have made gifts of $1 million or more.

J. Yule Bogue

Born near Dublin, Ireland, J. Yule Bogue forged lifelong ties with Northwestern's School of Music when he married Emily Boettcher (26, G28), a former School of Music faculty member and noted pianist. Bogue spent his career with companies that made significant scientific advances. In the 1940s he was a member of the team that developed a computer memory subsequently purchased by Remington Rand. At Imperial Chemical Industries, where at the time of his death in 1996 he was a retired deputy chair and technical director of the Pharmaceuticals Division, Bogue designed and supervised construction of pharmaceutical research laboratories and codiscovered an anti-epileptic drug. He served as a director of Cetus Corporation, a developer and manufacturer of pharmaceutical products for the treatment of cancer and infectious diseases, from its founding in 1972 until its merger with Chiron Corporation in 1991.

Bogue married Boettcher on October 5, 1938. A native of Montana, Boettcher studied at Northwestern with such eminent teachers as Arne Oldberg, Carl Beecher, and Peter Lutkin. In 1924 she became the first Northwestern student to be granted junior status during the first year of enrollment; she later became the first student to appear as a soloist with the Evanston Symphony Orchestra. Also a composer, Boettcher participated in the Northwestern Pageant and Pi Kappa Lambda, wrote the 1926 class song, and played at Northwestern's 1927 and 1928 Commencements. After completing her bachelor's and master's degrees at Northwestern, she studied in Europe. Her international performing career included appearances with the Chicago Symphony Orchestra and the London Philharmonic as well as recitals for the BBC and the British National Gallery.

After Boettcher's death on April 13, 1992, Bogue established the Emily Boettcher and J. Yule Bogue Endowed Fund for Graduate Students in her memory. The fund provides scholarships for deserving graduate students in the School of Music. In 1993 he founded the Emily Boettcher (Charlotte) and J. Yule Bogue Young Artists Performance Fund. Before his death on June 17, 1996, he gave the school several pianos and antiques from his personal collection. Bogue was a member of the John Evans Club.

Grace Fox Congdon

Grace Fox Congdon (G37) and her younger sister, Dorothy Fox Johnson (29), were born and raised on a farm near Britt, Iowa. Grace attended Cornell College before transferring to the University of Wyoming, where she earned a bachelor of music degree. After graduating she taught for a few years before deciding to further her music education career by pursuing a master's degree. Dorothy (see below) had earned an undergraduate music degree at Northwestern, and Grace decided to attend the University as well, attracted by the national reputation of its music education program.

Congdon's subsequent teaching career took her to Laramie, Wyoming; Benton Harbor, Michigan; and Shreveport, Louisiana. In Laramie and Benton Harbor she served as music supervisor in the public schools. During and after her days at Northwestern, she studied organ, playing for pleasure as well as performing. In 1960 Congdon moved back to the family home in Britt to care for her parents. She remained there until her death in 1993.

A generous patron of the School of Music, Congdon was an active and supportive member of the alumni community, endowing the Grace Congdon Endowed Scholarship Fund to benefit graduate students in the school.

Elsie S. and Louis Eckstein

Louis Eckstein made his fortune in the pharmaceutical business and then invested much of it in Chicago Loop real estate. At one time he also owned a chain of magazines, including *Redbook*. In 1911 he founded the Ravinia Opera, and under his artistic and financial guidance Ravinia Park became "the summer opera capital of the United States." Through his influence with New York's Metropolitan Opera Company, Ravinia hosted the greatest operatic stars of the day. During the Depression he underwrote the Ravinia Company's heavy deficits, and by the time the park closed in 1931, the Eckstein family owned 97 percent of the company's stock. In 1932 Eckstein became a director of the Metropolitan Opera, serving until his death in 1935.

His widow, arts patron Elsie S. Eckstein, was named honorary chair of the Ravinia Festival on its founding in 1936. The Eckstein family continued to own the Ravinia Park land until donating it to the festival in the 1940s.

At her death in 1950, Elsie Eckstein bequeathed $3.5 million to the School of Music. The Elsie S. and Louis Eckstein Northwestern University Musical Endowment Fund has funded scholarships, new equipment, facility renovations, library expansion, and new faculty hirings.

Dorothy Fox Johnson

Dorothy Fox Johnson (29) entered Northwestern in 1925 to study piano and composition. Shortly after graduating four years later, she married Carl Johnson, and they settled in Evanston. She regularly returned to campus to study with Carl Beecher and assistant professor Lowell Leslie Townshend in the 1930s, associate professor Stefan Bardas in the 1940s, and piano department chair Pauline Manchester Lindsey in the 1950s.

Both Carl and Dorothy Fox Johnson served Northwestern in various capacities, and they rarely missed home football and basketball games. Carl served for four years as head of the Northwestern Alumni Association, four years on the University's Board of Trustees, and twenty years on the board of directors of the NU Club of Chicago. A founding member of the John Evans Club — and for many years the club's vice chair or chair — Carl was also a charter member of the Northwestern Benchwarmers. He received the Alumni Service Award in 1947 and the Alumni Medal in 1961. Dorothy served as director of the Alumni Association, president of the Northwestern University Alumni Council, and president of the Alumnae of Northwestern. A member of the Board of Trustees for four years, she received the Alumni Service Award in 1955.

For the School of Music the Johnsons endowed the Dorothy and Carl Johnson Graduate Scholarship Fund. Dorothy established the Dorothy and Carl Johnson Visiting Artists Endowed Fund in 1988 and and provided for the School of Music generously in her will. She also helped establish the Dorothy and Carl Johnson Tennis Center, Northwestern's first indoor tennis facility, in 1993 and supported the renovation of Ryan Field.

The Picks and Staigers

Albert Pick Jr. and Charles G. Staiger helped the School of Music realize a longtime dream by funding the construction of its first concert hall. Named in honor of Pick's wife, Corinne Frada Pick, and in memory of Pauline Pick Staiger, Pick's sister and Staiger's late wife, Pick-Staiger Concert Hall was completed in the fall of 1975.

Corinne Frada Pick studied piano with Arne Oldberg at Northwestern in the early 1920s. Albert Pick Jr. was chair of the board of Pick Hotels Corporation, former president of the American Hotel Association, and a longtime supporter of the Ravinia Festival Association, the Auditorium Theatre project, and the Art Institute of Chicago. He was also a director of the Chicago Council on Foreign Relations and an Eisenhower appointee to the People to People program, an organization consisting of one member from each major U.S. industry.

In 1958 the Picks established the Corinne Frada Pick Scholarships, awarded annually to piano students in the School of Music. On their 50th wedding anniversary, Albert Pick told his wife that his gift to her would be a concert hall. Five years later that gift began to take shape when Charles Staiger agreed to join in financing it.

Pick's sister Pauline had died in 1931, a year after marrying Staiger, who kept in contact with the Picks after her death. As an executive with the Harry Winston diamond firm, Staiger sold jewels to many of the top names in the social registers and financial hierarchies in the United States and abroad. On his travels he collected Asian art and American and English antiques, and he later donated some of his Chinese art objects for display in the Pick-Staiger lobby.

Charles Staiger died on September 18, 1977, followed in death later that year by Albert Pick on December 11. Corinne Frada Pick died on January 18, 1989.

William Ragland

Soprano Edith Mason Ragland, wife of William Ragland, enjoyed a thriving operatic career in the first half of the 20th century. A native of St. Louis, she debuted in 1912 at age 20 with the Boston Opera Company as Nedda in *I Pagliacci*. After performing in France, Mexico, and Central and South America as well as at New York's Metropolitan Opera, she came to Chicago in 1921 to star in *Madama Butterfly* with the Chicago Opera Association at the Auditorium Theatre. She sang with the Ravinia Opera and Chicago Grand Opera until 1934, when she returned to the Met. Toscanini chose her to sing in Verdi's *Falstaff* at the 1935 Salzburg Festival. She retired in 1942.

In 1964 she donated her collection of costumes, hats, shoes, gloves, jewelry, and hand props to the School of Music's Opera Workshop. After her death in 1973 her husband established an opera fellowship in her honor; the Edith Mason Ragland Fellowship is awarded annually to a Northwestern graduate student. In 1983 William Ragland honored his late wife with a large endowment to fund Northwestern's opera program, which was subsequently named the Edith Mason and William E. Ragland Opera Theater.

Joseph and Helen Regenstein

In the 1970s the Joseph and Helen Regenstein Foundation helped meet the school's need for more space by donating funds to support the construction of Regenstein Hall of Music on the new lakefill campus. Named in honor of Mrs. Regenstein, who was fond of art and music, the hall was acoustically designed for the teaching, rehearsal, practice, and performance of instrumental music.

Founder of the Transco Envelope Company, Arvey Corporation, and Velsicol Chemical Company, Joseph Regenstein Sr. established the Joseph and Helen Regenstein Foundation in 1950 to support cultural, educational, and health organizations. On his death in 1957 the foundation passed to his widow, Helen Regenstein, who died in 1982, and his son Joseph Regenstein Jr., a Northwestern alumnus who was the foundation's president and director from 1982 until his death in 1999. Now named the Regenstein Foundation, the organization has also provided support for the Lincoln Park Zoo's Large Mammal Habitat, the Chicago Symphony Orchestra, the Regenstein Library at the University of Chicago, and Northwestern's Centennial Hall, Department of Cytology, Library Council Fund, and President's Fund.

Carol and Arthur Rice

Carol Rice (38) received a bachelor's degree in music performance from Northwestern. She and her husband, Arthur Rice, serve on the School of Music Visiting Committee. Retired president and chair of the Technical Publishing Company, he graduated from the University of Illinois but met his future wife at a party after a Northwestern football game. Throughout their 60-year marriage, the Rices have been ardent supporters of Northwestern University.

In 1993 Carol and Arthur Rice's interest in music and Northwestern led them to make a $2 million gift establishing the Carol F. and Arthur L. Rice Jr. Endowed University Professorship in Music Performance. Only the second Northwestern chair endowed at that monetary level, it enhances the School of Music's strong reputation by supporting superior performance and education in music. The inaugural chairholder is director of orchestras Victor Yampolsky. Subsequent Rice professors, like Yampolsky, will be artists and scholars of world-class stature.

Sanford and Jeanne Robertson

In 1999 Northwestern received a $1.5 million gift from Sanford and Jeanne Robertson to endow the Donald G. Robertson Director of Music Theatre Chair. The gift honors Sanford Robertson's late father, Donald G. Robertson, who as a Northwestern student wrote one of the University's most popular fight songs, "Rise, Northwestern" (also known as "Push On"). The inaugural chairholder is Dominic Missimi, professor of theatre and director of the Music Theatre Program.

Although he wrote the song in 1913, Donald Robertson did not publish it then because another Northwestern song, "Go U Northwestern," had been adopted the previous year. Upon its publication in 1916, "Rise, Northwestern" became popular immediately, and it remains in the Wildcat Marching Band's repertoire today. Robertson also wrote "The Wildcat Song," "Hail Alma Mater True," and "Because We All Like Old N.U." as well as songs for the Women's Athletic Association show, precursor of the Waa-Mu Show. He received the Alumni Service Award in 1944.

Sanford Robertson, a private investor, was a principal in the San Francisco firm of Robertson, Stephens & Co. until its sale to Bank of America in 1997. His wife, Jeanne Pollock Robertson, graduated from Northwestern's College of Arts and Sciences in 1955.

Richard and Helen Thomas

With their gift of $1 million in 1998, Richard L. and Helen Thomas of Winnetka, Illinois, have helped the School of Music's most talented graduate applicants make their educational dreams a reality. The Richard and Helen Thomas Fellowships for Principal Orchestral Players assist the school in its efforts to compete with peer institutions in attracting graduate students with high academic distinction and superior musical talent. Four endowed fellowships are awarded on an annual basis.

Richard Thomas, a graduate of Kenyon College and Harvard University, joined the staff of the First National Bank of Chicago in 1958. In 1974 he was named the bank's president, and in 1991 he was elected chairman and chief executive officer of First Chicago Corporation, the holding company for the bank and other enterprises. When he retired in 1996, a plaque was erected at First Chicago's downtown plaza. It reads, in part, "Together with his wife, Helen, he will long be remembered for a strong commitment to Chicago. His record of outstanding corporate and civic leadership will also endure as a continuing inspiration for all."

A longtime member and currently vice chair of Northwestern's Board of Trustees, Thomas serves on the board's executive committee and the Leadership Group for Campaign Northwestern.

Lifetime Gifts or Pledges of $50,000 or More to the School of Music

Estate of Margaret H. Akers
Anonymous
Estate of William Harrison Barnes
Warren L. and Eloise Batts
Dr. Jeanne M. Blanchet
J. Yule Bogue*
Harry R. Bornhoeft
Morris E. Brodwin
Patricia Holmes and A. C. Buehler Jr./
    ACP Foundation
Clifton A. Burmeister*
Lela H. Cady* Trust
E. Michael Carney III
Elizabeth F. Cheney Foundation
Estate of Fredrik A. Chramer
Edward J. Combs
Grace Fox Congdon*
Estate of Joyce Reed Cope
Helen Archias Cummings
Estate of Nora Dadian
Ken M.* and Ruth Dunbar Davee
Laurence D. Davis
Robert E. and Linda L. Davis
Estate of Carolyn S. Donato
Allan R. Drebin
C. P. Dubbs*
Estate of Frances C. Dunbar
Estate of Elsie S. and Louis Eckstein
Estate of Jack L. Elsley
Estate of Clarice Fine
Gene A. Fort
Ann and Gordon Getty Foundation
Marie L. Goyette
Richard A. and Monica Greenwood
Estate of Kathleen M. Haight
Bentley T. Handwork
Richard T. Holmberg
William T. Hopkins
Eugene and Ann Hoversen
Marie E. Howard* Trust
George R.* and A'Louise* Howerton
Dorothy Fox Johnson
Estate of Betty M. Kanable
Kemper Education and Charitable Fund
Dr. Jacqueline M. Krump
Estate of Aloha S. Lawver
Liberace Foundation for the Performing
    and Creative Arts
Estate of Pauline M. Lindsey
Henrietta Lundquist
Marjorie L. McKinney
Nancy L. Meendsen
Richard P. Menaul
Kenneth C. Merrill
Alvis J. Meyer
Norbert Molder
Muriel C. Nerad
Helen Heim Nichols*
Lynn M. Nothdurft
James J. and Ellen O'Connor
Mary S. Oldberg
Estate of Lucille T. Parkhill
Marietta M. Paynter
Albert* and Corinne Frada* Pick

Albert Pick Jr. Fund
Leslie B. Propp*
Estate of William E. Ragland
Regenstein Foundation
James T. and Laura C. Rhind
Carol F. and Arthur L. Rice Jr.
John M. and Priscilla Richman
Carole M. and Dr. Jerry N. Ringer
Jeanne and Sanford R. Robertson/
    San Francisco Foundation
Estate of Marian Brewer Rock
Ruth Wyatt Rosenson*
Rosemary J. Schnell
Estate of Helen M. Schockley
Charles E. and Elizabeth R. Schroeder
D. Gideon and Nancy S. Searle
George L. Siegel*
Alice V. Siorek
Estate of Berniece I. Smith
Spencer Foundation
Estate of Gertrude White Spencer
Estate of Charles G. Staiger
Estate of William G. Steigely
Estate of Martha R. Steinbach
Alan B. Stout
System Development Foundation
Estate of Helen L. Teich
Samuel* and Elinor Thaviu
Richard L. and Helen Thomas
Betty A. and Jerome W.* Van Gorkom
Helen Cottongim VanKirk*
Stanley J. Vesely Jr.
Estate of Dorothy Sidford Walker
Estate of Cecil M. Wimmer
Estate of Lotta Winkler
Estate of Russell C. Wonderlic
Estate of Marion Wurzburger
Estate of Harry N. Wyatt
Jay Maitland Young

*deceased prior to April 1, 2002

Bibliography

PRIMARY SOURCES

Northwestern University Archival Files
Alumni Biographical Files
Faculty Biographical Files
General Files, School of Music
Subject Files

Northwestern University Minutes of Meetings
Board of Trustees and Executive Committee (1851–present)
School of Music Faculty (1968–present)

Northwestern University Publications
Alumni Journal, 1914–21
Alumni News, 1921–69, 1971–87
Alumni News Letter, 1903–14
Northwestern Perspective, 1988–98
Northwestern University Bulletin, 1902–75
Northwestern University Catalog, 1856–present
Northwestern University Information: The School of Music
Northwestern University Observer, 1985–present
Northwestern University Register, 1940–63
President's Report, 1876–1948

Northwestern University School of Music Publications
Alla Breve, 1990–present
Fanfare, 1971–present
Musical Register, 1881–83
Noteworthy
School of Music Quarterly Bulletin, 1900–09
School of Music Announcement of Courses, 1892–1966

Northwestern University Student Publications
Daily Northwestern, 1910–present
Evening Northwestern, 1943–49
The Gadfly, 1933–34
The Northwestern, 1881–1910
Northwestern Magazine, 1904–16
Northwestern News, 1949–70
Northwestern University Record, 1893–96
The Northwestern World, 1890–92
Pandora, 1884
Profile, 1949–59
Purple Parrot, 1921–50
Scrawl: A Literary Quarterly, 1924–28
Syllabus, 1884–present
The Tripod, 1871–80
The Vidette, 1878–80

Other Periodicals
Evanston Index, 1872–1914
Evanston News, 1909–14
Evanston News-Index, 1915–42
Northwestern Christian Advocate, 1852–1940

Personal Papers
Beattie, John Walter
Boettcher, Emily
Carringer, Walter
Donato, Anthony
Fagg Jr., Fred Dow
Jones, J. Wesley
Knapp, Harold (scrapbook)
Lunt, Cornelia
Lutkin, Peter Christian
Mombaerts, Gui
Oldberg, Arne
Noelte, Albert
Scott, Walter Dill
Snyder, Franklyn Bliss
Wild, Payson

SECONDARY SOURCES

Barber, Carolyn A. "The Northwestern University Concert Band: A Conductor's Guide." Manuscript, Northwestern University, 1995.

Bateman, Newton, and Paul Selby, eds. *Historical Encyclopedia of Illinois.* Chicago: Munsoll Publishing Company, 1906.

Coe, George. *Sadie Knowland Coe, A Chapter in a Life, October 9, 1864–August 24, 1905.* Privately printed, 1906.

Deverman, John H. "Howard Hanson: His Life before the *Nordic* Symphony." Doctoral dissertation, Northwestern University, 1992.

Dorhout, Albert. "The Emergence of Music Education in the United States from the Tutor to the Bachelor of Music Education at Northwestern University." Student paper, Northwestern University, 1976.

Ebner, Michael H. *Creating Chicago's North Shore.* Chicago: University of Chicago Press, 1988.

Golinkin, Scott G. "Glenn Cliffe Bainum: Influence of His Charting Techniques on Big Ten Marching Bands." Master's thesis, Northwestern University, 1975.

Hurd, Harvey B., and Robert D. Sheppard, eds. *History of Northwestern University and Evanston.* Chicago: Munsell Publishing Company, 1906.

Kennel, Pauline Graybill. "Peter Christian Lutkin: Northwestern University's First Dean of Music." Dissertation, Northwestern University, 1980.

Morledge, Kirk W. *To the Memories: A History of the Northwestern University Waa-Mu Show, 1929–1980.* Evanston: Northwestern University, 1980.

Paulison, Walter. *The Tale of the Wildcats.* Evanston: Northwestern University, 1951.

Perkins, Margery Blair. *Evanstoniana, An Informal History of Evanston and Its Architecture.* Evanston: Evanston Historical Society, 1984.

Peterson, Doreen. "The Evolution of Northwestern University's Music Campus: An Architectural History." Student paper, Northwestern University, 1978.

Reeling, Viola Crouch. *Evanston: Its Land and People.* Evanston: Fort Dearborn Chapter, Daughters of the American Revolution, 1928.

Ritchey, Michael. "The Northwestern Strike of 1970: A Perspective." Student paper, Northwestern University, 1978.

Roe, Adam. "Movement Dreams: The History of Northwestern University's SDS, 1965–1970." Senior honors thesis, Northwestern University, 1992.

Scott, Franklin, D. *A Pictorial History of Northwestern University, 1851–1951.* Evanston: Northwestern University Press, 1951.

Thernstrom, Stephan. *A History of the American People,* 2nd ed., vols. 1 and 2. San Diego: Harcourt Brace Jovanovich, 1989.

Vespa-Papaleo, J. Frank. "Pride and Guts: A History of the Northwestern University Marching Band, 1887–1991." Student paper, Northwestern University, 1992.

Vincent, Esther, and Mary Oldberg. "Arne Oldberg, 1874–1962: Composer, Pianist, Teacher." Student paper, Northwestern University, n.d.

Ward, Estelle Frances. *The Story of Northwestern University.* New York: Dodd, Mead and Company, 1924.

Wilde, Arthur E., ed. *Northwestern University, 1855-1905,* 4 vols. New York: University Publishing Society, 1905.

Willard, Frances E. *A Classic Town: The Story of Evanston.* Evanston: Woman's Temperance Publishing Association, 1891.

Williamson, Harold F., and Payson S. Wild. *Northwestern University: A History, 1850–1975.* Evanston: Northwestern University, 1976.

Zalkin, Mark Wayne. "The History of Northwestern University A Cappella Choir, 1906–1970." Master's thesis, Northwestern University, 1971.

Photo Credits

263